Successful Garden[ing]
in the Greater Washington A[rea]

S0-DNL-196

Payment is enclosed for _____ copy/copies at $7.95 per copy plus postage and handling of $1.45 per copy for a total of $ _____

PLEASE PRINT

NAME _____

ADDRESS _____

CITY _____ STATE _____ ZIP _____

MAIL TO: Men's Garden Club of Montgomery County,
P.O. Box 34863, Bethesda, Maryland 20827

Successful Gardening
in the Greater Washington Area

$7 95

Payment is enclosed for _____ copy/copies at $7.95 per copy plus postage and handling of $1.45 per copy for a total of $ _____

PLEASE PRINT

NAME _____

ADDRESS _____

CITY _____ STATE _____ ZIP _____

MAIL TO: Men's Garden Club of Montgomery County,
P.O. Box 34863, Bethesda, Maryland 20827

Successful Gardening
in the Greater Washington Area

$7 95

Payment is enclosed for _____ copy/copies at $7.95 per copy plus postage and handling of $1.45 per copy for a total of $ _____

PLEASE PRINT

NAME _____

ADDRESS _____

CITY _____ STATE _____ ZIP _____

MAIL TO: Men's Garden Club of Montgomery County,
P.O. Box 34863, Bethesda, Maryland 20827

Successful Gardening

in the
Greater Washington Area

PUBLICATION COMMITTEE: John Edwards, Chairman
Allan E. Baker • Norton Boothe • Anthony R. Gould
Lynn M. F. Harriss • Eugene L. Hess • Ralph N. Ives
Frederick Jochem • Carl R. Mahder • Robert B. Melville
Sam Shiozawa • Howard Stagner

EDITORIAL COMMITTEE: Charles A. H. Thomson, Chairman
Henry E. Allen • John Edwards • John G. Shaffer

DISTRIBUTION COMMITTEE: John B. Toms, Chairman
Edmund C. Flynn

Men's Garden Club of Montgomery County

Publication History

Men's Garden Club of Montgomery County

*Ornamental and Flowering Plant Material which thrive in the climate and
soil conditions of Montgomery County, Md.* (mimeographed), 1948

A Garden Handbook of Ornamental Plant Material for the Greater Washington Area, 1955

Successful Gardening in the Greater Washington Area, first edition, 1969

Successful Gardening in the Greater Washington Area, second edition,
revised and enlarged, 1975

Successful Gardening in the Greater Washington Area, third edition,
new and enlarged, 1989; second printing, 1990

Price: $7.95

Cover Design: Jane Crawford
Front Cover Photo: Courtesy of Paul A. Zahl
  (Girl knee-deep in a field of Sweet William Phlox)
Back Cover Photo: Courtesy of B. Anthony Stewart
  (Dogwoods and azaleas in bloom at National Arboretum)
Map Inside Front Cover: Eugene E. Munn, Jr.,
  Frederick K. Hayes
Cover and Photo Coordination: William Whipple Abbe,
  Edmund C. Flynn, Cletis Pride, A. Blair Thaw
Composition: Wordworks
Printing: Colortone Press

Contents

About the Map

The map of the Greater Washington area inside the front cover is adapted from the plant hardiness zone map prepared by the U.S. Department of Agriculture. The USDA map shows the zones of average minimum temperature in the United States. It has served since 1952, with updates in the 1960s, as an approximate guide to what plants will grow and thrive in a given area.

Now, for the 1990s, a new and ongoing study by the U.S. National Arboretum is sharpening the familiar sweep of the zone lines. There will be more jagged lines and pockets of one zone, micro-climates, inside another. Information from weather stations and from professional and "keen amateur" observers is feeding into computers to pinpoint plant performance. New computer technology is bringing together millions of bits of data not previously available.

Temperature is a key to plant performance but there are other factors – sun, wind and rain, soils and altitude, and even density of population. All are taken into account in the new study which also broadens the USDA coverage to include Canada and Mexico. (See page 182.)

The area of our map – from Wilmington on the north through Baltimore and Washington to Richmond on the south, a strip 100 miles or more wide between the ocean and mountains – has high summer temperatures (30 to 40 or more days go to 90°F or higher each year), high humidity, and rainfall up to 40 to 50 inches annually, broken sporadically by drought. In spring and fall the weather is strikingly changeable. (Average freeze dates are shown on the chart inside the back cover.)

This is an area rich in horticultural variety. Nearly every garden has its private micro-climate with special quirks for the gardener. Here one is aware of the fact that gardening is an art to be practiced with as much knowledge, understanding, sensitivity and skill as the gardener can muster.

Contributing Authors

Successful Gardening in the Greater Washington Area, Editor of *The Saturday Leaning Post*, and a former President of the Men's Garden Club. He worked on newspapers and radio in the midwest before joining the original CBS News staff in New York and later spent 25 years as Washington and White House correspondent for ABC. He is a Master Gardener.

Robert Alde is a Consulting Rosarian for the American Rose Society and past President of the Potomac Rose Society, a member of the Men's Garden Club, and a Master Gardener. He is a retired electronics engineer for the National Security Agency.

Henry E. Allen, a retired U. S. Foreign Affairs officer, grew up in Montgomery County. Gardening has been a lifelong hobby. In addition to vegetables – *Washingtonian* magazine called him "Mr. Vegetable of Washington" – he has a wide range of gardening expertise. He is a former President of the Men's Garden Club and a Master Gardener.

Allan E. Baker is a past President of the Men's Garden Club and a Master Gardener. He had a long career with the U. S. Information Agency. At retirement he was chief of Near East and South Asia language broadcasts for the Voice of America.

Edward A. Behr is retired after a career as a newspaperman in New York and Washington; he was with *The Wall Street Journal* in Washington for many years. He is a member of the Men's Garden Club.

Els Benjamin has been a horticulturist at Brookside Gardens since 1975 and the Director since 1979.

Henry Marc Cathey, Ph.D., is Director of the U. S. National Arboretum. Before his appointment in 1981, he was in charge of florist and nursery crops at the USDA experiment station in Beltsville for 25 years. He is a former President of the American Horticultural Society.

George Coffee, D.V.M., died as this book was going into print. He had been retired from the District of Columbia government. He and his wife had spent 40 years developing their plantings of daylilies, companion annuals and perennials, hollies and vegetables at Ashton, Maryland.

John Edwards is Publication Chairman of

Jacob B. Engle is a former President of the Potomac Valley Chapter of the American Rhododendron Society and a former President of the Men's Garden Club. A retired editor in the Washington Bureau of the Associated Press, he has gardened in the area for 60 years.

Stanton Gill was a member of the University of Maryland team that pioneered the Integrated Pest Management program. He was Extension Agent/Urban Horticulture in Montgomery County for 11 years and now holds a new position as Area Specialist for commercial nurseries, greenhouse operations and commercial landscape operations, headquartered in Clarksville, Maryland.

Anthony R. Gould, a retired Vice President of *U. S. News and World Report,* has been the sparkplug of the Men's Garden Club. He was one of its founders in 1946, its President in 1950, founder of *The Saturday Leaning Post* in 1958 and its editor for 25 years, and Editorial Chairman in 1969 of the first *Successful Gardening in the Greater Washington Area.*

Carl R. Hahn is chief of the natural resources division at the Maryland National Capital Park and Planning Commission. He is a former Director of Brookside Gardens and garden writer for the *Washington Evening Star.*

Lynn M. F. Harriss is a Fellow of the American Society of Landscape Architects. He has been a practicing landscape architect in California and has served as landscape architect for the National Park Service and the Department of Housing and Urban Development in Washington and elsewhere. He is a former President of the Men's Garden Club and a Master Gardener.

Rick Heflebower was an Extension Agent/Urban Horticulture in Montgomery County for several years and is now Extension Agent/Horticulture at the Hagerstown office in Washington County.

William M. Hoffman, now deceased, had a long and distinguished career with USDA and EPA for research in pesticides and fertilizers.

He was a pesticide extension agent for the University of the District of Columbia. He was a President of the Potomac Rose Society and the Takoma Horticultural Society.

Wallace F. Janssen has had a lifetime career as a writer and editor. He is a former Director of Public Information and now Historian for the Food and Drug Administration. He is a former President of the Men's Garden Club.

Roland M. Jefferson for many years was a botanist with the U. S. National Arboretum. Now retired, he lives in Seattle, Washington.

Frederick Jochem, a retired art historian and USIA public affairs officer, became a gardener when he moved into a new house in the McLean, Virginia area. What taught him the most and fastest, he says, was "the hilly, unplanted lot and the Men's Garden Club." He is a former President of the Club.

Diane Lewis is a native Washingtonian and a gardener and wildflower enthusiast since childhood. She is a photographer and a landscape design critic.

Conrad B. Link, Ph.D., now retired, was a Professor of Horticulture at the University of Maryland for many years. Before coming to Maryland in 1946 he was a horticulturist at the Brooklyn Botanic Garden.

Pamela Marshall is an Extension Agent with the University of the District of Columbia. She is an instructor at George Washington University and a frequent host on WGTS-FM.

Robert S. Melville, Ph.D., is a biochemist whose career has included posts with the Food and Drug Administration, National Bureau of Standards, and Veterans Administration. He is a former President of the Men's Garden Club and a Master Gardener.

Erik Neumann is head of education and public services at the U. S. National Arboretum. He was formerly with the New York Botanic Garden.

George Ring, a rhododendron grower and hybridizer, is a former President of the American Rhododendron Society and of the Potomac Valley Chapter. He is a civil engineer with the transportation research board of the National Academy of Sciences.

Frederick John Rosenthal is a Consulting Rosarian for the American Rose Society, a past President of the Potomac Rose Society and member of the Men's Garden Club. Now retired from the staff of the Library of Congress, he lives in Asheville, North Carolina.

John G. Shaffer became a landscape architect after retiring from the Central Intelligence Agency. His garden in Potomac was cited in 1986 for having "the best garden design by its owner" by *Garden Design*, the quarterly of the American Society of Landscape Architects. He is a former Editor of *The Azalean*, the newsletter of the Azalea Society of America, and a former President of the Men's Garden Club.

Holly Harmar Shimizu is public programs specialist at the U.S. Botanic Garden. Formerly with the National Arboretum, she was the first curator there of the National Herb Garden.

Emerson P. Slacum is a retired public school principal in Montgomery County. A winner of many awards for his chrysanthemums at shows of the Potomac Chrysanthemum Society, he is a former President of the Men's Garden Club.

Edward L. Stock, Jr., after earning a degree in horticulture at Cornell University, has spent more than a half-century in nursery and landscape contracting and maintenance in the Washington area. He is one of the founders of the Men's Garden Club.

Charles A. H. Thomson, Editorial Chairman for *Successful Gardening in the Greater Washington Area*, a post he also held for the 1975 edition, died during a trip to India in early 1989, a few hours before a scheduled visit to the Taj Mahal and its gardens. Col. Thomson, a retired political scientist, had been a Washington area lecturer, teacher, writer and radio co-host dealing with gardening since 1942 with time out for a nine-year stint in California and visits to world gardens "to give him perspective." He was an early President of the Men's Garden Club in 1951.

Thomas R. Turner, Ph.D., is an Associate Professor of Agronomy at the University of Maryland. He has been dealing professionally with turf grasses and turf management for nearly 20 years.

Michael J. Zajik, once a high school English teacher, has practiced in landscaping and horticulture in the area since 1972. He is now landscape supervisor at Brookside Gardens.

Dedication

Joe is the mascot of the Men's Garden Club of Montgomery County. He is the woebegone little man on the title page of this book. His usual home is the masthead of our newsletter, *The Saturday Leaning Post.*

The little man

It is said of Joe that his doleful look comes from the burdens he shares with all of our members. When he sows grass seed the birds hold a convention. The Japanese beetles feed on his roses. He has the most crabgrass and it all goes to seed. The moles use his lawn as if they were tunneling a new terminus for Metro. In winter his garden is the coldest and in the summer the driest.

Joe did not spring into life at once. Like Topsy he "growed." He is the brain child of Founding Member Anthony R. Gould, who also founded *The Saturday Leaning Post* and was its editor for 25 years. The first issue in June 1958 was a page of garden notes on a Club letterhead. By the second issue in July the newsletter had acquired its name and a masthead depicting a little man with a hoe – a "leaning post." He appeared each month thereafter for nearly five years. Then a new masthead and a new image of the little man were introduced in May 1963 with this note from Editor Gould: "The little man at the top of the page is such a faithful worker for the Garden Club he should have a name. Let's call him 'Joe'."

Joe's opinions and observations began to appear from time to time. In October 1964 the first of the "Joe says" comments was printed: "Joe says that work fascinates him; he could watch it all day." Since then *The Saturday Leaning Post* has been brightened regularly with the sayings of Joe.

This was a favorite one years ago: "Joe says that if you are resting on your laurels you are wearing them in the wrong place." A typical one about gardening: "Joe says that you can't live off your garden without living in it."

Joe: since 1963

Our last edition in 1975 of *Successful Gardening in the Greater Washington Area* was dedicated to Tony Gould – he's Andy to many old-timers. For this new edition we honor Tony's friend. This book is dedicated to Joe.

John Edwards

John Edwards
Publication Chairman

The Rembrandt Peale portrait, "Rubens Peale With a Geranium," has been described as celebrating "the science of horticulture as much as the art of portraiture."

The National Gallery of Art paid $4,070,000 for it in December 1985 – a record auction price for an American painting – using private funds from a new Patrons' Permanent Fund. The Gallery has called the 28¼-by-24-inch portrait "one of the most important, and most movingly beautiful, American paintings."

It was painted in 1801 when Rembrandt Peale was 23 and his younger brother, Rubens, only 17. Rubens already had a reputation as a botanist and, according to tradition, cultivated the first geranium in America. Rembrandt and Rubens and their brother Raphaelle, also a painter, were sons of Charles Willson Peale, the 18th century artist-patriot famous for his many portraits of George Washington.

Foreword

This book is for all gardeners in the Greater Washington area, but chiefly for beginners: those beginning to garden, and those who have gardened elsewhere but are beginning to garden in our area. Its purpose is to give good advice about what grows best here and how best to grow and to use plants in the special climate and soils of our area. We also want it to be helpful to experienced gardeners.

This book is the fifth in a series. The first, mimeographed and of only 83 letter-sized pages, appeared in 1948. It concentrated on ornamentals. The second appeared in 1955, with 98 pages, still dealing with ornamentals and making no mention of vegetables. The third appeared in 1969 with 128 pages. Vegetables appeared for the first time. The fourth was published in 1975 with 176 pages. Vegetables got a big play.

Reading these books shows permanence and change – permanence in much of the basic cultural instructions; change in varieties, estimates of hardiness, and in cultural practices.

This book embodies more change. Camellias, for instance, described in 1975 as "the easiest of shrubs" we now know to be of doubtful hardiness here after the devastating winters of the late 1970s. We also know that breeding at the National Arboretum has given us and will give us more dependably hardy shrubs with good flowers. There has been great change in available varieties of many plants and in cultural materials and practices, notably in varieties of grasses, vegetables and ornamentals, and of fertilizers. Even more notable is the revolution in methods and materials for controlling pests embodied in Integrated Pest Management.

While several of our authors are not members of our club, they all bring special expertise. There are four women among them. All of our authors base their views on substantial local experience.

Recognizing past change, this book features information about Where To Go For More – especially to plant societies, extension services, arboreta, and horticultural communicators, as well as the best references. Assiduous use of these resources will help gardeners here to keep up with the changes certain to come.

Our purpose, however, remains the same: to give the best advice to Greater Washington gardeners about successful gardening in our richly endowed but sometimes tricky area.

Charles A. H. Thomson

Charles A. H. Thomson
Editorial Chairman

ix

Down to Earth with the Home Gardener

By John Edwards

George Washington, an early home gardener in this area, had a favorite garden book. It was Batty Langley's *New Principles of Gardening*, which he ordered from London when he was 27 and newly married to Martha. The book had been a major influence in changing English tastes from formal to natural gardens. It became a major influence at Mount Vernon.

As a home gardener today you have a valuable guide in *Successful Gardening in the Greater Washington Area*. It is unique because it deals with the special characteristics of gardening in this area. We hope it will become one of your favorite garden books and a major influence in your gardening.

This book, as Charles Thomson states in the foreword, is for all gardeners but is aimed at the beginner – the serious beginner. The advice given by our authors is good advice based on years of experience here. As you gain in your own experience, as you profit from successes and failures, you will begin to rely more on your own judgment and good sense.

First in importance to most home gardeners is their lawn. This advice is basic: Try to mow it regularly. Mow it high – two and a half to three inches from early summer into fall. Keep your mower blades sharp. If you seed, from scratch or to patch up what you have, the best time

PHOTO COURTESY OF PAUL A. ZAHL

◀ **Come spring and the enthusiasm of the home gardener runs high. There is much to do. But many serious gardeners favor fall over spring as the time to plant certain trees and shrubs. And turf experts say that in this area the time to reseed or rehabilitate a lawn is late August through September, and the time to fertilize is fall.**

is late summer. When you fertilize, do it in the fall. When you water, deep soaking is essential. Avoid light sprinkling. Hopefully, as a serious gardener, you will learn early that one of the causes of failure in gardening is a lack of good watering practices.

About the Lawn-Care Services

Raising a good lawn in this area can be difficult even for an expert. It is no surprise that some homeowners turn to a lawn-care company. This is a subject that is highly-charged and controversial and there is nothing elsewhere in this book about it. So let's get "down to earth" with it here.

A fact to begin with: There are "responsible" and "irresponsible" lawn-care companies. They are highly competitive, big ones and small ones alike, offering many different services in many different ways. Collectively they represent a multi-million-dollar business, adept at high-pressure promotion and advertising.

The complaints against them cite heavy fertilizing in spring in disregard of good cultural practices – ("The customer wants a green lawn, we give it to him") – a frequent misuse of herbicides, and billing practices that sometimes border on trickery. The "responsibles" emphasize that there is a legitimate need and demand for their services, and claim their image is being tarred by the sins of the "irresponsibles."

How to Pick a Lawn Service

If you want a lawn company, ask around for a recommendation. Get estimates from several; the cheapest offer is not necessarily the best. If possible,

1

know in advance exactly what you want, and don't be talked into "add-ons" you don't want. Make sure the company is licensed. Check its complaint record. If you are uncertain about the type and timing, especially the timing, of their chemical applications, check with your Cooperative Extension Service. Finally, be sure of the terms of your contract.

The Council of Better Business Bureaus, a national headquarters in Arlington for about 200 local bureaus, has published for local use a leaflet on "Lawn Care and Lawn Care Services." Not all the lawn-care tips apply to this area but the tips on services are excellent. You can get a copy here from the Better Business Bureau of Metropolitan Washington. Advice also is available from consumer offices. In Montgomery County the Office of Consumer Affairs has a good leaflet on lawn services.

A final tip: If you are physically able to do the work yourself, you can save a lot of money.

Something New in Pest Control

There is no doubt that too many homeowners use chemicals improperly. As a beginning gardener, you should learn immediately about the exciting new concept called Integrated Pest Management (IPM). The University of Maryland was among the leaders in its development. You will find it discussed by Stan Gill ("Pest Control in Your Landscape") and Henry Allen ("Vegetables in the Home Garden").

IPM recognizes that no garden pest can be eradicated entirely and that trying to do so can upset an ecological balance. So the goal is to control pests at a level where they cause minimal damage. This means a reduced use of chemicals. The ones you use must be target-specific and applied when the pest is most vulnerable.

Planning and Planting the Garden

The Washington area is a great place to garden. It is host to a rich diversity of native plants and plants introduced from around the world. As a beginning gardener you are urged to start with the "safe" ones with a record of doing well here, and wait until later to experiment with the plants considered chancy.

In planning your garden, it's a good idea to work from a plan on paper but one in your mind will do. Before you ever set a tree or shrub or other plant in the ground, visualize what it will look like as it grows and reaches full growth, and what it will look like in relation to other plants and to such elements as your house or a walk or a fence. Buy good nursery stock and buy from a reputable supplier. If you want an "instant" garden, you'll have to pay dearly for it. It's better to plant smaller and therefore less expensive plants and have the pleasure of watching them grow. Plant properly. Another fact you'll learn soon enough is that a major cause of failure in the garden is improper planting. You will read the admonition in this book to plant high. How high is high? Common sense will tell you in each case. You might note that the entire azalea collections at Brookside Gardens were planted above ground and then heavily mulched.

Don't Worry About Jargon

Beginning gardeners sometimes complain that too many experts use too many terms that are not familiar. That's often true. Don't let it intimidate you. You'll pick up these gardening terms and botanical names as you need them. Make friends with them. They bring order into gardening.

A note about the botanical names in this book: Styles listing them differ. For consistency we have followed *Hortus III*. This dictionary of cultivated plants in the United States and Canada is the product of a continuing study in horticultural nomenclature at Cornell University.

And a last word: There is an allure to gardening some of us feel and it helps to keep us young. Everything in gardening is a beginning; even an ending opens the way to a new beginning. Every seed you plant or seedling you put in the ground is a beginning. It's a beginning when you dig a furrow, trim a hedge, divide a clump of daffodils, or rake up leaves for compost in the fall. It's a beginning when you use this book as a valuable guide. Enjoy it!

The home gardener wants low-maintenance plantings for himself but admires the gardens of others that demand a lot of work. This gem in the late Beatrix Farrand's plan for Dumbarton Oaks in Washington is an ellipse with an airy pleached hedge, not a common sight in the United States because of the maintenance required. It is formed by 68 American hornbeam or ironwood trees *(Carpinus caroliniana)*, pleached above 10 feet. The upkeep calls for three gardeners working five days, twice a year. The guide books seldom note that Dumbarton Oaks' 12 acres of formal gardens are the work of one of America's foremost landscape architects. If your out-of-town guests are gardeners, here is a choice sightseeing attraction.

Words of Warning

Many gardeners from other parts of the country may be distressed to find that plants that did well "back home" do not do well here. Other plants call for a special selection of varieties and careful placement. Comments:

Bamboo (Common and Sacred): Spreads, moving underground.

Begonias (tuberous): Need cool place, overhead light, coddling – and luck.

Bermuda Grass (Common): Spreads underground.

Black Walnut: Large and messy. Roots deadly to rhododendrons, tomatoes and others.

Delphiniums: Rarely good, die quickly. Treat as biennials, provide sweet soil and sharp drainage.

Gingkos: Fruits of female are messy and malodorous.

Japanese Honeysuckle: A vicious, invasive vine here. Puts down roots at every node.

Lilacs: Only fair. Mildew. Need full sun and good air circulation. Korean cultivars are best here.

Lombardy Poplars: Short-lived. Invasive roots love sewer pipes and will go far to find and foul them.

Lupines: Very difficult. Not the lush plant of New England.

Peonies: Very beautiful, very chancy. Many herbaceous varieties don't bloom well here. Blooming season short at best. Diseases mar summer foliage.

Sweet Gums: Messy, prickly profusion of seed balls.

Sweet Peas: It gets hot too early here. Vines and flowers burn up.

West Coast Natives: In general, plants native to Japan and China do better here than natives of our own west coast.

Willows: Vigorous roots invade sewers, out-compete nearby plants.

Violets: Invade new territory by sneaky seed-popping.

Soils - Fertilizers - Mulches - Compost

By Conrad B. Link, Ph.D.

Soil consists of mineral particles: "decayed" or broken down rock, organic matter, enormous quantities of micro-organisms and water. Soils vary widely in their mineral and nutrient composition and in the sizes of their particles. A soil that has been cultivated changes gradually – when it has been fertilized, had additions of organic matter and had plants growing in it. If this is to be done properly, the soil improves constantly for the growing of plants.

SOILS

Soil Texture and Structure

The physical characteristics of soil are referred to as texture and structure. Texture reflects the percentage of each of the major soil particle sizes, from largest to smallest: sand, silt, or clay in a soil. Soil types range from a sandy loam with the highest percentage of sand and lesser amounts of silt and clay to a loam, a silt loam, a clay loam and a clay soil which has the highest percentage of clay particles. To the gardener, soil texture is important since it influences the aeration, moisture supply and mineral materials that may be available to the plant.

Soils with the highest percentage of clay particles are referred to as a heavy soil. It is one that holds moisture tenaciously, sticks together when wet, and on drying often develops large cracks. To prevent heavy clods from forming, it must be cultivated or tilled when not excessively wet. The lighter textured soils are the sandy loams or loam soils. They are more loose and friable, they fall apart when spaded or cultivated. To change the soil texture it is necessary to add liberal quantities of sand to a heavier soil or to add clay to a lighter textured soil.

Structure refers to the arrangement of the soil particles into small clumps or "crumbs." A soil that has produced a crop of grass for many years is likely to have a good structure since millions of tiny roots have broken up the soil mass and provided conditions so it will form clumps. A clay soil that is cultivated or spaded when wet will have this structure destroyed so that it becomes "puddled:" that is, the clay particles are broken apart so they act as tiny individuals rather than forming "crumbs." Good gardening practices will improve the structure through cultivation, the addition of organic matter and perhaps the addition of lime as indicated by a soil test.

Soil Air and Drainage

A plant root requires air in the soil in order to grow. Good aeration is found when the soil is well drained and by making certain that water does not stand for a long time after a rain. Some plants will tolerate a poorly drained soil, but the majority of garden plants will not. If a plant root is in a poorly drained soil too long it stops growing, the intake of water and nutrients is slowed down; it may be attacked by decay organisms, foliage may become yellow green and growth is stunted. You may observe this in a lawn or a field where the growth of the plants is shorter in and nearest the poorly drained spots or in a house plant that is over-watered and its leaves drop. It is important to maintain good soil aeration.

Soil Reaction

The soil reaction or pH is important since it influences the availability of the soil mineral nutrients. Plants may vary in their tolerance of soil acidity, but most kinds will grow in a wide range of acidities as long as the necessary nutrients are present. A few kinds grow best in a certain soil-reaction range but this is probably due to their greater demand for certain minerals that are available in this acidity range.

Soils are classified as acid, neutral or alkaline. When a test is made, the results are reported by the letters pH (potential of hydrogen) and then a number. The symbol pH 7 is the neutral point. The numbers smaller than 7 being acid soils and those above 7, alkaline. For practical purposes, soils are identified as follows:

Extremely acid	less than 4.5 pH
Very strongly acid	4.5 - 5.0
Strongly acid	5.1 - 5.5
Medium acid	5.6 - 6.0
Slightly acid	6.1 - 6.5
Very slightly acid	6.6 - 6.9
Neutral	7.0
Very mildly alkaline	7.1 - 7.5
Mildly alkaline	7.6 - 8.0
Moderately alkaline	8.1 - 8.5

In general, the elements from the soil that are required for growth are all available in the pH range 5.0 to 7.5. They may be in greater abundance at a higher or lower pH but in this medium range they are at least available in adequate amounts. This probably is the reason why most plants grow well in this acidity range. Plants requiring more acid soil conditions or more alkaline conditions have a greater need for certain elements that are more available in these more extreme pH ranges. For example, iron becomes more available in increasingly acid soil. Plants such as azaleas, pieris and blueberries – acid loving plants – grow best in medium soils which may be due to the greater availability of iron. In very acid soils many elements become less available or some such as aluminum become available in quantities which make them toxic to plant growth.

When it is desirable to make the soil more acid, finely powdered sulfur or aluminum sulfate is used. Table 1 will serve as a guide in the use of these materials.

One pound of sulfur will lower the pH about as much as six pounds of aluminum sulfate. Do not use more than one pound of finely-powdered sulfur per 100 square feet at a time. If more is needed, allow eight to 10 weeks between applications. This should be based on a soil test.

When Lime is Added

When it is desirable to make the soil less acid, then finely ground limestone or hydrated lime is used. If the soil test also indicates that magnesium is low, then use dolomite limestone which contains magnesium as well as calcium. (See Table 2).

Lime should be applied to the soil when it is prepared for planting, and spaded in thoroughly as should be done when materials are used to lower the acidity. If such applications are necessary on established plants, then the material is applied to the surface of the soil and watered in. If the plants do not have extensive roots near the soil surface, then a light cultivation may be made. The acidity may be maintained in the soil by adding organic matter and by using a mulch. This is not difficult in the greater Washington area since the soil is naturally acid. Gypsum – calcium sulfate – is used in garden soil as a soil conditioner to loosen heavier soils, but has little or no effect on lighter tex-

Table 1. Number of Pounds of Aluminum Sulfate to Apply to 100 Square Feet to Lower Soil Acidity (Loam and Silty Loam)

Present pH	Desired pH	
	to pH 4.5	to pH 5.5
5.5	3	none
6.5	6	3
7.5	10	6

Table 2. Number of Pounds of Ground Limestone to 100 Square Feet of Area to Raise the Soil pH

Present pH	Desired pH			
	On a sandy loam		On a silty loam	
	to pH 6.0	to pH 6.5	to pH 6.0	to pH 6.5
6.0	none	2.0	none	4.0
5.5	2.0	4.0	4.0	7.0
5.0	4.0	6.0	7.0	11.0

tured soil. It supplies calcium to the soil without influencing the soil acidity. A safe rate of application is one to three pounds per 100 square feet.

Organic Matter

Organic matter is an essential part of good soil. It helps to improve the soil structure, as it is mixed in, by providing weak areas between the soil particles. It loosens the soil, increases its water-holding capacity and aids drainage. As organic matter decomposes it releases nitrogen and other elements into the soil and the decomposition organisms acting upon it release certain acids that make other soil minerals available. In this way the organic matter furnishes the food materials for the micro-organisms. However, the greatest value of organic matter to soil is that it improves the soil structure, influencing its physical properties. Its value as a source of nutrients or as a fertilizer is a secondary value.

Organic matter as used in relation to soil refers to organic matter of plant or animal origin. The kinds commonly available include fresh or partially decomposed leaves, grass clippings, plant refuse, straw, animal manures and peat. Fresh succulent materials such as grass or other plant materials when added to the soil decompose rapidly whereas matured plant refuse, such as leaves or straw, rot more slowly. Animal manures and the accompanying litter decompose rather rapidly when incorporated into the soil.

In adding organic matter to the soil as it is prepared for planting, use a kind that is partially decomposed rather than fresh. If fresh material is used, then add some fertilizer along with it to aid in the decomposition. When fresh organic matter is added to the soil there is a rapid increase in the rate of decay and the decomposition organisms draw on the supply of soil nutrients. With this large demand, there may be a temporary loss of these to the plants and hence a need for the fertilizer. As decay continues and these organisms die, the mineral nutrients are released back into the soil.

FERTILIZERS

Fertilizers are materials added to the soil to supply the plant with available mineral elements for growth. They supply or supplement those minerals already available in the soil. There are two general kinds of commercial fertilizers based on their origin: (1) organic fertilizers derived from natural sources, either plant or animal, and (2) inorganic fertilizers, often called chemical fertilizers, that are mined and processed or manufactured.

Fertilizers of organic origin may supply one or more nutrients to the soil. They are slowly available since they first must be decomposed and because of this are not likely to cause any injury if used in excess. The inorganic or chemical fertilizers are generally more concentrated depending on their degree of refinement. They may be of a water-soluble form so that they are available almost as soon as they become dissolved in the soil water. A newer technique is to process these fertilizers into forms that are slow acting and become available over a long period of time.

For a fertilizer to be of use to the plant, it must be broken down, get into the soil water and in this way become available to the plant roots. The origin of the nutrient, whether organic or inorganic, makes no difference to the plant in its absorption.

"Complete" Fertilizers

Some fertilizers are sold that supply only one of the nutrient minerals. Others are "complete" fertilizers, a mixture of materials that, together, supply nitrogen, phosphorus and potassium, the three most commonly lacking soil nutrients.

When you buy a bag of fertilizer the analysis of the contents is given on the bag or on an attached label. For example, an analysis such as 5-10-5 indicates the presence and ratio of the available materials. The first figure indicates the amount of nitrogen; the second the amount of phosphorus as phosphoric acid (P_2O_5); and the third the amount of potassium (K_2O). These figures also indicate the amount of pure minerals thus: 5-10-5 means that in a 100-pound bag there are five pounds of available nitrogen, 10 pounds of available phosphorus, and five pounds of available potassium.

Other materials may be present in a complete fertilizer which supply the minor or trace elements, the ones needed for normal growth but required in very low amounts. An example of a single fertilizer is one that supplies only one nutrient, such as superphosphate that supplies only phosphorus, or ammonium sulfate or nitrate of soda that supply only nitrogen.

Any mineral materials that are claimed as a fertilizer must be indicated on the bag or label as to the amount present.

Fertilizer Sources

Some of the common sources of nitrogen are ammonium nitrate (32% to 33%), ammonium sulfate (20.5%), sodium nitrate (16%), ureaform (38%), and urea (45%). Phosphorus is supplied primarily as superphosphate (18% to 48% phosphorus) and potassium is supplied as sulfate of potash (48% to 52%). A few ferti-

lizers may contain two or more nutrients such as diammonium phosphate (21% nitrogen and 52% phosphoric acid) or potassium nitrate (13% nitrogen and 44% potassium). Some organic fertilizers which vary in their composition include dried blood (12% nitrogen and 2% phosphoric acid), cottonseed meal (6% nitrogen, 3% phosphoric acid and 2% potassium), and raw bone meal (4% nitrogen and 22% phosphoric acid). Most bone meal commonly available today is steamed. It is finer in structure than raw bone meal and tests only 0-11-0. It takes months for it to become available to plants. Raw bone meal takes even longer.

Minor or trace or micro-elements include those nutrients needed by plants in very small amounts. They are found in most soils but occasionally are unavailable. They include iron, copper, zinc, boron, magnesium and manganese. Many fertilizers carry them as natural impurities of the materials used. Some trade-name fertilizers may have them added specifically in which case they will be identified on the label. Trace elements also may be purchased as a separate material or in mixtures. As a general rule, additions of trace elements are not needed in garden soils that have been fertilized regularly and had organic materials added. Use them when a soil test indicates they are needed. Excess use, especially of boron, may become toxic to plant growth.

How to Use Fertilizers

Dry fertilizers, to be most effective, should be incorporated into the soil. Broadcast the fertilizer uniformly and spade or cultivate it into the upper four to six inches when the soil is being prepared for planting. On established plants, the fertilizer is broadcast around the plant and cultivated in, being careful not to go so deep as to damage the roots. Plants growing in rows may have the fertilizer applied in a band or strip alongside the row and cultivated in. At the time of sowing seed in rows, a band of fertilizer may be made two or three inches to one or both sides of the row and at the same or approximate depth at which the seed is sown. This is a common method in the commercial planting of row crops.

Completely water-soluble fertilizers have become a useful way of fertilizing in the intensive conditions of a garden. They are usually complete fertilizers such as 10-10-10, 20-20-20, or 15-30-15, or some other special formulation. While they may be used in dry form and watered in, it is difficult to spread uniformly the small quantity required. The soluble fertilizers should be used in solution, and the directions followed. Small quantities may be dissolved in a sprinkling can and applied to the soil or a proportioning device – attached, say to a hose – can be used when larger quantities are required.

Certain soluble fertilizers may be used for spraying on the foliage – foliar fertilization. It is essential that the concentration and directions be carefully followed. The fertilizer is absorbed by the leaf. This method of fertilizing should be supplementary to that applied to the soil and used in a limited way to correct certain nutrient problems or to supplement a normal soil application where a rapid boost in growth is wanted. This may be a way of correcting some of the minor element deficiencies, but is effective often only on those leaves sprayed.

Soluble fertilizers also are used as a "starter fertilizer." They are added to the water used following planting or transplanting, especially of annuals. It insures that the roots have at least a little fertilizer as the new roots get started. One precaution: Follow the directions with the fertilizer, especially with the more concentrated kinds. If one pound is recommended, use that rate or less; two pounds may cause plant injury.

Slow or controlled-release fertilizers are one of the useful recent developments. They are designed to be a uniform product, formulated so nutrients become available to the plant within a certain period. Osmocote is a water-soluble fertilizer encapsulated into plastic resin pellets that in contact with moist soil gradually absorb water, and the fertilizer is released into the soil solution. The thickness of the coating determines the rate at which this fertilizer becomes available. Some forms are identified as three-to-four-month materials and others for longer periods. An advantage is that they are gradually releasing the fertilizer and there is long value to it. A disadvantage is that several weeks elapse before it becomes available. Also it must have a moderately moist soil to be effective. Cool or cold temperatures slow down the rate of release. At present they are somewhat expensive for general garden use and have found their greatest use for such specific purposes as plants indoors and in nursery container growing.

Another type of slow-release materials is products that are formulated to gradually dissolve. Magamp – magnesium ammonium phosphate is such a product – produced in a uniform size for easy and uniform distribution.

Urea-formaldehyde is a synthetic organic fertilizer that is a slow-release nitrogen source. Slow-release fertilizers may be added to the soil when a plant is planted without danger of any damage to the new roots.

MULCHES

Mulches in the garden perform many functions. They aid plant growth; they save labor; and when used sufficiently deep they retard or eliminate weed growth. Organic matter mulches will add organic matter to the soil as well as some mineral nutrients when they are completely decomposed. Mulches retard the rate of drying and conserve soil moisture. Mulches also may be important in giving the garden a finished, well-cared-for look.

Two major groups of materials are used for mulching, those of organic origin and those that are inorganic.

Organic Mulches

Historically, the commonly available organic mulches have been straw, fresh or partially decomposed leaves, and animal manures, together with the usual litter. Peat, of sphagnum or sedge origin, is recommended often as a mulch for garden purposes. But it should not be allowed to form a dry crust that prevents the passage of water into the soil. If too dry it becomes flammable. Peat is much more valuable in the soil than on it.

Residues from plants that have been thrashed or processed are sometimes available such as buckwheat, rice, peanut hulls, or ground corn cobs. In recent years chipped bark or wood have been available. Sugar cane after crushing is dried and sold as "bagasse." Even shredded paper or newspaper may be used with proper precautions. Use only the black-and-white print.

Mulches of organic origin should be partially decomposed so they do not compete with the plants for soil nutrients. This is the disadvantage of using freshly cut lawn clippings or newspaper as a mulch directly on the soil. If it is added to an already existing mulch then this may be less of a problem. Where an application of a fresh material is used, a light application of a complete fertilizer to the soil is made before the mulch is added to prevent this competition for available nutrients.

Inorganic Mulches

Inorganic mulches may be used for permanent year-round purposes, especially when a special effect is to be developed. These materials usually are small-sized gravel or crushed stone of certain sizes or colors. To be effective, the mulch should be at least two to three inches deep, depending on the texture of the materials. The use of such a mulch on top of black plastic will eliminate weed growth. These types of mulches may be used on woody trees or shrubs.

Black plastic film is used in the vegetable or cutting garden. If it is used where appearance is important it should be covered with another mulching material. In using these the gardener must be sure that adequate water supply gets to the plant roots.

Selecting a Mulch

When selecting a mulch, consider where it is to be used and its appearance. Consider the texture. It should be coarse enough so water will drain through without compacting the material, or com-

pressing or sticking together if it becomes dry. This tendency to crust over may occur on very fine peat, fine sawdust or lawn clippings as they wilt and dry. The addition of some coarser material will tend to prevent this. A light raking or stirring will break up such crusts. Coarse-textured bulky materials as corn stalks or garden refuse may be suitable for the vegetable garden but not in the landscaped area.

Very light-weight materials may blow or be washed around until they become moistened thoroughly and then stay in place.

Materials that decompose rapidly should have a light sprinkling of a fertilizer to the soil before being applied, especially if they have not been decomposed. This provides mineral nutrients to the decomposing microorganisms.

When to Apply a Mulch

Mulches may be applied at any season of the year. However, a permanent year-round mulch usually is applied in the spring after planting and additions made

Sand in Your Soil Mix

At a meeting of the Men's Garden Club, our speaker, an academic soil scientist, mentioned in passing that we never should add sand when preparing planting sites. Many sets of eyebrows took off to mid-forehead. Most of us have been telling hearers and readers that we should use sand – sharp, coarse builder's sand – to loosen up the clay. And we should add plenty of organic material so that our mix will have three parts of clay, two parts of compost, and one part of sand. The trick, we maintain – and our speaker's peers generally agree with us – is in the quantity of organic material. The caution is this: Organic material tends to disappear from our soil mixes and we should replenish it. The clay and sand will remain; the humus will pass away.

– **Charles A. H. Thomson**

PHOTO BY EDMUND C. FLYNN

Good gardeners do not overlook this valuable source of organic matter available to them at no cost beyond time and effort: leaves, spent plant material, grass clippings, pruning residues, and kitchen wastes. Proper recycling or "composting" can produce the equal of the finest animal manures. There are many ways of composting. This gardener built an eight-foot-high wire "compost pen" in a ravine at the back of his property. He uses what he calls the "trap door" to bring out decayed materials into the ravine for immediate use or further composting.

in a succeeding spring or fall.

Permanent mulches are useful on perennials and shrubs, especially on shallow-rooted rhododendrons and pieris. Mulches on herbaceous perennials or bulbs should be loose-textured so the new growth will come through without becoming crooked. Coarse-textured bark or wood chips are not used on areas planted with bulbs for this reason.

Temporary or Summer Mulches

A summer mulch is especially useful on annual flowers and vegetables. Such mulch is applied after planting or when the plants are several inches high. After the growing season is over and when the soil is again prepared for the planting, the organic matter is incorporated into it. You have the benefit of the mulch in conserving water and controlling weeds and then soil improvement when incorporated into the soil.

A summer mulch is the gardener's way of reducing some garden labor during the summer. For such purposes, select materials that will be incorporated easily into the soil later.

Plastic film or aluminum foil may be a temporary summer mulch material, but since they do not decompose, they have to be removed and disposed of at the end of the growing season. They are not easy to salvage for another season's use. Black plastic mulches are commonly used for certain vegetables, melons and strawberries. Aluminum foil has been used to disorient moths that produce squash vine borers.

Mulches that are used for winter pro-

PHOTO BY EDMUND C. FLYNN

This gardener built a sturdy three-bin composter – each bin four by four by four feet – from plans in *Crockett's Victory Garden*. The late James Crockett called it his "brown gold Cadillac." Not all plant materials should be composted. Exceptions include leaves and stems of plants that may carry diseases over winter and infect plants the next spring. Do not compost tomatoes, peppers or plants of the cabbage family, or such plants as peonies, roses or hollyhocks, and do not compost grass clippings from a lawn that had a weed killer used on it.

tection are temporary, applied in late November or early December, and removed in early spring. These may be fresh undecomposed materials such as leaves or other coarse materials. Then, when removed, they should be added to the compost pile.

COMPOST

Compost refers to decomposed organic matter together with inorganic materials such as sand or soil. Compost is produced commercially from animal manures, peat and other organic materials and sold in bags. It often is mixed with soil and perhaps other materials to produce mixtures for specific horticultural uses such as for house plants, or by formula for young seedlings. For the gardener, a compost pile is an effective way of disposing of organic matter which later can be used in the garden.

To make compost, select an area in the garden where it is least obvious or conceal it with a fence or planting of evergreens or other woody plant material. With limited space, construct an enclosure in which the compost is placed. This may be made of wire fencing, cinder blocks, boards, or whatever your skill and materials may provide.

In the fall there is an abundance of organic materials available as leaves and the tops of plants after the frost has killed them. Such materials are spread in the enclosure six to 12 inches thick and then covered with an inch or more of soil. This compresses the material as well as providing an abundance of micro-organisms which will inoculate the material and hasten decomposition. A light sprinkling of a complete fertilizer is made over the soil. A 10-6-4 is good for this purpose; its function is to supply mineral nutrients for the decomposition process. Next add another layer of organic materials and soil and repeat until the pile is three to four feet high or a convenient height to work. Sprinkle each layer as it is added to moisten the materials and help start the decomposition process. When the materials are coarse and bulky, tramp each layer to make a more solid pile with good contact between the several parts. Pull the old annual plants and add both the tops as well as the roots with as much soil as will stay with the roots.

At other seasons, any fresh or dried materials may be added as they are available. Many times there is refuse from the kitchen which is excellent such as peelings, waste leaves from lettuce or cabbage, or other organic materials. Such materials will decompose rapidly. One precaution: Do not add disease or pest-infested plant parts; this material belongs in the trash. Adding it to a compost does not kill the organisms and they later may become available to infect other plants.

Turn the Compost Pile

To hasten decomposition and to have a uniform material as quickly as possible, the pile should be turned. This may be done as often as every four to six weeks. If left undisturbed, the pile rots more slowly, although the center of it may be ready to use in several months. If you have sufficient area, several piles may be made. After the first has been made, then start another as materials are available and perhaps a third. By the time the last is completed, the first may be ready to use.

In the process of decomposing, considerable heat will be generated which helps to destroy weed seed and disease organisms. This will be greatest in the center of the pile. There will be a lot of shrinkage and settling as the organic matter is broken down and the pile becomes more compact.

Some instructions for making compost include the addition of lime to the pile. This is not necessary for general garden use and would be undesirable if the compost is to be used on azaleas and rhododendrons or other plants requiring an acid soil.

Composted sewage sludge is becoming available to gardeners. This is excellent organic matter for gardens, especially if it comes from a sewage treatment that does not add excessive amounts of lime to the dewatered sludge in the processing. Sludge composted with wood chips and then screened when ready makes a uniform, odorless and safe material for gardens. With improved industrial treatments and the reduction or elimination of potentially injurious minerals and chemicals from the industrial waste, the composted sludge is safe to use, even in a vegetable garden.

Commercially available sludge from sources with a high incidence of unwanted chemicals may be used best on lawns and flower beds or around shrubs. Sewage sludge, unlike other composts, may contain low but significant amounts of nutrients.

Do's and Don'ts

DO bring in your green tomatoes in the fall. Wrap them in newspaper to ripen where it is dark and warm.

DON'T leave your row covers on vegetable crops that require pollination after the blossoms are set.

DON'T try to grow vegetables out of season like beans in spring and cabbage in summer. Time your crops to their requirements.

DON'T use a chemical pesticide until you know what pest you are dealing with and have exhausted all other remedies. Then use a target-specific and biodegradable control. Regular preventive applications are not good, except for controlling black spot on roses and for eliminating pests prior to planting in your vegetable garden. Do go for the pest when it is getting out of hand. Don't panic at the sight of a Japanese beetle.

Planning the Home Grounds

By Lynn M. F. Harriss

This is written with the beginning gardener in mind: perhaps a young couple who buy their first piece of residential property, and have high hopes of developing it with a minimum of mistakes, after-thoughts, back-tracking and doing over. But the principles apply to those who buy small tract-type houses or those who can acquire larger acreages in our pastoral hinterland.

Phase 1: Divide into Land-Use Areas

The first vital steps are to identify and partition the various areas of the property, use by use, before even the house is designed or located. Of course, we actually visualize the house in the back of our minds as we work on every step. It is easier to change things on paper than on the ground. There are many important things that influence the location and design of the house itself.

Entrance and Service Areas come first as they probably come nearest to the street. Get a sheet of plain paper, or a print of the lot if it's of a convenient scale – an inch equals 30 feet or thereabouts. Lay out the street at one edge. Indicate which way is north. Draw a rough oval near where you think your driveway will come. If yours is to be a compact house in town, the oval will be small, bearing in mind the expense of driveways and entrance walk, minimum setback requirements and the like. If it's a larger place you might envision a long, tree-bordered drive with a longer oval. Just bear in mind that everything has its cost and an exceedingly long driveway will involve a lot of expense, not only in the initial construction but in the maintenance with periodic patching, sealing and snow removal.

The **Service Area** is one of the most important and frequently omitted areas. It can serve as a storage area for extra lumber, equipment, bulk supplies such as sand, gravel and mulches, as well as a source of cut flowers for the house without denuding the formal garden. How big should it be? That depends on the uses for it you have in mind and how much space you can spare.

Outdoor Living Area will be directly adjacent to the future house and set aside for: (1) entertaining, (2) showing off flowers and flowering shrubs or trees, or (3) indulging in something more active such as swimming or badminton. Call this Patio Garden, Terrace or just plain Garden. Bear in mind that this and the entrance area will be the most intensively maintained of any in the place. So be cautious about getting it too big. For now just draw an oval next to where the house might be.

Other Areas may be as many as you have room for: a vegetable garden, a rose garden, a place for dogs, an herb garden. They can be written in with ovals or not as you wish. They may be of lower priority and may have to wait any actual construction.

Phase 2: Lay Out and Locate House

Now get a sheet of coordinate paper, perhaps on which a design can be placed at a scale of a quarter-inch equalling one foot. Even if you eventually want to hire an architect, it is worthwhile to get your ideas down on paper first. The design and location of the house is best done at the same time as the design of the grounds. The living areas of the house then can be arranged to relate with the Outdoor Living area, and the service portions of the

13

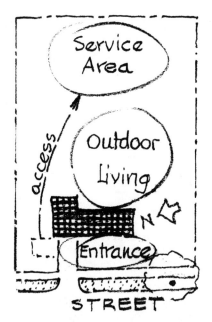

Figure 1. Preliminary land use study — city property.

house – kitchen, laundry, garage – can be linked up with the functional service of the grounds. There are no hard or fast rules about this. Much depends on your life-style.

Placing the kitchen near the front door might save a lot of steps answering the door to callers and deliverymen. But for a large house, the two might be separated, the entrance via a less-obvious route for guests, and deliveries made in another area. In this case the kitchen might be placed there, or equidistant. Or perhaps you hope to do a lot of barbecuing. Then you might want the kitchen to meet the patio at floor level. Or, with children in the family, the mother might want a kitchen to overlook a play area. Or perhaps, it should face the best view, for the enjoyment of the cook. If there is a "should-do" in all this, it would be to make the garage and entrance driveway have more-or-less direct access to the service area, so that bulk materials can be delivered easily.

Resist the temptation to set the house down right in the middle of the lot. Maybe that would be the best place for a terrace or a garden, and it might therefore make more sense to locate the house to one side, or nearer to the street. Don't be afraid to use several sheets of studies on the coordinate paper. You will come closer to your goal if you have several alternate layouts to choose from. Don't be afraid of funny-looking shapes. Sometimes they are the only way to get the relationships you want.

Phase 3: Planning the Garden

Now get some coordinate sheets, preferably of a size on which you can show your property at a scale of one-eighth inch equalling one foot. Set down your boundaries from the official plat, indicate the bordering street and show which way is north. This is important in orienting rooms of the house, trees and gardens toward exposure to sun. Some like it hot, some like it shady.

While this is written as if one step followed another in a logical sequence, there is no law that says you can't telescope some of the steps. You might have engaged an architect by this time, and/or a landscape architect, and made some studies of the house, its placement on the property, the entrance and service areas, as well as the all-important Outdoor Living Area. But if you have a house plan reasonably to your liking, show it on the Landscape Plan lightly in pencil, and see how that fits the Outdoor Living or Terrace Area. Is the area big enough for the type of entertaining you do? Remember to keep it as small as will fill the bill. You don't have to extend it to the lot line. You can use a boundary fence or wall inside the lot boundary, and plant flowering trees between the two to be seen from the garden. You might even want to provide for service access (viz. by wheelbarrow) along the same strip. Just remember that the Outdoor Living Area will be the most intensively maintained area in the place, so don't make it so large that it will become burdensome.

The **Service Area** is a must, even on the smallest lot. From your earlier sketches, lay it out so as to be convenient to the driveway and garage, but not conspicuous from either the street or from the house. Remember that it can be combined with a dog-run (see Figure 6) or with vegetable and cutflower gardens (see Figure 3) and such.

The **Entrance** can be simple, but also imaginative. Guests can come to the front door through a grape arbor or a forecourt garden. There might be restrictions imposed either by your city or county jurisdiction, or in a neighborhood association, so better check with them first. In any case, avoid unnecessary "wiggles" in the entrance walk. The same goes for the driveway. The most direct access is best. Under some circumstances you may want to provide some off-street parking, perhaps with a circular drive. Just be sure to include curvatures that cars, even trucks, can easily negotiate, and that you get the necessary permits. Be sure to include an area for dumping and tempo-

rarily storing bulk materials such as sand, topsoil, wood chips or leafmold without impeding access to the garage. Of course, if you don't mind parking your car elsewhere for a time, there is no real reason outside of appearance why such materials cannot be dumped in the driveway itself. But if a small area of, say, 12 by 15 feet can be added to the driveway, to receive such deliveries, having at least wheelbarrow access to the Service Area, it can be mighty handy. Lay it out so that a truck can back into it, but hidden from most direct view from the street with a barrier or planting or both (see Figure 6). Don't say to yourself "I'll never have deliveries like that." *You will.*

Connecting Links and Boundaries. You will want to have easy access throughout the area. If the roof has an overhanging eave of three feet or more, a convenient place for a walk is right under

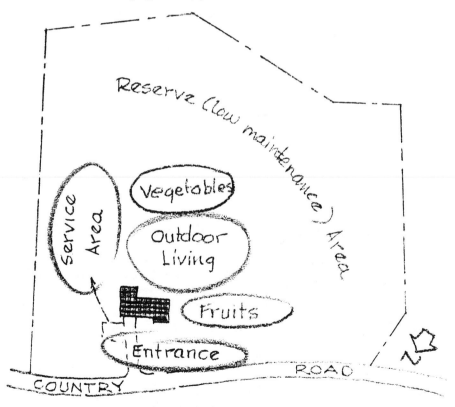

Figure 2. Preliminary land use study – country property.

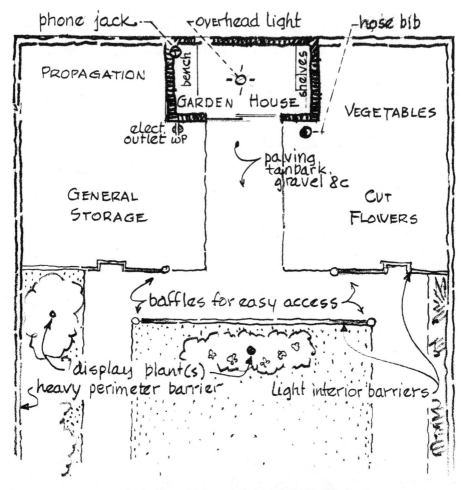

Figure 3. A service area and garden house.

this eave. For one thing, it keeps plants, which might otherwise be located against the house and under the same eaves, from drying out and perhaps dying. For another, it tends to keep the walks, and you, dry and free of ice. Foundation planting, you will find, is every bit as attractive when placed on the outside of this peripheral walk as when placed on the inside. For other walks, keep them as simple as possible. At first, they may be surfaced with wood chips or gravel. This will not only help your budget, but also allow for after-thoughts which require digging trenches across the path, such as

an additional water or electric line, a run of drain tile to dry out a marshy spot, or the like. After a time, when all things are working well and the ground settled, you can think about paving. Hard-burned brick (not soft common brick which tends to spall and wear unevenly), laid in your choice of a variety of patterns, is a good, permanent do-it-yourself material.

Steps. These sometimes necessary evils should be treated as the hazards they really are. Never – repeat never – introduce a single step in a walk unless going into a building. Instead, when steps are unavoidable, grade the area so as to group the steps in a flight of three or four or more at a conspicuous place, such as from one area into another. Build cheek and retaining walls on each side, and equip each side with a louvre light, plus at least one handrail. Flatten the areas of the walk at the top and bottom of the steps. If there is a likelihood that rainwater may flow from above down and over the steps, occasionally freezing, make a shallow reverse grade at the top landing, picking up the drainage in a strip drain, or conduct it aside if such can be done without causing erosion (Figure 7). Then plant small ground cover and accent plants on the adjacent slopes to highlight the fact that "Here is a flight of steps. Be careful."

Boundaries. You will have to be the judge whether or not to enclose the whole property with a fence or wall. In the average case, probably not. But enclosing the interior areas is something else again. They should be enclosed, and perhaps some of these enclosures can do double-duty by forming a barrier against adjacent properties or the street. Fences, or walls, or hedges, can be used. But stay away from clipped hedges if you want to conserve maintenance. And stay away from unclipped hedges if you want to conserve space. Walls cost quite a bit, so most of us use fences.

But why have a fence in the first place? There are several good reasons. In the first place, it will keep your neighbor's well-intentioned St. Bernard out, plus rabbits and deer. Secondly, it gives a sense of privacy while entertaining, sunbathing or swimming. If you do plan to have a pool, a strong fence is a must to protect yourself against lawsuits based on the principle of "attractive nuisance." Thirdly, the fence acts as an elegant background for your display plants: your azaleas, tulips, lilies, and also clematis and other showy vines. Fourthly, it acts as a "micro-climate buffer," tempering wintry winds or providing summer shade. Finally, there is the all-important aspect which is frequently overlooked: masking nearby clutter and focussing the eye on the more distant view (Figure 4), of trees, woods, hills, sky, clouds.

Figure 4. A fence enhances a distant view while displaying your choice plants (left) and concealing nearby clutter (right).

Figure 5. For terrace shade, try a seat-wall planter. The walls should be 15 to 17 inches high and should enclose the planting area which could be circular, rectangular, or any shape you choose. Waterproof inside of wall with bituminous paint. Provide weepholes for drainage.

Figure 7. When steps are unavoidable, dramatize them.

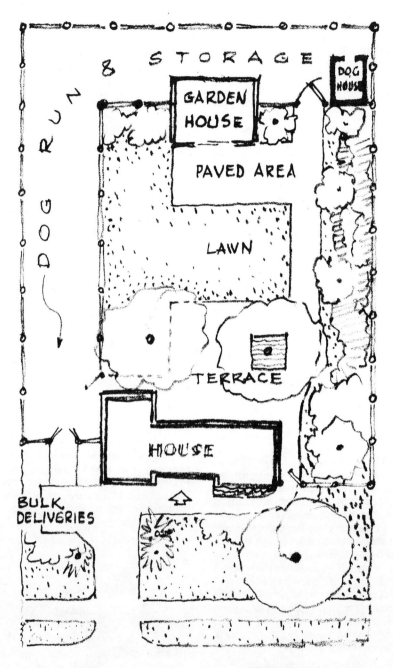

LINE DRAWINGS BY LYNN M. F. HARRISS

Figure 6. A storage area doubles for a run for the dog.

Placing Your Plants

By Edward L. Stock, Jr.

So you are going to landscape your new house grounds or redo an old one. The first thing you will need is a plan for the job.

Unless you already know about landscape architecture and design, read something about it, beginning with the article on "Planning the Home Grounds" in this book. If the job is too difficult, consult a landscape architect or a landscape designer from a landscape contractor organization. Whatever you do see that the placement of your trees and shrubs is going to accomplish what you want before you get a shovel in the ground.

Read the article in this book on "Shrubs and Trees for Your Garden." These growing elements, shrubs and trees, are what you need to accomplish your landscaping purposes. Walls, fences, pools and patios also come within the realm of the landscape architect.

Not all plants do well everywhere. Many have environmental constraints and this is especially important in the Washington metropolitan area – important because here we are able to grow both many southern and many northern plants. Camellias, magnolias, and crape myrtles may do well south and east of Washington or in protected mini-climates in Washington. They most likely will suffer severely north and west of Washington and in exposed places.

Environmental Constraints

Some plants require full light intensity to thrive and flower. They get this in full sun or the unshaded north side of a building, at least where the light intensity is sufficient. Other plants prefer some shade – that is, less light intensity – to thrive. We must remember, too, that when we place plants under trees, the trees will get first call on moisture and plant food in the soil. The underplantings will suffer unless we feed and water and mulch supplementally. In the woods decaying leaves from the trees furnish mulch and additional nourishment and so they will in your yard.

Next, there is the matter of subsoil drainage. Some plants will tolerate "wet feet." Some like it or even require it. Others must have perfect subsoil drainage. Know what your chosen plants require and see that they get it. For instance, many hollies, viburnums, willows and shrubby dogwoods like or will stand poor drainage but, curiously, hemlocks, yews, pieris and lilacs want their roots to be in well-drained soil. Incidentally, in judging drainage, remember that the side of a hill does not necessarily mean good subsoil drainage.

Finally, in this list of environmental constraints comes soil acidity or alkalinity, known as pH. Many plants do well in soils of varying acidity; others are very particular. For example, such plants as azaleas or rhododendrons prefer or even demand that the soil be acid but yews and lilacs prefer alkaline soil. That says: Do not plant azaleas and lilacs in the same place. Have your soil tested for its pH if you are uncertain.

Consider the Growth Rate

In choosing plants for your landscape plan don't forget the rate and habit of growth. Some plants are slow growing and will take a long time to do what you want them to do. A beech or a white oak takes much longer than a honey locust or tulip poplar to create any shade and an

COURTESY OF COOPERATIVE EXTENSION SERVICE

Ornamental trees and shrubs are expensive. To invest your money wisely, buy quality plants and plant them properly. They come in three forms: bare-root, balled and burlapped, and container grown.

Bare-root (left): Only small deciduous trees and shrubs can be transplanted successfully as bare-root – that is, without a ball of earth around the roots. They must be planted when they are dormant, in late fall, winter or early spring. The planting holes should be dug large enough to permit the roots to extend downward and spread in a normal manner without cramping.

Balled and burlapped (center): All ornamental trees and shrubs, regardless of size, can be transplanted throughout the year as balled and burlapped plants. The nylon cord fastening the burlap to the trunk must be untied to avoid any chance of the tree suffering suffocation. If the burlap is really burlap, you don't have to remove it all the way, but if it is a synthetic that won't rot, you should pull it away so the roots can penetrate easily into the surrounding soil.

Container grown (right): Plants grown in containers may be transplanted throughout the year. It is important to cut any roots that wind around the root ball. Then score the sides of the ball with a sharp knife or spade, and cut an X across the bottom and through the lower third of the ball. The practice in recent years of butterflying the roots is no longer recommended.

English boxwood takes far longer than a globe arborvitae to become effective.

In other words, are you planting for the long pull and do you have enough money to buy immediately effective large plants or do you want later effect at lower initial cost? Remember this adage: "Plants either grow or die." Eventually even a beech or an English boxwood will get too large for the place chosen for it. *Horribile dictu!*

Dig Plant Hole Properly

When you know what you're going to plant, what its needs are, and where you would like to plant it, the next vital step is to test that place for drainage. Dig a hole

24 inches deep and fill it with water. If the water has not drained away in 24 hours, you need to correct the drainage. If the water has drained away, fill up the test hole. Then dig your planting hole about 12 inches wider than the ball of dirt or the container, or, if it's bare root, the spread of the roots.

This is the hard part but it's also the fun part. Your hole should be as deep or somewhat less than the ball of soil, container or bare-root depth. Tamp down the bottom of the hole so the plant will not sink. Work into the soil you removed from the hole from 25 to 50 percent of humus – leaf compost, well rotted manure or other organic soil amendment. The quantity of amendment depends on the quality of the soil in which you are planting.

Then test the amended soil for acidity or alkalinity. If you had the basic soil tested through your Extension Service, add the amounts of lime needed for raising the pH or the amounts needed to lower it.

Once the plant is located in the hole to its best visual advantage, back-fill with the enriched soil. Tamp it in place around the plant ball or roots thoroughly. Air pockets around the roots are disastrous. Leave a little berm or ring around the edge of the hole you dug to hold water and then water the plant thoroughly, once every two weeks. Rainy weather does

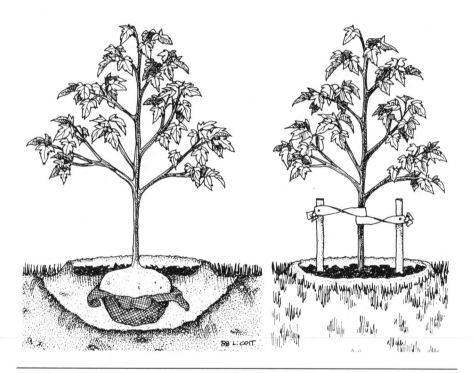

88 L. COIT

COURTESY OF AMERICAN HORTICULTURAL SOCIETY AND LAURA COIT

Dig a wide, shallow hole rather than a deep hole to plant your trees. The newest research emphasizes that the primary roots are in the top eight to 18 inches of soil. A spokesman for the International Society of Arboriculture recommends a "satellite dish" hole: "twice the width of the root ball is good, three times is even better."

Plant high, at least six inches above ground level. The slight mounding of the soil – an old English technique called "planting proud" – is acceptable in most areas. In the Washington area it is important. Dr. Francis Gouin of the University of Maryland says more newly-planted trees have died within five years or so because they were planted too deep, or had sunk down, than for any

other single reason.

The ancient lore says when you plant a tree, especially if it is bare-rooted, you should stake it for the first season or two, until the roots have a chance to anchor themselves in the soil. More recent tests have shown that staking may not help and the tree will take hold more successfully if it is subject to some stress. If you fear that winds may be too strong, and tend to tear out the roots, erect a windbreak.

Summed up: Plant high. Water and feed, especially the first two seasons. Protect from strong winds. And stake if you take more stock in the ancient lore than in the newer recommendations. Tender, loving care may not be necessary but it helps.

Windows are intended to let light through and to see through, not to be covered by plants that are out of place. The best advice here is to take out the old plants and start over with low-growing new ones.

not always suffice for newly-planted plants but over-watering also can be harmful.

Always Plant High

If you need to correct drainage, dig the hole for the plant a foot or so deeper than the ball to ensure that moisture will drain away from it. Fill the hole to a few inches below the planting depth with pea gravel or other coarse material. Then fill to the planting depth with prepared soil and set your plant so that the top of the ball is somewhat higher than the surrounding terrain. Err on the side of planting *high*.

It is not necessary to remove the burlap from a root ball but it is necessary to be sure that the cords tying the ball to the trunk are untied, especially if these cords are nylon. When you plant a shrub or tree from a container be sure the roots are healthy and not winding around the root ball. Cut away any broken or diseased roots, and unwind or cut off any that are winding around it. If the root ball is compacted, roughen up the sides and the bottom a bit. It is not necessary to "butterfly" the root ball as sometimes recommended. This in some instances may do more harm than good. Then complete the planting as described above.

You also might want to stake or guy a tree, and to wrap the trunk with burlap or similar material to help get the plant through its first stressful year. Be sure the plant never lacks adequate water – and equally be sure that it does not get too much. Be sure it is protected from drying winter winds and heavy snow. Mulch the plant with two or three inches of appropriate material, but do not cover the trunk itself. Pray.

Shrubs and Trees for Your Garden

By Erik A. Neumann and Roland M. Jefferson

The home grounds can be landscaped effectively with woody plants alone. Large deciduous trees and conifers can be used to provide all-important shade and background. The small flowering trees and shrubs give seasonal displays of great beauty, and the highly adaptable broad-leaved evergreens add quality to any landscape.

This article covers selection, culture and maintenance of a wide range of trees and shrubs suitable for the average suburban lot of a quarter to a half acre in the Greater Washington area. Articles on specific woody plant groups such as azaleas and rhododendrons will be found elsewhere in this book.

What to Consider

The vast array of woody plants described in books and nursery catalogs seems to offer the suburban gardener endless choices. But when the gardener considers his landscape needs and the availability of plants his choices are rapidly narrowed. For example, if the gardener wants a small tree with yellow flowers in July, he or she has but one choice for this area; the Golden-rain tree *(Koelreuteria paniculata)*.

In addition to the usual reasons for selecting a particular plant, i.e. color of flowers and leaves, fruit and habit, one should carefully consider the following factors:

Beginning gardeners should always make their basic plant selections from known cold-hardy varieties. Failure to do so can lead to bitter disappointment and delay. After the cold-hardy types have been established, then try the borderline and perhaps more unusual and appealing varieties.

Relative Freedom from Insects and Diseases. No matter how desirable a variety may be, it is not worth growing if it must be sprayed frequently to keep it attractive. For example, Dutch elm disease on the American elm *(Ulmus americana)*, sweet gum blight on Sweet-gum *(Liquidambar styraciflua)*, the mimosa webworm on Honey Locust *(Gleditsia triacanthos)*, preclude these species from consideration in this area at this time.

Year-round Attractiveness of the Plant. Too many plants are selected on the basis of a single-season landscape value with no regard for their appearance at other times of the year. Although very attractive when in flower, Beauty Bush *(Kolkwitzia amabilis)*, Weigelas, most Mock-oranges *(Philadelphus)* and Deutzia are unattractive when not in bloom. Our native flowering dogwood *(Cornus florida)* is attractive at all seasons of the year with white "flowers" in spring, good foliage in summer (some variegated), bright berries in fall, and interesting branch structure in winter.

Availability. Although it is exciting and often rewarding to track down rare plants, it is not a good practice for the beginning gardeners to choose such plants for basic landscape needs. Local nurseries in most cases will have on hand, or can easily obtain, those plants that do well in the gardener's area. From these one can establish a landscape without going through the frustrating experience of compiling a long list of plants only to find them difficult to locate.

Ease of Culture. It is foolhardy for the beginning gardener to select plants that are difficult to grow. Although the experienced gardener may scoff at forsythia and Hinodegiri azaleas in their landscape scheme, he could hardly deny the encouragement value of such plants. Early success is very heartening. Large-flowered clematis, most of the Ghent and Mollis hybrid azaleas and many rhododendrons may best be left to the more experienced gardeners. Fortunately, local gardeners can choose from a long list of easily grown plants.

Troublesome Plants. Avoid selecting plants that may become weeds in your own garden as well as in your neighbor's yard. Although Hall's honeysuckle *(Lonicera japonica* cv. *Halliana)* is recommended for northern gardens because it is kept in bounds by winter killing of its stems, it is not so contained in this area and will soon become a pest.

The true bamboos *(Phyllostachys* spp.), Mexican bamboo or Japanese knotweed *(Polygonum cuspidatum)*, and Harlequin-bush *(Clerodondrum trichotomum)* may invade areas where they are not wanted by sending up shoots from their spreading roots. Box elder *(Acer negundo)* is a heavy seed producer, and attracts hordes of box elder bugs. Some fast-growing trees like silver maple *(Acer saccharinum)* are brittle, littering the ground with twigs and branchlets the year round and are short-lived and susceptible to major wind damage.

Culture and Maintenance

Fertilizing. Most well-established trees and shrubs will respond favorably to a single annual application of fertilizer put on in late fall or early spring before growth starts. A 10-6-4 50-percent organic fertilizer applied as directed on the bag will usually be adequate for most ornamental plants that are not fussy about acidity or alkalinity of the soil. Other fertilizers especially prepared for broad-leaved evergreens and other acid-loving plants, or for lime-loving plants like lilacs, should be used instead. Beginning gardeners can generally rely on the manufacturer's recommendations or the advice of experienced gardeners. Be suspicious of excessive and often contradictory claims for special formulations.

Fertilizers should be used sparingly; over-fertilization can cause excessively rapid growth or death. Young plants that have been properly fertilized when planted should require no more food until they show signs of healthy growth. The first application should be made in early spring (March) and the second in fall after the first heavy freeze. Care should be taken to keep the fertilizer from direct contact with the base of the tree or shrub. Fertilizer for shade trees can be spread over the soil on grass surfaces beneath the span of its limbs and beyond. It need not be placed in holes.

Pruning. Most shrubs need regular pruning to improve their appearance and usefulness. All dead, diseased and weak branches should be removed when first noticed. Newly transplanted trees and shrubs should be pruned to prevent excessive water loss and to balance roots with top growth. Pruning also should be used to direct the growth of young trees and to prevent the formation of narrow crotches. Always prune rubbing cross branches.

The time to prune varies with the plant. Plants which flower on the previous season's growth should be pruned immediately following flowering. Summer-flowering kinds, i.e. those that flower on spring growth, should be pruned in late winter or early spring. Deciduous trees and conifers can be pruned at any season of the year.

Plants to be pruned after flowering include Azalea, Bridal Wreath Spirea, Common and Persian Lilacs, Deutzia, Dogwood, Early-Flowering Quince, Forsythia, Fringe-Tree, Honeysuckle, Kerria, Magnolia, Mock-orange, Pearlbush and Rhododendron.

Plants to be pruned in late winter or early spring include Barberry, Butterfly Bush, Coralberry, Cotoneaster, Hibiscus, Hydrangea, Crape Myrtle, Indigo Bush, Rose of Sharon, Snowberry, Viburnums, and Vitex.

Insects and Diseases. Insect and disease problems of woody plants are too many and varied to be dealt with in any general discussion. Specimens showing insect or disease symptoms should be taken to your local Cooperative Extension Service or to a local plant clinic for identification and suggested controls.

Hedges

Hedges are primarily used to obtain privacy and a formal appearance on the small home grounds. Hedges also are useful as windbreaks and barriers.

Size of Plant to Buy. To grow a uniform dense hedge, buy only small (18 to 24 inch) well-branched plants. Young plants usually make new growth from the base when pruned, assuring a hedge well-branched to the ground.

Trimming. Although hedges may vary in outline according to taste, they always should be slightly wider at the base. This is particularly important for evergreens, since their branches quickly drop their needles once they become too shaded.

Young developing hedges are best pruned during active growth. When your succulent shoots are cut in half the lateral buds in the axils or leaves will immediately start growing. With hedges at their desired height, trimming is best done after new growth has fully developed for the year. Pruning should extend back slightly into the old wood.

Pines can be made to branch by cutting back the new growth (candles) approximately in half in early summer. The remaining conifers can be made to branch simply by pruning the ends of the branches at almost any time of year. To encourage dense branching to the ground, begin pruning conifers when the plants are three to five years old, depending on species. It is important to establish the desired shape early in the plant's development.

Plants For Hedges That Can Be Held Under Three Feet

Deciduous: Crimson Pygmy Barberry, Dwarf Ninebark, Dwarf Cutleaf Stephanandra, Dwarf European Cranberry Bush.

Evergreen: Kingsville Dwarf Boxwood, Heller Japanese Holly.

Plants For Hedges That Can Be Held At From Two To Five Feet

Deciduous: Slender Deutzia, Bush Cin-

quefoil, Potentilla or Buttercup Shrub, Spirea Anthony Waterer, Dwarf Arctic Willow, Dwarf Burning Bush, Flowering Quince.

Evergreen: Chenault Barberry, Warty Barberry, Varda Valley Boxwood, Privet Honeysuckle, Japanese Skimmia.

Plants For Hedges Five Feet and Taller

Deciduous: Glossy Abelia, Japanese Barberry, Mentor Barberry, True-hedge Barberry, Regel Privet, Hardy Orange, Tall Hedge Buckthorn, Rugosa Rose, Arrowwood Viburnum.

Evergreen: Wintergreen Barberry, Leyland Cypress, Burford Holly, Japanese Holly, American Holly, Amur Privet, Hatfield Yew, Hicks Yew, Canadian Hemlock.

RECOMMENDED PLANTS

The plants in the following lists were selected because they grow well in the Washington area. Buying selections from these lists should make it possible for the gardener to meet almost all initial woody plant needs. The reader is referred to the selected references on plants at the end of this article to supplement these lists.

Heights given are the maximums expected under cultivation in this area.

Flowering Deciduous Shrubs

Glossy Abelia (6 feet)
Abelia grandiflora
Very free flowering shrub covered with pinkish-white blossoms all summer. The decorative red calyces are attractive along with and after the flowers drop. Its glossy dark green foliage persists until late fall in the Washington area.

Red Chokeberry (9 feet)
Aronia arbutifolia
A multi-season native shrub featuring white flowers in spring, red and orange fall foliage color and brilliant red fruit holding well into winter.

Summersweet (6 to 9 feet)
Clethra alnifolia
Excellent shrub for fragrant summer bloom in shady moist sites. Flowers white in spikes four to six inches long. Variety *rosea* with pink flower spikes. Autumn foliage is yellow to orange.

Springtime blossoms are a decoration for a tiny home in a flowering apple tree.

Smoketree (10 to 15 feet)
Cotinus Coggygria
Foliage and feathery purplish flowers give the effect of a dense cloud of smoke during June and July. An excellent shrub for summer color beginning in early June, and brilliant autumn coloration. It requires full sun and plenty of space.

Warminster Broom (4 to 6 feet)
Cytisus x praecox
This plant has spectacular lemon-yellow, pea-shaped blooms in May, and pendulous evergreen branches. It is dense, free-flowering and easy to maintain.

Burning Bush, Winged Euonymus (9 feet)
Euonymus alatus
An easily grown shrub valued for its brilliant, scarlet autumn foliage and scarlet fruit which attracts birds in fall and winter. Its unique horizontal branching and twigs with corky ridges are also of interest. The variety 'Compacta' is outstanding as a specimen or a hedge. It reaches nine feet at maturity.

Showy Border Forsythia (9 feet)
Forsythia x intermedia 'Spectabilis'
Perhaps the most widely grown of all shrubs. Since its flower buds are not killed by

Washington winters, it can be depended upon for a mass of golden blooms each year in early April. It should be pruned but not sheared.

Alabama Fothergilla (6 feet)
Fothergilla monticola
This native of the lower Smokies is deserving of wider use. The large white terminal flower clusters in early May and the brilliant yellow to scarlet autumn foliage make this an outstanding ornamental.

Chinese Witch Hazel (15 to 30 feet)
Hamamelis mollis
Bright yellow, ribbon-like fragrant flowers bloom as early as February. A wide-spreading shrub which thrives in full sun or light shade and prefers growing in a moist, sandy, peat soil. Foliage turns deep yellow in the autumn.

Common Witch Hazel (10 to 15 feet)
Hamamelis virginiana
A native American shrub with yellow ribbon-like flowers blooming in late fall making it the last shrub to bloom in this area. Good in full sun or shade and recommended for moist locations. Autumn foliage color is yellow.

Hibiscus syriacus 'Diana' (8 feet)
A National Arboretum introduction producing large white, long lasting blooms throughout the summer. A dense shrub with rich green foliage, it is immune to air pollution injury. It makes few if any seedlings.

Peegee Hydrangea (20 feet)
Hydrangea paniculata 'Grandiflora'
An extremely popular shrub producing large showy white clusters of flowers in late summer, when few other shrubs are in bloom.

Big Leaf or House Hydrangea (12 feet)
Hydrangea macrophylla
Large blue or pink flowers in rounded heads blooming in late summer. Color depends on cultivar and soil acidity. Many good named varieties are in the nursery trade. Its glossy green leaves make it a good shrub for the shady garden.

St. John's-wort
Hypericum patulum 'Sungold'
A compact plant with bluish-green foliage that produces large (2 ½ inches in diameter) yellow flowers during late June and July.

Virginia Sweetspire (3 to 9 feet)
Itea virginiana
An attractive native shrub for summer and autumn interest. Its fragrant creamy white flowers are borne in dense racemes in June and July. Its brilliant red fall foliage make this little-known native shrub a desirable addition to the Washington garden.

Winter Jasmine
Jasminum nudiflorum
Among the earliest of all plants to bloom, its yellow flowers begin appearing in late February and continue till early April. Its arching branches make it particularly useful for wall or bank planting.

Kerria (4 to 6 feet)
Kerria japonica
A good choice for the foreground of shrub borders or in deep shade. Cheerful yellow flowers appear in late April to early May, on bright green slender branches which remain colorful through the winter. To maintain vigor this plant needs renewal pruning. The double form 'Pleniflora' has yellow, globe-shaped flowers which remain attractive on this plant longer than on the species.

Beauty Bush (8 to 10 feet)
Kolkwitzia amabilis
A vigorous, upright shrub with arching branches and light pink, bell-shaped flowers in late May to early June. It grows almost anywhere, even in poor, sandy, dry soils. Its autumn color is reddish.

Crape Myrtle (20 feet)
Lagerstroemia indica
Profuse summer-flowering shrub available in white and various shades of pink with some bordering on lavender and red. Its habit is often tree-like and it can be trained as a small flowering tree. Several new cultivars produced at the National Arboretum offer wider color range and better disease resistance. Dwarf forms also are available.

Star Magnolia (18 feet)
Magnolia stellata
Although this large shrub is prized for its early April show of white flowers it also can be recommended for its foliage. The dark-green tightly-packed foliage makes a pleasing green mass throughout the summer. In some years, blooms may be killed by late frosts.

Buttercup Shrub (4 feet)
Potentilla fruticosa
An excellent summer flowering shrub that blooms profusely from May till frost. Early grown and pest free, it does well in full sun or partial shade. It may be used as a low hedge plant, in edging and foundation plantings or in perennial borders. Named varieties range in color from yellow to white and gold.

Pyracantha 'Teton' (12 feet)
A new Pyracantha introduction from the National Arboretum with a distinct vertical form producing a dense, columnar shrub 12 feet high and four feet wide. It is disease resistant and winter hardy. Evergreen, it can be used as a screen, hedge or as a specimen plant. It produces white blooms followed by yellow-orange fruit.

Virginia Rose (6 feet)
Rosa virginiana
This is a very useful plant because it is interesting in more than one season. It has single pink flowers in late May and June, glossy dark-green leaves in summer, with bright red fruit, red autumn foliage and red stems in winter.

Thunberg Spirea (5 feet)
Spiraea Thunbergii
This neat billowy plant is the first of the spireas to bloom. It is covered in mid-April with small white blossoms. Its very fine texture and soft reddish-brown foliage in the fall are other points of interest.

Chinese Lilac (15 feet)
Syringa chinensis
This species along with the equally attractive Persian Lilac *(Syringa persica)* are the most satisfactory lilacs for general landscaping. Although the rose-purple flowers of the Chinese lilac, coming in early May, do not approach the beauty and fragrance of the blooms of the best varieties of the common lilac *(Syringa vulgaris)*, its better foliage and more graceful habit make it more desirable. The Korean lilac *(S. patula)* x 'Mis Kim' blooms later, and is a smaller, better-shaped shrub that lengthens the lilac blooming season.

Fragrant Snowball (7 feet)
Viburnum x. carlcephalum
Judd Viburnum (8 feet)
Viburnum Juddii
These fragrant viburnums feature pinkish-white daphne-like flowers in April. Both are more resistant to disease than the old Korean fragrant viburnum *(Viburnum carlesii)* and are better for our area.

Double-file Viburnum (8 feet)
Viburnum plicatum cv. *Tomentosum*
A high quality deciduous shrub that should be used more. Flat white flower clusters appear in early May on the upper surfaces of horizontal branches. Bright red clusters of berries are produced in early fall, followed by velvety red autumn foliage. This plant is attractive at all seasons of the year. It is most effective when planted near the base of a slope where it can be viewed from above.

Evergreen Shrubs

Japanese Aucuba (8 feet)
Aucuba japonica
Aucuba is dioecious like holly, and both sexes must be present if red berries are de-

sired. The shrub may have large green or variegated leaves and will grow well despite shade and root competition.

Warty Barberry (4 feet)
Berberis verruculosa
This barberry is a neat, low plant. Its small yellow flowers are followed by blue-black fruit and the small leaves give it a tailored appearance.

Wintergreen Barberry (6 feet)
Berberis Julianae
Yellow flowers in spring, bluish-black fruit in summer and fall and vigorous growth characterize this plant. Spines on its branches should discourage all unwanted traffic.

Thorny Elaeagnus (10 feet)
Elaeagnus pungens
This plant makes a good barrier, even in poor soil. The silver evergreen leaves and small fragrant flowers in the fall give this plant special interest.

Burford Holly (20 feet)
Ilex cornuta 'Burfordii'
A fast growing holly, good as a hedge or screen, this plant should be placed well away from the house walkways or driveways because of its large ultimate size. Not always hardy in exposed colder locations.

Dwarf Chinese Holly (4 to 5 feet)
Ilex cornuta rotunda
This is a slow-growing holly reaching five feet in width. It grows in a globe form and requires little pruning.

Heller Japanese Holly (5 feet)
Ilex crenata 'Helleri'
A fine textured, very slow-growing plant, just right for under low windows, whose size can be easily controlled by shearing or pruning.

Mountain Laurel (12 feet)
Kalmia latifolia
A good native evergreen for woodsy and partly shaded situations. Pink to white flowers occur in late spring. The plant benefits from yearly light applications of an oak leaf or pine needle mulch. Leaf-spot occurs on plants in full sun, and in nutrient-deficient soils.

Oregon Grape (3 to 4 feet)
Mahonia aquifolia
Bright yellow flowers in April are followed by blue grape-like fruits in summer. Foliage is spiny, lustrous, and evergreen, turning bronze-red in autumn.

Leatherleaf Mahonia (4 to 10 feet)
Mahonia bealei

This plant has holly-like evergreen leaves that do not change color in fall. Yellow, fragrant flowers appear in spikes followed by grape-like fruits. An excellent shrub for partial shade.

Heavenly Bamboo (8 feet)
Nandina domestica
Nandina features long large terminal clusters of white flowers in July, followed by red berries and scarlet leaves in the fall. New leaves possess a pink hue in the spring. A nice specimen plant to flank a doorway or main entrance.

Dwarf Chinese or White Spruce
(10 to 15 feet)
Picea glauca conica
A slow growing dwarf form of native White Spruce with a compact pyramidal habit, and light bluish-green needles.

Japanese Andromeda (9 feet)
Pieris japonica
This plant produces an abundance of pendulous white clusters of flowers in early spring. The plant resists lacebug if planted in part shade. New growth on some cultivars is reddish-orange all summer long.

Cherry Laurel (15 feet)
Prunus laurocerasus
This is a useful plant for hedges and windbreaks. The dwarf variety 'Otto Luykens' has dark green glossy leaves and white flower racemes in late May.

Japanese Skimmia (2 to 3 feet)
Skimmia japonica
This dense compact shrub thrives in shade producing fragrant clusters of creamy-white flowers in spring and red berries in fall. Dioecious, plants of both sexes must be present for the females to set berries.

For a more detailed discussion of the species covered, the reader is referred to the selected references at the end of this article and to the wealth of bulletins available from local Extension Services.

Small Flowering Trees

Red Buckeye (30 feet)
Aesculus pavia
A small attractive tree with crimson flowers that open in late May or early June.

Shadblow Service Berry (45 feet)
Amelanchier canadensis
A slender tree, often growing in clumps, that is best used against an evergreen background to bring out its delicate white flowers in early spring and its red and yellow autumn

foliage and gray trunks.

Chinese Fringe Tree (20 feet)
Chionanthus retusa

A beautiful large shrub or small tree with a profusion of attractive white flowers in June or July and showy black fruit in the fall.

White Fringe Tree (20 feet)
Chionanthus virginicus

One of the most beautiful native American flowering trees. Each spring it has a mass of showy white pendant blossoms that appear in great profusion.

American Yellow-wood (50 feet)
Cladrastis lutea

A handsome tree with fragrant Wisteria-like flowers that hang in clusters, and attractive foliage that turns orange-yellow in autumn. It has smooth light gray bark.

Flowering Dogwood (20 feet)
Cornus florida

One of our most useful native plants. It is attractive at all seasons of year. The white "flowers" of spring, the red foliage and fruit of fall and its picturesque branching habit have endeared this plant to millions. Pink-flowered forms are also widely available in a number of different clones.

Franklinia (20 feet)
Franklinia alatamaha

This beautiful tree has large fragrant white flowers in late summer. Its bright green leaves turn a very beautiful scarlet before falling in autumn.

Golden-rain Tree (45 feet)
Koelreuteria paniculata

The main value of this tree is its yellow flowers of late June and July when few other woody plants are in bloom. It grows well in any type of soil.

Arnold Crab Apple (20 feet)
Malus x *atrosanguinea*

An attractive round-headed tree, which is covered with beautiful pink and white blossoms in spring.

Carmine Crab Apple (20 feet)
Malus x *atrosanguinea*

Has pleasing carmine colored flowers in the spring and attractive glossy leaves throughout the summer.

Japanese Flowering Crab Apple (30 feet)
Malus floribunda

Particularly attractive flowers, deep pink to red in bud, fade to white as they open in mid-April. Its yellow and red fruits are effective in early fall.

Tea Crab Apple (30 feet)
Malus hupehensis

The most picturesque of all crab apples, its long wand-like branches are covered with white flowers that are pink in the bud stage in late April.

Sweet Bay Magnolia (35 feet)
Magnolia virginiana

One of the best flowering trees for swampy locations, it has fragrant white flowers in early summer and broad green leaves that are white on the under surface.

Sourwood (30 feet)
Oxydendrum arboreum

One of the best native trees for crimson fall color, it has drooping racemes of white flowers that are very showy in late summer when few kinds of perennials are blooming. It grows best in acid soils.

Weeping Higan Cherry (30 feet)
Prunus subhirtella f. pendula

One of the earliest ornamental cherries to bloom, abundant pink blossoms hang from long graceful, drooping branches.

Yoshino Cherry (45 feet)
Prunus yedoensis

These are the Japanese cherries surrounding the Tidal Basin. Their delicate pink to white flowers in early April are beautiful but, unfortunately, short-lived. The double flowering varieties of *Prunus serrulata*, 'Kwanzan' (pink) and 'Shirofugen' (white), are later flowering and effective over a longer time. Stiff habit of branching, interesting flowers.

PHOTO BY SAM SHIOZAWA

This 25-year-old Japanese cut-leaf maple (*Acer palmatum*) is one of many cultivars grown in this area. It is pruned lightly once a year to keep it from growing over the entranceway to the house.

Stewartia (35 feet)
Stewartia monadelpha or *S. pseudocamellia*
This summer-blooming (July) tree belongs to the same family as camellias. It is columnar in habit, has white flowers, red autumn foliage and attractive mottled bark. Needs moisture during dry periods.

Japanese Snowbell (30 feet)
Styrax japonica
Since this tree blooms in mid-May after the leaves have come out, it is best viewed from beneath. The flowers are white and bell-shaped.

Fragrant Snowbell (30 feet)
Styrax obassia
An excellent ornamental with large leaves that partly hide the showy fragrant white flowers.

Natchez Crape Myrtle (25 feet)
Lagerstroemia hybrid cv. 'Natchez'
A disease resistant multi-stem tree with very showy white flowers and beautiful mot-tled light tan and cinnamon colored bark. A National Arboretum introduction.

Galaxy Magnolia (60 feet)
Magnolia hybrid cv. 'Galaxy'
A single trunk tree with excellent branching habit. Its attractive reddish purple flowers open late enough to escape most late frost damage. A National Arboretum introduction.

Whitehouse Callery Pear (30 feet)
Pyrus calleryana cv. 'Whitehouse'
A very upright fireblight-resistant tree that produces early white flowers and has beautiful purple and red leaves in the fall. A National Arboretum introduction.

Milky Way Dogwood (20 feet)
Cornus kousa cv. 'Milky Way'
This tree produces large pure white petal-like bracts in June that remain attractive for several weeks. In autumn it bears a heavy crop of large red raspberry-like fruits that are enjoyed by birds. Its exfoliating dark and light gray bark becomes more attractive as the tree matures. This is one of the finest Chinese dogwoods available.

Shade Trees

Red Maple (100 feet)
Acer rubrum
A good compromise between the faster growing but less durable Silver Maple *Acer saccharinum* and the slower growing but sturdier Sugar Maple *Acer saccharum*. The clean gray bark of the upper limbs, its red flowers and young fruits in spring and the red or yellow autumn foliage are all of landscape merit. Roots are invasive. Good for wet sites.

Katsura Tree (70 feet)
Cercidiphyllum japonica
A beautiful, often multi-stemmed tree with drooping branches and spirally twisted, furrowed trunks. The attractive heart-shaped leaves, similar to those of the Redbud *Cercis*, turn bright yellow or partly scarlet in autumn.

Maidenhair Tree (45 feet)
Ginkgo biloba cv. 'Autumn Gold'
This highly disease-resistant tree has interesting fan-shaped leaves that turn a beautiful yellow in autumn. Since the fruit has an obnoxious odor and becomes untidy after falling, non-fruiting varieties like 'Autumn Gold,' 'Lakeview,' 'Mayfield,' 'Palo Alto,' and 'Santa Cruz' are recommended.

Mountain Silverbell (75 feet)
Halesia monticola
This little-known native tree of the Smoky Mountains is deserving of wider use. Its small white bell-shaped flowers in early May are

FOREST SERVICE COLLECTION, NATIONAL AGRICULTURAL LIBRARY

The tupelo or black gum is an excellent ornamental that can grow to 100 feet. Widely found in eastern woodlands, it has an attractive pyramidal shape, lustrous dark green foliage in summer, and orange to scarlet color in the fall. Because of a prominent taproot, it does not transplant easily.

particularly attractive when seen from below.

Tupelo, Black Gum (100 feet)
Nyssa sylvatica
This native of the east coast is recommended for its glossy summer foliage and brilliant fall color. Since it is difficult to transplant it should be moved only as a young balled and burlapped tree.

Bradford Pear (45 feet)
Pyrus calleryana 'Bradford'
A most useful, moderate size tree with year-round interest. White spring flowers, disease-free summer foliage and red to orange fall color are among its attributes.

Northern Red Oak (75 feet)
Quercus borealis f. *maxima*
A very popular fast-growing oak. It is easily transplanted and develops into a beautiful tree that turns red in autumn.

Willow Oak (75 feet)
Quercus phellos
A dense tree with glossy willow-like leaves that turn yellowish-orange in the fall. Its drought resistance offers many advantages for landscape planting over otherwise satisfactory Red Oak *(Quercus borealis maxima)* and Scarlet Oak *(Quercus coccinea)*.

Japanese Pagoda Tree (80 feet)
Sophora japonica
The pale yellow flowers are followed by three-inch pods. Tolerant of soils, symmetrical form.

Littleleaf Linden (40 feet)
Tilia cordata
A small tree with fragrant yellow flowers in late May or early June. It makes a fine street or lawn tree and is resistant to many adverse city conditions.

Chinese Elm (50 feet)
Ulmus parvifolia
Although the Siberian Elm *Ulmus pumila* is more widely used it is decidedly inferior to the Chinese Elm. The dark green foliage, exfoliating bark and fast growth make the Chinese Elm desirable as a shade tree for the home grounds.

Japanese Zelkova (90 feet)
Zelkova serrata
A graceful shade tree with growth habit and foliage similar to that of the American Elm, *Ulmus americana*. It is resistant to Dutch Elm disease and is often substituted for the American elm in street plantings.

Paperbark Maple (25 feet)
Acer griseum

An outstanding small tree that has beautiful exfoliating reddish brown bark. Its attractive green compound leaves turn red and scarlet in autumn.

River's Purple Beech (80 feet)
Fagus sylvatica cv. 'Riversii'
A large wide spreading European beech tree with beautiful dark purple leaves and smooth gray bark. It should be grown in well-drained locations. It does well in both acid and alkaline soils.

Conifers

Silver Fir (75 feet)
Abies concolor
One of the best firs for areas with long hot summers. Its long bluish-green needles and soft pyramidal outline make it a more desirable accent tree than the coarse blue spruces which it somewhat resembles.

Blue Atlas Cedar (80 to 100 feet)
Cedrus atlantica 'Glauca'
An attractive blue-needled conifer of pyramidal form that becomes flat-topped with age. This is a fast growing, low maintenance plant.

Deodar Cedar (100 feet)
Cedrus deodara
The most graceful of the true cedars and the best conifer for the southeastern states in the Washington area, it is damaged in severe winters. The closely-related species Atlas Cedar *Cedrus atlantica* and Cedar of Lebanon *Cedrus libani* are less graceful but still highly desirable.

Hinoki Cypress (60 feet)
Chamaecyparis obtusa
A dark glossy green foliage plant, with compact columnar habit and relatively slow growth make this species much more desirable than the often-planted Sawara False-cypress *Chamaecyparis pisifera*. The variety *Chamaecyparis obtusa nana* is an excellent dwarf shrub which grows up to three feet.

Leyland Cypress (75 feet)
Cupressocyparis leylandii
This narrow columnar evergreen can grow two to three feet in a season, even in clay. Excellent choice as a screen or windbreak.

California Incense Cedar (60 feet)
Calocedrus decurrens
An excellent narrow columnar tree with dark green foliage. Since it does not turn brown in the winter, it is recommended over the more frequently planted American Arbor-vitae *Thuja occidentalis*.

Oriental Spruce (60 feet)
Picea orientalis

The best of the spruces for planting on small properties. Its slow growth rate, small, dark green needles and dense graceful habit of growing make it a highly desirable ornamental. The equally attractive Serbian Spruce *Picea omorika* is not widely available.

Lace-Bark Pine (30 to 60 feet)
Pinus Bungeana
A picturesque multiple stemmed tree with attractive mottled bark which becomes chalk-white and exfoliates as the tree matures. It becomes flat topped with advanced age.

Eastern White Pine (120 feet)
Pinus strobus
The soft delicate texture of this pine makes it an excellent background tree for flowering shrubs and trees. The Himalayan Pine *Pinus wallichiana* with long blue-green drooping needles is also an excellent evergreen, but its wide-spreading branches preclude its use on the small property.

Canada Hemlock (90 feet)
Tsuga canadensis

Carolina Hemlock (75 feet)
Tsuga caroliniana
There is little difference in the landscape merit of these two excellent evergreens. Since the needles on the Carolina Hemlock are more nearly at right angles to the twig it has a softer more feathery appearance than the flat-sprayed arrangement of the needles on the Canada Hemlock.

References

Dirr, Michael A.: *Manual of Woody Landscape Plants*, rev. ed. Stipes, Champaign, IL, 376 pp., 1983.

Hillier and Sons: *The Hillier Colour Dictionary of Trees and Shrubs*. David and Charles, Inc., North Pomfret, VT, 323 pp., 1983.

Wyman, Donald: *Trees for American Gardens*. Macmillan, NY, 502 pp., 1965.

Wyman, Donald: *Shrubs and Vines for American Gardens*. Macmillan, NY, 613 pp., 1969.

PHOTO BY EDMUND C. FLYNN

A 20-foot hemlock hedge served as the boundary for a patio-swimming pool-vegetable garden area until it was decided to make use of the narrow strip behind that dropped off sharply to the property line. In the newly-terraced strip, try-outs are being given a row of blueberries and a row of asparagus.

Hollies: A Sight to See

By Anthony R. Gould

George Washington searched the woods for young plants of native holly with red berries and evergreen spiny leaves and had them moved to the borders on both sides of the land approach to Mount Vernon. There they could be admired by visitors and provide winter greens for the house. Two of them are still growing 200 years later.

American hollies *(Ilex opaca)* grow wild not only in the Washington area but from Cape Cod, down the eastern seaboard to Florida and around the gulf to Texas. Hollies have penetrated to the higher areas of the Appalachians. They obviously are tolerant of our acid clay soils, our violent winter winds and our hot and humid summers.

George Washington was not the first and certainly not the last to bring hollies from the woods. Today it is well nigh impossible to find wild hollies with berries. The berries appear only on trees with staminate flowers (female) while trees with pistillate (male) flowers will have none. The search for female plants not only has reduced the proportion in the world but has left fewer and fewer sources of seeds.

New Plants from Nurseries

Because of the popular demand for plants with berries, nurseries have learned to propagate new plants from cuttings taken from favorite trees. Some have darker leaves, more spines, and redder berries; some have yellow berries. Some are more slender, others bushy, and these qualities, including sex, are repeated in new trees. These frequently are named and sold. Popular in the Washington area are 'Delia Bradley,' 'Emily,' 'Farage,' 'Jersey Princess,'

'Manig,' 'Miss Helen,' 'Old Heavy Berry,' 'St. Mary,' and 'Satyr Hill.' These are all female, berried varieties.

Because of their value in winter, American hollies often are planted as specimen trees in the lawn or border. They also serve well as screens such as can be seen beside the roads leading to the Kennedy Center where they are 20 feet high. At Williamsburg they often have been planted close together and sheared to three-foot hedges, serving as fences between properties.

Plant in Early Spring

Hollies are best planted in early spring so that the new roots can reach into the natural soil before hot weather sets in. Planted in early fall they should be shielded the first winter from harsh winds and strong sun with snow fencing or burlap fastened to stakes. In any event they should be watered generously the first summer if there has been no rain for seven days.

No fertilizer should be used in the new hole nor during the first year. Thereafter fertilize if you want more rapid growth with a cup of 10-6-4 or 10-10-10 for a three-foot tree and two cups for a five-footer.

Mulching with twigs, chips or partly-decayed leaves protects the roots from extremes of both heat and cold just as the roots were protected in the woods. The lower branches should be left to shield the roots from direct sunlight. While the roots should be shaded, the tree itself will bloom and berry much better in full sun.

Male Hollies for Pollination

In subdivisions developed from woods there probably are male hollies within

PHOTO BY JOHN EDWARDS

The 'Nellie R. Stevens' holly is one of the most popular in the nursery trade. Discovered by chance in the mid-fifties in the waterside lawn of Miss Nellie Stevens in Oxford on Maryland's eastern shore, it was called to the attention of the National Arboretum. After years of uncertainty, the Arboretum is now convinced that it is a cross between *Ilex aquifolium* and *I. cornuta*. Specimens of the widely-grown holly are found today throughout Oxford. This one stands outside the historic Robert Morris Inn.

500 feet that will pollinate a staminate tree. But in areas that have been fields it may be necessary to plant a male for adequate pollination. Of course you could give one to your neighbor to screen your compost pile from his patio.

One of the reasons to plant holly is to have material to decorate the house at Christmas. When your tree is small, don't prune off the ends of branches if you want the berries that will set on the new twigs that will grow from those ends. My rule is to prune my older and larger trees the week before Christmas. Then I have

little trouble disposing of the "rubbish" to friends and neighbors.

Before permitting your neighbors to help you prune be sure they know where to cut. Insist that they cut above a leaf, not below. The new growth next spring that will bear the flowers comes at the juncture of leaves and stem.

Do not be surprised if in spring or fall the older leaves turn bright yellow and fall off. Hollies are evergreen meaning always green. This does not mean that every leaf stays on forever – only for two or three years.

Other Hollies Grow Here

American holly – *Ilex opaca* – is only one of the many specimens of holly that grow in the Washington area. These other hollies are not native to our soils and climate. Not all do well. Our bitter winds and long hot summers with high humidity often do them in. *Ilex opaca* has survived such ordeals for thousands of years.

The cut holly sold at Christmas often is called Oregon or English holly because it is grown commercially in Oregon. It is *Ilex aquifolium* with dark shiny leaves and plump berries. This has been crossed with other species such as *I. pernyi* from China with small leaves to form a slender tree known as *I. aquipernyi*. Dr. Henry Skinner, the former director at the National Arboretum, crossed *I. opaca* with another holly from China, *I. cornuta*, resulting in the hybrids named 'Lydia Morris' and 'John Morris.'

That brings up *I. cornuta*, a fast-growing holly with dark shiny leaves. One that is popular here has only a terminal spine and is known as 'Burfordii' or Burford. This cultivar sets berries without a male.

Japanese Holly Popular

The holly most used here by landscape gardeners comes from Japan – *I. crenata*. It has small leaves, no spines and is usually a bush but does grow as a tree and can be trimmed as a tight hedge or used in foundation plantings. It looks much like boxwood but is even more resistant to disease. The cultivar 'Helleri' can be kept under one foot. If there is a male around the berries will be black.

I. aquifolium has been crossed by Mrs. Kay Meserve of Long Island with *I. rugosa* to produce a very hardy race referred to as the "blue hollies" *(I. Meserveae)*.

Female hollies resulting from crosses usually set berries with pollen from either species.

Our *I. opaca* has not responded well to crossing but a very popular one is the Foster holly, a cross with a southern holly, *I. cassine*, with good red berries and less aggressive spines.

There are native hollies with red ber-

In the female holly the dark center is the ovary and, when pollinated, will become the berry. The bloom comes early in May, the color in September.

PHOTOS BY ANTHONY R. GOULD
The male holly flower will not set berries. Instead of a dark center the anthers are conspicuous and stand up to brush pollen on visiting insects.

ries on gray twigs that lose their leaves in the fall, *I. decidua* and *I. verticillata*, and one from Japan, *I. serrata*.

There are many more kinds to meet every need and enough to start with if that should become your hobby. Once you have established holly in your garden you can enjoy your private supply of Christmas greens. When a guest exclaims, "Where did you find such fresh holly?" you can reply casually, "In our garden."

Do's and Don'ts

DON'T over-fertilize. Remember that more is not necessarily better.

PHOTO BY GEORGE TALOUMIS

The most beautiful and most widely grown of the Clematis are the large-flowered hybrids. In one group of these is the *C. Jackmanii* on the author's list of best vines. In another group, blooming on old wood, is the double, pure white 'Duchess of Edinburgh,' pictured above.

The Versatile Vines

By Michael J. Zajic

What is a vine? It is any plant that depends on its environment for support. Vining plants are from many different genera. They can be woody or herbaceous, annual or perennial, tropical or hardy.

Vines have many uses. The happy blend of the practical and the aesthetic makes vines extremely valuable in the garden. They are deep-rooted, vigorous of growth, and require less coddling than most other garden plants. Vines can grow up walls and fences; can cover an unsightly stump, dead tree, or shabby building; can dance down over walls and ledges; can provide low maintenance ground cover and erosion control; can provide a quick screen; and can provide ornament and shade on an arbor, trellis, pergola or porch. A deciduous vine on the south-facing wall of a house can provide cooling shade in summer and allow the bare wall to absorb heat in winter.

How Vines Support Themselves

Vines have different methods of supporting themselves:
1. Twining the main stem about a narrow support. Examples are morning glory and honeysuckle.
2. Grasping any nearby narrow upright support with twining tendrils or leaf petioles. Examples are pea, grape and clematis.
3. Clinging to an upright surface by aerial rootlets that secrete an adhesive glue. Examples are English ivy, Virginia creeper, and trumpet vine.

You must provide adequate support for your vine. Sometimes the support is a given situation for which you specifically chose the vine. For example, a stone or masonry wall calls for a vine that clings by rootlets, while a wire fence is suitable for either a twining or grasping vine. Otherwise you may design and provide special supports such as trellises, pergolas and archways.

Good Drainage Needed

Provide good drainage for your vine. Most vines require this. Here is how to do it. Dig your planting hole about a foot and a half deep and fill with water. If there is any water still in the hole after two hours, your drainage is unacceptable. A better location should be sought and tested. Or, try growing a vine in a half barrel with holes drilled in the bottom and filled with soil that drains well.

Prepare the soil for your vine. In the list here of vines, few are fussy about soil type or fertility. Clematis is the chief exception; it requires rich organic alkaline soil. Any vine you plant, however, should have the soil dug deep and broad (perhaps two feet by two feet and two feet deep). Sand and organic matter should be added.

BEST VINES FOR WASHINGTON AREA

Here is a list of the choicest vines for our area. Washington gardeners can choose any perennial vine with Zone 7 hardiness and many tropical vines as summer annuals. However, the vines in the following list are known to perform particularly well here and to have superior cultural or ornamental qualities. These vines are selected because they need relatively little maintenance and they are mostly disease and pest free.

Kolomikta Actinidia – *Actinidia Kolomikta.* Perennial. Woody. Deciduous. To 50 feet. Valued for foliage. Part shade or shade. Good

PHOTO BY GEORGE TALOUMIS

The popular Climbing Hydrangea is a superior clinging vine that can grow up to 60 feet. Valued for both flowers and foliage, it does well in sun or part shade.

screen on walls and fences.

Trumpet Creeper – *Campsis radicans.* Perennial. Woody. Deciduous. Clinging to 30 feet. Valued for flowers, berries. Sun. Cut root suckers.

Oriental Bittersweet – *Celastrus orbiculatus.* Perennial. Woody. Deciduous. Tendrils, to 40 feet. Valued for berries, foliage. Part shade or sun. Plant both sexes.

Jackman's Clematis – *Clematis Jackmanii.* Perennial. Woody. Deciduous. Tendrils, to 10 feet. Valued for flowers. Part shade or sun. Five-inch purple flowers bloom from June to September.

Sweet Autumn Clematis – *Clematis paniculata.* Perennial. Woody. Deciduous. Tendrils, to 15 feet. Valued for flowers, foliage. Part shade or shade. Requires rich, well-drained soil. Blooms August and September.

Cup and Saucer Vine – *Cobaea scandens.* Annual. Herbaceous. Grasping, to 20 feet. Valued for flowers. Sun. Flowers June to September. Use no fertilizer.

Hyacinth bean – *Dolichos Lablab.* Annual. Herbaceous. Twining, to 20 feet. Valued for flowers, berries, foliage. Part shade or shade.

Fast growing. Great red-purple color. Pest free.

English Ivy – *Hedera Helix.* Perennial. Woody. Evergreen. Roots in soil. To 50 feet. Valued for foliage. Part shade, or shade. Covers structures, trees. Used as ground cover.

Climbing Hydrangea – *Hydrangea anomala petiolaris.* Perennial. Woody. Deciduous. Clinging, to 60 feet. Valued for flowers, foliage. Sun or part shade. Covers walls, sturdy structures.

Moonflower – *Ipomoea alba.* Annual. Herbaceous. To 20 feet. Valued for flowers. Part shade or shade. A night bloomer.

Morning Glory – *Ipomoea purpurea.* Annual. Herbaceous. Twining, to 25 feet. Valued for flowers. Sun. Poor soil, no fertilizer.

Coral Honeysuckle – *Lonicera Heckrottii.* Perennial. Woody. Deciduous. Twining, to 8 feet. Valued for flowers, berries. Sun or part shade. A neglected marvel. Watch for mites.

Boston Ivy – *Parthenocissus tricuspidata.* Perennial. Woody. Deciduous. Clinging, to 60 feet. Valued for foliage. Part shade. Walls, trellises, porches. Control pests.

Silver Fleece Vine – *Polygonum Aubertii.* Perennial. Woody. Deciduous. Twining, to 25 feet. Valued for flowers. Sun. Flowers, September and October.

Black-eyed Susan Vine – *Thunbergia alata.* Annual. Herbaceous. To 8 feet. Valued for flowers, foliage. part shade. Summer bloom.

Japanese Wisteria – *Wisteria floribunda.* Perennial. Woody. Deciduous. Twining, to 30 feet. Valued for flowers. Sun. Needs strong support structure.

———

References

Howard, Frances: *Landscaping With Vines,* Macmillan, New York, 1959.

Cravens, Richard G., ed.: *Vines,* Time-Life Books, Inc., Morristown, N.J., 1979.

———

Do's and Don'ts

DON'T assume that a plant on a slope will not have a drainage problem. A plant hole on a slope can hold water as long as a bucket, especially if the soil is clayey.

DO throw plants away when they prove to be weak, slow, disappointing or greedy unless you enjoy challenges for the sake of a challenge.

Primer for a Beautiful Lawn

By Thomas R. Turner, Ph.D.

A beautiful lawn is certainly possible in this area with proper attention. A good lawn is not only aesthetically pleasing but it also sets off ornamentals, acts as a natural air conditioner, reduces soil erosion, and can add substantially to the value of your home.

The first step in obtaining a satisfactory lawn is understanding why lawns in the Washington area often fail or deteriorate. Some of the most important reasons for poor lawns are:
1. The wrong turf grass species or cultivar.
2. Poor quality seed.
3. Too little or too much lime or fertilizer.
4. Fertilizing at the wrong time of the year.
5. Watering indiscriminately.
6. Too much shade.
7. Poor soil conditions.
8. Too much traffic.
9. Damage from insects or disease.

To obtain a quality lawn there are five main keys: These are a) choosing the proper grass, b) preparing the seedbed properly, c) proper mowing, d) proper fertilization, and e) proper watering. Other practices that may be needed are weed control and dethatching.

Choosing the Proper Grass

Washington is in a climatic transition zone. We are a little too far north for ideal growth of warm season grasses (bermudagrass, zoysiagrass) and too far south for ideal growth of most of the cool season grasses (Kentucky bluegrass, perennial ryegrass, fine-leaved fescues). Selection of the proper type and variety of grass thus becomes very important.

Kentucky bluegrass generally will provide us the highest quality lawn in full sun or light shade, but it also must be intensively maintained. Periodic deep watering and relatively high fertility levels are required, as well as periodic dethatching. Recommended bluegrass varieties for this reason are: 'America,' 'Aspen,' 'Blacksburg,' 'Bristol,' 'Cheri,' 'Eclipse,' 'Enmundi,' 'Georgetown,' 'Gnome,' 'Majestic,' 'Merit,' 'Midnight,' 'Plush,' 'Sydsport,' 'Trenton,' and 'Victa.'

Not all of these are available singly; seed companies usually offer blends of several, so if one cultivar fails, others will take over. In any case, your mixture should contain a blend of at least three varieties seeded at a rate of one and a half to two pounds per 1,000 square feet. You can be sure of quality seed (good germination, few weeds) by buying seed boxes bearing the Maryland-Virginia Recommended Label.

The ideal seeding time is late August through mid-September for all cool season grasses. Another acceptable but less desirable time is mid-February through late March. Kentucky bluegrass sod is also available and can be laid almost anytime that the soil is not frozen. However, if it is put down in the summer, watering must be available.

Fine Fescues Recommended

Fine fescues are especially good for shady areas. They are fine textured, have bristly leaves and produce a dense sod in medium shade. Fine fescues cannot take excessive water or heavy nitrogen fertilization and will not perform well if mowed lower than one and a half inches. Currently, the fine fescues recommended for use in Maryland are 'Flyer,' 'Pennlawn,' 'Longfellow,' 'Victory,' 'Aurora,'

Table 1. Fertilizer Programs for Maintaining Kentucky Bluegrass and Fescues

Time to Apply	Readily Available Nitrogen Program (less than ½ water insoluble N)	Slow Release Nitrogen Program (more than ½ water insoluble N)
	Pounds Nitrogen per 1,000 Square Feet	
September	¾ to 1½	2 to 3
October	¾ to 1½	—
November	¾ to 1½	—
Mid-May	0 to ¾	0 to 1½

'Reliant,' 'Spartan,' 'Waldina,' 'Scaldis,' and 'Big Horn.' Different fine fescue species, such as creeping red fescue, Chewings fescue and hard fescue should not be mixed together. Use only one.

Tall fescue is a coarser-textured, perennial turfgrass which tolerates a wide variation in soil and shade conditions. It has become a popular species in Maryland because of its adaptability to a wide range of soil and sunlight conditions and good resistance to insects and wear. Kentucky 31 (K-1) was the most commonly used cultivar in the past, but it is a very coarse textured bunchgrass. Many finer textured cultivars have been developed in recent years that provide aesthetic cover and are highly recommended for home lawns as well as athletic fields, play areas, and utility sites. These include 'Adventure,' 'Apache,' 'Arid,' 'Bonanza,' 'Finelawn I,' 'Falcon,' 'Houndog,' 'Jaguar,' 'Mustang,' 'Olympic,' 'Rebel,' and 'Trident.'

When tall fescue is properly mowed and fertilized, pesticide use can generally be reduced by 50 to 75 percent compared to Kentucky bluegrass or perennial ryegrass. Water requirements of tall fescue also are reduced when compared to the two aforementioned grasses. Tall fescue is resistant to most common turfgrass diseases except brown patch and netblotch. However, fungicide applications are rarely needed for these diseases. Tall fescue is not compatible with Kentucky bluegrasses or other species. Tall fescue, therefore, should be seeded alone at rates of five to eight pounds per 1,000 square feet to achieve a stand with the most desirable texture and overall quality.

Perennial ryegrass has received increasing attention in recent years as a lawn grass. Its biggest advantage is its rapid germination and excellent seedling vigor. It is often a component of lawn seed mixtures, although it should never exceed 10 percent of the mixture. Although perennial ryegrass is now being used successfully on many golf courses, its use on home lawns is *not yet recommended* because it is very susceptible to many diseases.

Zoysia A Summer Grass

Zoysiagrass must be established from plants in the form of sprigs, stolons, plugs or sod rather than seed. It is an excellent summer grass for areas with full sunshine and heavy wear. The chief disadvantages are that it is slow to become established, the turf becomes straw-colored with the first heavy frost, it does not regain color until late spring and it tends to build up thatch rapidly if overfertilized or mowed too high.

'Meyer' (Z-52) is the preferred variety in Maryland. 'Emerald' is fine textured and makes a slightly thicker turf, but is less winter hardy. 'Belair' is slightly more aggressive than 'Meyer,' more resistant to rust, coarser, easier to mow with a rotary mower and darker grass. Zoysia requires a completely different type of management than bluegrass and fescues.

Bermudagrass is also a warm-season perennial which grows naturally in eastern and southern Maryland. Native bermuda, often called "wiregrass," is usually found on dry soils where it is difficult to grow cool-season species such as blue-

Table 2. Fertilizer Programs for Maintaining Bermudagrass and Zoysiagrass

Time to Apply	Readily Available Nitrogen Program (less than ½ water insoluble N)	Slow Release Nitrogen Program (more than ½ water insoluble N)
	Pounds Nitrogen per 1,000 Square Feet	
April to May	1	2 to 4
June	1	—
July	1	0 to 1
August	1	—

grass and red fescue. Bermudas are not shade tolerant and, like zoysias, turn straw-colored with frost in the fall and remain brown until late spring.

Several cultivars of improved, fine-leaved, high-quality turf bermudas are available. All bermudas except Common must be sprigged, plugged or sodded. The best bermudas for use in the Washington area, because of their winter hardiness, are 'Tufcote' and 'Midiron.' 'Midiron' is more winter hardy than 'Tufcote.' The ideal time to establish zoysia or bermudagrass is in late spring or early summer. 'Vamont' fills in more quickly than 'Midiron' and is more winter-hardy than 'Tufcote.'

Establishment

The second step toward a quality lawn is preparing a good seedbed or sod-bed. There are no easy shortcuts. You must devote enough time, effort, and money to ensure proper soil preparation, grass selection and planting in order to avoid many problems later on.

A level, firm and fertile seedbed is essential for successful, long-term turfgrass quality. Here is a step-by-step approach to seedbed preparation:

1. Stockpile the topsoil (four to six inches).
2. Subgrade or grade the lawn area (one percent grade with no pockets or depressions recommended).
3. Remove all debris (bricks, rocks, boards, sticks).
4. Redistribute topsoil to grade.
5. Mix in lime and fertilizer according to local university soil test recommendations. If no soil test is run, add 50 pounds limestone and 40 pounds 5-10-10 fertilizer per 1,000 square feet.
6. Rake and roll soil so that the surface is level and smooth.
7. Seed, plug or sod area – apply one half of the seed then the other half at a right angle direction. Zoysia or bermuda plugs should be planted six to 12 inches apart.
8. Roll the area again.
9. Water thoroughly.
10. Mulch seeded areas, using weed free straw mulch at a rate of one bale per 1,000 square feet.

It is critical that the area remain moist but not saturated for the first month to six weeks after seeding or sodding, especially in warmer weather. Failure to do so can result in almost complete failure.

Mowing the Lawn

Although mowing is often taken for granted, the proper mowing height, mowing frequency, and a sharp blade are very important aspects of a quality lawn program and can help avoid both short and long term damage.

Mowing height is especially critical for cool season grasses. Kentucky bluegrass and finer leaved fescues should be mowed two to three inches, while tall fescue should be between two to four inches in height. Mowing these grasses at lower cutting heights can stress the turf seriously, resulting in thinner turf and a large increase in weeds. During the summer months, mow your lawn about a half-inch higher than the rest of the year. For bermudagrass and zoysiagrass, a three-quarter-to-one-inch mowing height is recommended.

Frequency of mowing can be as critical as the mowing height. Try not to remove more than one-third of the leaf area at one time. For example, if you mow your lawn at two inches, do not let it grow to more than three inches before mowing again. Although it is difficult to keep up with the cool season grasses in the spring and bermuda-grass in the summer, this is one of the most important things you can do for the health of your lawn.

Although the benefits of a sharp versus dull mower seem obvious, many homeowners forget to check the blade periodically. Sharpen the blade at least annually for best results. Not only is the general appearance of the turf diminished when a dull blade is used, but several turf disease problems have been shown to increase. A reel mower generally will do a better mowing job than a rotary mower, but the expense of obtaining and maintaining a quality power reel mower is usually prohibitive for the average homeowner.

Removing Clippings

When mowing, clippings do not have to be removed unless 1) you have not kept up with the mowing and have excessive clippings or 2) you have an existing thatch problem. Otherwise, return of clippings causes no problems and may be beneficial by recycling nutrients.

Great good can be done for the lawn by proper fertilization, while improper fertilization can be as detrimental as no fertilizer at all. To determine the right combination of nitrogen, phosphorus, potassium, and limestone, have a soil test run by your local university. In lieu of a test, try a fertilizer with ready-release nitrogen (less than 50 percent water-insoluble nitrogen) at such ratios as 3-1-2, 3-1-1, or 4-1-2, and apply 25 to 50 pounds of ground limestone every other year. The numbers on fertilizer bags (such as 10-5-5) represent the percentage by weight of nitrogen, phosphate and potash. Thus a 50-pound bag of 10-5-5 has five pounds of nitrogen, two and a half

pounds of phosphate, and two and a half pounds of potash.

Many of the most popular lawn fertilizers will have ratios like 28-3-3. Some of the slow-release fertilizers are pelleted, and the fertilizer is released only when warmth and moisture penetrate the covering of each pellet. Controlled rate of release accounts for the difference in recommendations about how much fertilizer to apply and when (see Tables 1 and 2), between ready- and slow-release formulations.

Nitrogen Use

Nitrogen has the most dramatic effect on turfgrass performance of all these nutrients. Applied in the correct amounts and at the proper times, nitrogen will improve the density, color, and overall vigor of the lawn. However, applied at the improper time or at excessive rates, drought stress and disease problems can be increased, and the overall quality of the lawn reduced. For most home lawns, about four pounds of nitrogen per 1,000 square feet annually is sufficient to provide a high quality lawn. For tall fescue or zoysia lawns, two to three pounds nitrogen is usually sufficient. The recommended rates and timing of all applications are shown in Tables 1 and 2.

Ideally, to prevent fertilizer burn, fertilizer should be applied when the grass blades are dry, soil moisture adequate, and temperatures less than 90°F. If possible, water the fertilizer in immediately after application. Also, apply one half of the total amount of fertilizer in one direction, then the other one half at right angles. This will help prevent fertilizer skips, which can be very unsightly.

Watering

Once a lawn is established, water it only during excessively dry periods. In hot weather, heavy footprinting and a blue-gray coloration of bluegrass and fine fescue turf indicates that it has reached the wilting point and should be watered. However, if you start a regular watering program in early summer, continue the program throughout the summer. If you do not, you might lose much of your lawn

Table 3. Common Broadleaf Weeds and Chemicals for Their Control

Weed	2, 4-D	2, 4-D + 2, 4-DP	MCPP	Dicamba
Chickweed				
common	R	S	S-I	S
mouse-ear	I-R	S	S-I	S
Clover, White	I	S	S	S
Dandelion	S	S	S	S
Garlic, Wild	S-I	I	R	S-I
Ground Ivy	I-R	I	I	S-I
Healall	S	S	R	S-I
Henbit	I	S	I	S
Knotweed*	R	I	I	S
Oxalis	R	S	R	I-R
Plantains	S	S	I-R	I-R
Spurge**	I-R	S-I	I	S-I
Red Sorrel	I-R	I	R	S
Speedwell (Veronica)***	I-R	I	I-R	I-R
Thistles	S-I	S-I	I	S
Wild Strawberry	R	I	R	S-I

Response: R = resistant, S = susceptible, I = intermediate
 * very young plants (2-3 leaves) in spring can be controlled with 2, 4-D
 ** some species controlled with preemergence application of dacthal
 *** some species controlled with postemergence application of dacthal

during long dry periods. Tall fescue can usually survive the summer without irrigation.

When you water your lawn, give it only as much water as the soil can absorb. Moisten the soil to a depth of four to six inches. This usually requires the equivalent of one-half to one inch of rainfall. One method to determine when the root zone is moist enough is to push a screwdriver into the soil. When it can be pushed to a depth of four to six inches easily, the area has been sufficiently watered.

Frequent shallow watering on established turf should always be avoided. This practice causes shallow rooting, invasion and encourages disease.

Since most cool-season grasses become semi-dormant, growing very slowly, during hot, dry summer months, watering at that time to force or increase growth can weaken the turf and permit crabgrass to spread.

Since zoysia and bermudagrass grow the most during summer, they can benefit from regular watering. However, they will tolerate dry weather better than the cool-season grasses.

What is the best time of the day to water the lawn? Night irrigation is discouraged because it may encourage diseases, particularly when night temperatures exceed 69°F. The best time to irrigate is during the coolest part of the day when there is no wind. These conditions usually occur during early morning or late afternoon, and help conserve water by reducing evaporation. Conversely, mid-day irrigation during hot, sunny or windy days should be avoided because of increased evaporative losses of water. Furthermore, water that collects in low areas and inundates the turf may cause scald injury during sunny, hot periods.

The best form of weed control is proper management. Yet even the best maintained lawns will develop weed problems occasionally. Chemical control differs for broadleaf weeds (dandelion, plantain,

Table 4. Pre-emergence Crabgrass Herbicides Available

Chemical Name	Trade Names	Weeks Before Reseeding Possible	Other Comments
benefin	Balan	8 weeks	Usually two applications 6-8 weeks needed for season-long control.
benesulfide	Betasan, Presan	16 weeks	One application usually sufficient.
DCPA	Dacthal	10 weeks	Two applications. The second at ½ rate, usually needed to ensure season-long control.
pendemethalin	Ronstar	16-18 weeks	One application sufficient.
siduron	Tupersan	—	Only chemical that can be applied to a new seeding. Two applications recommended if used. Control in Washington area usually not as good as other chemicals.

etc.) and annual grass weeds (crabgrass).

Four primary broadleaf weed chemicals are available to the homeowner: 2, 4-D; 2,4-DP; MCPP (mecoprop); and dicamba. A combination of two or more of these chemicals will control most broadleaf weeds; however, a few weeds such as oxalis and wild violets are difficult to control although 2,4-DP will give moderate control. Also, dicamba should never be sprayed under the dripline of trees or shrubs as it can be absorbed by their roots and damage these ornamentals. As a result, a few weeds such as ground ivy and wild strawberry, for which only dicamba gives excellent control, become a particular problem in shady areas. Table 3 shows the susceptibility of the most common broadleaf weeds to the chemicals that are available.

Read Labels Carefully

Always follow herbicide label directions carefully. Apply broadleaf spray herbicides when there is no wind, when soil moisture is adequate, and when the weeds are actively growing (best months are April, May, September, or October).

Crabgrass and other annual grasses are best controlled by pre-emergence herbicides, i.e., herbicides applied prior to weed seed germination. Although there are chemicals to control mature crabgrass, they can be difficult for the homeowner to use successfully.

Five different pre-emergence crabgrass herbicides available to the homeowner are listed in Table 4. They all should be applied by April 1 to April 10 in the Washington area to ensure they are on before crabgrass germinates. Any crabgrass that germinates before the herbicide is applied will survive. Also, any mechanical action that disturbs the soil surface, such as dethatching or aerification, will also break the pre-emergency herbicide barrier, allowing crabgrass to germinate and mature. All the pre-emergence herbicides should be watered-in if possible, and some need a second application for season-long control.

Nutsedge is a difficult weed to control selectively, although success has been achieved with the chemical bentazon (Basagran). The chemical is relatively expensive and label directions must be followed very carefully for good control. Apply bentazon in mid-June or after most of the nutsedge has emerged.

Clumps of tall fescue, orchardgrass, quackgrass, and bermudagrass in a bluegrass lawn cannot be selectively controlled. However, they can be killed with spot spraying of glyphosate (Roundup, Kleenup), allowing for reseeding. Remember that glyphosate is nonselective. It will kill any green and growing plants it is sprayed on. Only spray where you intend to overseed and follow label directions carefully.

Thatch

Thatch, an accumulation of organic matter consisting of dead stems and roots between the soil and green vegetation, is often a major problem in Washington area lawns. Many lawn problems can be related to excess thatch (more than one-quarter- to one-half-inch thick), including greater disease, insect and weed problems, reduced effectiveness of pesticides, lower heat and drought tolerance, and inefficient use of water and fertilizer.

There is no simple method of controlling thatch development. Preventive thatch management should involve proper nutrition, cultivation, mowing and irrigation. The pH of the thatch layer appears to be important to thatch decomposition, with 6.2 to 6.4 the most desirable range. Light annual applications of agricultural ground limestone (10 to 25 pounds per 1,000 square feet) may help to speed up thatch decomposition.

Aerification and topdressing also speed up thatch decomposition. The soil brought to the surface through the aeration process increases microbial activity and improves moisture retention in the thatch layer. A vertical mower that cuts through the thatch down to the soil surface, or very heavy raking with a thatch rake to remove the thatch materials, are about the only other ways to get rid of this organic matter. This should be done in the fall on bluegrass lawns and in the summer on bermuda or zoysia lawns. Tall fescue produces very little thatch compared to most other grasses.

Shade

One of the major problems in establishing grass is shade. Even with good management, it often can be difficult to maintain quality grass. There are, however, several things that can be done to enhance the chances for good turf.

First, and most important, select a grass species that is adapted to shady conditions. For most situations, the best choice is fine-leaved fescue, such as Pennlawn creeping red fescue. If the soil generally remains very moist, then *Poa trivialis* will usually persist best, although it easily spreads and becomes a weed on drier, sunnier locations of the lawn. Tall fescue also will perform better in the shade than most other grasses.

After getting a shade tolerant grass established, following these guidelines will help it to persist longer:

1. Mow the grass slightly higher than is normal for sunny areas.
2. Rake leaves off the grass periodically during the fall to prevent smothering the grass.
3. Water infrequently but deeply when you must water. Light, frequent watering will encourage shallower tree and turf rooting.
4. Apply the recommended amount of nitrogen or less. Higher amounts will encourage disease. Maintain soil pH, phosphorus and potassium levels as recommended by soil tests.
5. Improve light penetration and air movement through selective pruning of trees and shrubs. Also prune shallow roots of trees and shrubs if possible.

Diseases and Insects

Numerous diseases can affect Washington area home lawns. Some of the most common are helminthosporium leaf spot on bluegrass and fescues; summer patch on bluegrass; brown patch on tall fescue and perennial ryegrass; dollar spot on bluegrass, fine fescues, and perennial ryegrass; red thread on perennial rye-

PHOTO BY LONDON TOWN PUBLIK HOUSE AND GARDENS

London Town Publik House and Gardens is a double attraction on Maryland's South River at Edgewater, near Annapolis. The restored Publik House, built in the 1760s, is a national historic landmark. London Town Gardens is one of the most pleasing small public gardens in the East and the Men's Garden Club has followed its development with close interest. The view above is from a woodland height, rich in native and exotic plant species, looking down into an area where every species of North American azaleas east of the Rocky Mountains can be found.

grass, and powdery mildew on bluegrass.

Unfortunately, diseases are very difficult for homeowners to diagnose and by the time they realize they have a problem, it is often too late to treat them. Therefore, the homeowner's best defense against diseases is using grass varieties recommended by the local universities and using sound cultural practices, particularly fertilization, watering, and thatch control.

Even the best managed lawns in the Washington area will suffer occasionally from insect problems. Among the most important is the damage caused by the feeding activity of larvae (grubs) or certain beetles (particularly chafers and Japanese beetles), chinch bugs, sod webworms, and billbugs (particularly in zoysia grass). As chemical control recommendations change periodically, it is best to contact a local extension agent for the most up-to-date recommendations. One chemical that you may want to keep on hand is diazinon. It will control the most common turf insects if used properly and at the correct time. Dursban also will do a good job on sod webworms but will not be very effective against grubs if there is much thatch.

In conclusion, maintaining a healthy, attractive lawn is much like maintaining your own good health. No matter how good your intentions, the quality and health of your lawn will fluctuate with weather and unexpected problems. However, following the basic guidelines for proper establishment, grass selection, and maintenance will give you the best chance for a long-lived, attractive turf.

A Philosophy of Ground Cover

By Frederick Jochem

Ground cover, whether it's vegetable or mineral, is indispensable to most Washington area gardens. It can take care of places where lawn grasses will not do well. And it can cut down the areas of lawn, thus reducing mowing and pest control and otherwise simplifying maintenance.

Not all ground covers grow. Washed gravel and crushed stone, especially if there is plastic beneath them, keep out weeds and outline buildings nicely. You must consider your walks and drives as special cases. Paved walks can be enhanced by fragrant, low-growing herbs – thymes, especially.

The term "ground cover" means to me:

1. Plants to cover banks or other spaces you cannot or would not mow, or where grasses or other plants will not grow.

2. Small plants to shade out weeds around and under larger ornamental plants that cannot do this for themselves.

A ground cover should be presentable all year long, ideally. But it should be modest, not calling attention to itself. A ground cover can add interest to otherwise waste places, providing contrasts in size, form, leaf shape and color.

I see no reason to plant annuals as a ground cover except while waiting for something better and less care-intensive to grow up.

References

de Wolf, Gordon P., et al.: *Taylor's Guide to Ground Covers, Vines and Grasses.* Houghton Mifflin, 1987.

Dimond, D. and M. MacCaskey: *All About Ground Covers.* Ortho Books, 1982.

Ground Covers for the Area

Bearberry (Kinnikinick) – *Arctostaphylos uva-ursi*
Native low-spreading evergreen, excellent for large areas. Pinkish-white flowers, glossy-green leaves bronze in winter, scarlet berries. Full sun.

Creeping Thyme (Mother-of-Thyme) – *Thymus Serpyllum*
Evergreen 2-to-6 inch edging plant. Small rosy-lilac flowers. Leaves aromatic.

English Ivy – *Hedera Helix*
Large, five-pointed leaves, purple in winter. Vine starts flat but must be kept pruned down.

Spring Heath – *Erica carnea*
Evergreen. Leaves form 6-to-12 inch mats in full sun. Rosy flowers late winter to April.

Japanese Spurge – *Pachysandra terminalis*
Excellent under plants and some shade. Shiny 6-to-8 inch leaves evergreen or streaked with white; creamy flowers.

Junipers – *Juniperus* species
Juniperus horizontalis (Creeping Juniper) is a popular U.S. native. 'Bar Harbor' from Maine is prostrate. So are 'Waukegan' and 'Douglasii' named for the Douglas nursery in Waukegan, Illinois. 'Emerson' is steel-blue. 'Plumosa,' from the Andorra nursery in Pennsylvania is feathery purple in fall. 'Wiltonii' was found on a Maine island by someone from Wilton, Connecticut. It has blue color lasting all winter and also is known as 'Blue Rug.' *J. chinensis procumbens* 'Nana' (dwarf Japanese Garden juniper) has branches with distinctive shelving effect.

Lily-of-the-Valley – *Convallaria majalis*
Fragrant flower clusters above 8-to-10 inch leaves. Likes mostly shade. Ratty leaves in midsummer.

Myrtle (Periwinkle) – *Vinca minor*
Prostrate creeping vines with shiny dark

leaves, blue flowers prominent March-May (others have white or pink). Attractive almost anywhere.

Plantain Lily – *Hosta*
Excellent low-or-zero-maintenance hardy perennials with lily-like white or purplish flower spikes in summer over striking green or variegated leaves. Small (8 inch) to large (4 feet). Snails love them.

St. John's-wort – *Hypericum calycinum*
Sub-shrub to 12 inches for shade, yellow flowers to 3-inch diameter July to fall, 3-to-4 inch leaves purplish in fall. Does well even in sandy soil. Easy to cut back or root.

Wild Strawberry, Sand Strawberry – *Fragaria virginiana, F. chiloensis*
Small creepers, thick green leaves, stocky runners, five-petaled little flowers, inedible red fruits.

Stonecrop – *Sedum* species
Tiny evergreen leaves form low, flat mats. Grows even in full sun among hot rocks. Flowers pink to red.

Thrift – *Armeria maritima*
Perennial 6-inch herb with small pink flowers in spring. Does well in sandy soil, full sun.

Wintercreeper – *Euonymus Fortunei*
Evergreen vine with shiny green myrtle-like leaves grows fast in any soil, sun or shade. Purple stem. Prune to keep in bounds. Creeps or climbs.

Wild violets – *Viola* species
Blue, yellow, pink or white, they will volunteer, often in grass. Can make colorful carpet in part shade.

Forget-me-not – *Myosotis* species
Volunteers under trees, in grass, damp spots, or mulch in expanding drifts. Can be attractive after 2 to 3 years.

Carpet Bugleweed, Geneva Bugle – *Ajuga reptans, A. genevensis*
Popular and vigorous but invasive. Many varieties – blue, rose, red or white flowers, green to purple leaves, some variegated. Varietal plantings in a few years can yield plants like the species not the variety.

Minority View

One reason I attended a Longwood Gardens seminar on ground covers was to learn whether any of the specialists conducting it knew how to eradicate myrtle, *vinca minor*. Unhappily they didn't. The problem with this plant – why I wanted to get rid of it – is that it's overly eager. Give it full credit for being handsome with a lustrous leaf and an attractive spring flower but it's also very competitive against less invasive plants I'd rather grow.

Will Roundup kill it? Not my vinca. Not even a double-strength second application. A phone call to the Monsanto Company confirmed the failure. "You'll notice that we don't label it for vinca," a spokesman said. So I grubbed it out by hand, tediously since it grew in a mat under the azaleas and tried to smother the bearberry. I now know vinca never will be entirely gone but at least the first victory was mine.

The Longwood seminar did recommend some less usual ground covers including several on Fritz Jochem's list. I'll add one more, a real aristocrat:

Wild Ginger *(Asarum europaeum)*, so refined it allows itself to spread only a few inches a year. Expensive but worth it. A marvelously shiny green-leaved ground cover which will knock them dead if you have the right cultural conditions: A moist, well-drained, woodsy acid soil, partial shade. Fertilize with blood meal.

– John G. Shaffer

Junipers: A Short Tale

Junipers like sun, non-acid soil and free drainage. They are useful for checking erosion and traffic, especially on steep banks, and they come in a wide choice of heights, shapes and colors.

We planted bluish-green Pfitzers *(Juniperus chinensis)* across the top of the steepest bank and just below *J. horizontalis* 'Plumosa,' the Andorra juniper, which is gray-green in spring, purplish in fall. Then came *J. Sabina* 'Tamariscifo-

A 26-foot bed of pachysandra encircles an old red maple. Something besides grass at the base of a tree in the lawn is more than a decorative accent. It protects a tree from lawn mower injury, makes mowing easier, conserves moisture around tree roots, and reduces weed growth. Only a small bed is necessary. Ground covers are popular but stones, gravel, bricks and wood chips also are widely used.

lia,' which is dense and light green; *J. chinensis procumbens*, the Japanese Garden juniper, which is dark green and a foot high, and at the bottom *J. horizontalis* 'Bar Harbor' and 'Wiltonii' to give two shades of blue-green.

With lime and pine bark mulch plus a 10-10-10 fertilizer after growth started, we checked erosion in three months. After two years neither children nor dogs could get through, up or down, nor did they want to. It was a lovely sight – for a while.

Then the white pines, the deodar cedar and the other trees we planted began to shade out the junipers. Our basic plan is still there but it's a sorry sight and substitute plantings are called for.

Moral: (1) Junipers need sun. (2) Never turn your back on your plantings. (3) Never plant trees and shrubs that compete with each other.

– Frederick Jochem

Do's and Don'ts

DON'T plant your vegetable garden too early. A tomato plant set out on May 21 will be just as far along on June 21 as one set out May 7.

DO plant the whole Jiffy pot if the roots of your seedlings have grown through the top. Research has shown that pulling off the pot can damage the roots.

DO stake your high-growing flowers and vegetables when you plant them, or at least before they reach six inches in height.

DO allow the leaves on your bulbs after flowering to wither naturally in order to store up energy for next year's bloom.

DON'T be afraid to use ground covers instead of grass. They are attractive in all seasons, require minimum care, and are useful in shady areas.

Growing Annual Flowers

By Charles A. H. Thomson

Annuals are plants that germinate, grow, flower, go to seed and die in a single season. Biennials take two years for the same cycle. Perennials can repeat season after season.

Annuals are treated here as plants featured for a single season. They may be biennials like foxglove 'Foxy' that will bloom from seed the first season if started early. Or they may be perennials like delphiniums that can be started from plants and give at least one season of good bloom before they succumb to our heat and diseases. Mostly they are true annuals like marigolds and zinnias.

Most annuals do well here. The main climatic condition governing their selection and use is our relatively short spring followed soon by hot and humid summers. Hence some cool-season plants like stock or sweet peas rarely do well. Those that do bloom well, like Shirley poppies, are likely to be cut down by early summer. The warmth lovers like petunias and marigolds can take our summers, and some will go well into fall, particularly if they are protected for a day or so against our early frosts. Others, like annual chrysanthemums, get past such frosts by themselves.

For Almost Every Need

Annuals available to us make it possible to meet almost every need of the gardener or landscaper. Flowers in brilliant hues and more delicate tints abound. Vines give flowers and make screens. Bushy plants make colorful hedges. Low plants are available for edging. Medium-sized plants grace the middle of the flower border. Tall plants provide excellent accents and striking backgrounds. Annuals give us fine cut flowers ranging from those that last for a day to the everlasting. Annuals are well suited to pots, containers, and window boxes. The former let you put your plants where they will do well and can be moved around to what you want, say in decorating.

Annuals are great bridgers, useful for filling in gaps between well-spaced perennials and shrubs, especially those that have not reached their full size. They bridge the times and spaces between the disappearance of spring bulbs and the arrival of summer and fall flowers and foliage. Annuals can also provide a succession of flowers and foliage to brighten the whole gardening season.

Timing a Factor

Having plants available in timely fashion is necessary for getting the most out of annuals in our area. This means starting or buying your cold-tolerant plants early in the season, and setting them out so they can enjoy whatever cool there may be in spring, or sowing them the preceding fall (larkspur, Shirley poppies). Warm weather plants also like to be in place when the weather turns favorable and stable for them. Some, like impatiens, will self-sow and come up at the right time. It does not pay to rush the season. Annuals, like most plants, need to be grown on without setback for best results. Late May and early June are propitious times in most years to set out the warmth-lovers.

Plan for the Whole Year

It is well to have a plan for the whole year's garden, and to see how best you can use annuals to carry it out. One advantage of annuals is that the gardener

All America Selections, the seed industry cooperative, celebrated its fiftieth anniversary in 1983 by naming the popular 'First Lady' marigold as its "all-time, first-place winner."

can obliterate his mistakes and cover them with later choices, assuring good balance of color, texture, leaf and plant form. For example, if the earlier garden is fading beforetimes in mid- to late-summer, ornamental kale can be set out to provide color when the weather turns cool and keep on with green and lavender and white until heavy freezes. In planning, think about the ultimate spacing of plants prior to setting them out, given their ultimate size, and the possibility that some plants may be placed thickly to be thinned out as the season progresses.

Most Annuals Like Sun

Most annuals like sun, gentle slopes, a lean to moderately fertile soil, and a pH from 6.0 to 6.5. Some, like larkspurs, like a sweet soil; others, like cleome, will do well almost anywhere, including the acid soils of azalea beds. Too much nitrogen encourages too much leaf and weak stems; too little means stunted growth. Cautious feeding with balanced fertilizers is in order, adjusting pH and time of feeding to the needs of companion plants as well as the annuals themselves. After

the first flush of bloom of plants that will repeat their flowering, the gardener might give them a light meal of balanced fertilizer. Or if he has used a slow-release fertilizer in preparing his planting sites, he may not need even that.

Most annuals grow well under mulches. They profit from the lack of competition whether from weeds or from their own kind. Grooming is important not only for appearance, but also to keep plants from setting unwanted seed and hence encouraging them to cease flowering. Taller sorts may require staking, although the garden designer Gertrude Jekyll planned some of her most effective gardens by putting larger later flowering plants back of earlier, smaller ones so the rearward plants could be draped forward over the declining foliage and spent bloom of the shorter ones. As in vegetables, flowers should be harvested at the peak of perfection; but if the peak be missed, harvest anyway to prevent setting seed.

Disease-Free Varieties

Control of pests and diseases must always be assured. The first move is to select varieties that are relatively disease-free and not attractive to insects or other pests. Cleome is a good example. The second move is to space your plants so as to assure good air circulation. This will help avoid mildews (to which zinnias are on occasion prone). The third is to give them good culture, moving in on pests as soon as pest infestation threatens. Some preventive dusting or spraying may be in order, as for example using systemic insecticides and fungicides for bedding dahlias, and dusting zinnias and other susceptible plants to ward off mildew and leaf-spotting. Sulfur is useful for this provided the temperature does not go above the mid-80's.

CHOICES FOR THE GARDEN

Choices among annuals are literally legion for the Washington gardener. To provide an initial guide, the following list of sure-fire choices is offered (with a code indicating their uses):

Ageratum (non-rampant) (B, E, S, PS)

Begonia semperflorens (B, E, S, PS)
Cleome (CF, S, PS, V)
Coleus (B, E, P, PS, SH)
Impatiens sultani, balsamina (B, E, P, PS, SH)
Ipomoea **Morning Glory** (S, PS)
Marigold (B, CF, V, P)
Nicotiana (F, PS, SH)
Petunia (B, F, P, S, PS, V)
Sweet Alyssum (B, E, S, PS)
Zinnia (B, CF, E, P, S, PS, V)

B = Bedder	C = Climber
CF = Cut flowers	E = Edger
F = Fragrant	P = Pots,
PS = Part sun	containers
S = Sun	SH = Shade
V = Versatile	VI = Vine

For sunny areas the following can be substituted for the shade lovers:

Centaurea – **Bachelor's Button, Cornflower** (V)
Cosmos (CF, S, V)
Digitalis – **Foxglove,** Biennial self-sower. The cultivar 'Foxy' will bloom first year from seed. **Excelsior** mix, florets stand at right angles to stem.

For those who wish to go further afield, the following list of species will perform well under the conditions mentioned. As for the best varieties, watch the ever-changing parade rated by local observers.

Armeria – **Thrift, Sea Pink.** E, borders, rockery. Drainage important.
Brassica oleracea acephala – **Ornamental kale.** Late colorful B, E, P.
Capsicum annuum – **Ornamental pepper.** E, P, S.
Consolida orientalis, formerly *Delphinium ajacis* – **Larkspur.** Good annual self-sower. CF, PS, S.
Dimorphotheca sinuata – **Cape Marigold.** S, V for hot dry situations.
Geranium *(Pelargonium* x *hortorum)* – Striking flowers and leaves, until frost. B, E, P, PS, S.
Gypsophila – **Annual Baby's Breath.** B, PS, S. For dried arrangements.
Helianthus annuus – **Sunflower.** Seeds, height, backgrounder. S.
Helichrysum – **Everlasting Flower, Strawflower.** For dried bouquets. S.
Iberis umbellata – **Globe Candytuft.**

PHOTO BY GEORGE TALOUMIS
The flowering tobacco hybrids developed in recent years have given the gardener a delightful new bedding plant. The sweet-scented Nicotianas hold their color from early summer to frost.

White, colored flowers. B, P, PS.
Iberis amara – **Rocket Candytuft.** White. CF, C.
Kochia scoparia – **Summer Cypress, Burning Bush.** Annual hedge, fall color.
Limonium – **Sea Lavender.** Everlasting dried flowers. S.
Lobelia erinus – **Edging Lobelia.** Var *pendula,* for hanging baskets. Cool season.
Papaver – **True poppies.** (1) *nudicaule.* **Iceland Poppy.** Biennial grown as annual. Sow in fall or early spring. Excellent variable form and color. S. (2) *rhoeas.* cvs **Shirley Poppy.** Annual, short season. Self sower. S.
Portulaca grandiflora – **Rose Moss, Eleven O'clock.** Rockery, edging, dry banks. P.
Salvia – B, E, mid-border accent. (1) *farinacea* – **Mealy-cup.** Perennial grown as annual/biennial. Blue, white forms. (2) *splendens* – **Scarlet Sage.** Various red, pastels, early, midseason. P, PS, S.
Sanvitalia procumbens – **Creeping Zinnia.** B, E, P, rockery.
Scabiosa atropurpurea – **Mourning Bride.** Varied heights. CF, PS, S. *Stellata* – **Starflower.** Everlasting flower heads for dried arrangements.
Thunbergia alata – **Clockvine, Black-eyed Susan.** Ground Cover, E, boxes, V;, arbors, trellises.
Torenia fourniera – **Wishbone Flower.**

Early cool-season edger, rockery, P.

Verbena x *hybrida* – **Garden Verbena.**
Creeper, edger, P. Fragrant. Perennial grown here chiefly as annual.

Note above the absence of annual asters, nasturtiums, phlox, and sweet peas. They can be grown here but it is not always rewarding because of diseases, insects, and summer heat.

Almost any listing of preferred varieties, or even species, is likely to go out of date. In recent years plantsmen have been producing many new cultivars, extending the range of available colors, plant heights, flower and foliage forms, and desirable garden behavior. Three examples: (1) *Portulaca*, or Rose Moss, used to go to sleep by early afternoon. Now it has brilliant new colors and doubled flowers that stay open all the sunny day. (2) Mule marigolds (triploids) put all their strength into making flowers, not seeds. They will bloom well into early fall. (3) Geraniums, horticulturally *pelargoniums*, now come in short to tall varieties. Colors range from classical bright red through pink to white and rose, in solid colors or with white eyes. Leaves often have strong zoning. They are easy from seed. Although they are tender perennials, mostly used as annuals, they can be overwintered in the house and propagated by cuttings.

Consider plants labeled All America Selections (AAS). They have been tested for good performance in many parts of the country, but that does not mean they will be outstanding here. Be on the lookout for varieties that have been bred for improved resistance to diseases, reduced attractiveness to pests, longer growing seasons, and reduced requirements for maintenance and care. To keep up with these developments, consult the latest and best catalogs and garden magazines.

Good references

de Wolf, Gordon P. Jr., et al: *Taylor's Guide to Annuals*. Houghton Mifflin, 1987.
Rockwell, F.F. and Esther C. Grayson: *The Complete Book of Annuals*. Doubleday, 1955.
Sinnes, A. Cort, and Michael D. McKinley. *All About Annuals*. Ortho Book, 1981.

PHOTO BY SAM SHIOZAWA

". . . as high as an elephant's eye." One of our members was given seed for this corn (Hawaiian Super Sweet No. 9), developed at the University of Hawaii, and tried it out in a decorative planting by his house. The tallest stalk is 13 feet.

Do's and Don'ts

DON'T buy plants described with words like "gigantic," "miraculous," "stupendous" or some similar superlative. And do remember that bargain plants often are no bargains.

DO buy first-class nursery stock from reputable sources. Do get expert advice before buying: on ultimate size, placement, maintenance requirements (sun, shade, soil, food, pH), and whether it's pest prone. Do visit a neighbor's garden to see how the plant behaves. Is it hardy in this area? Drought-resistant?

Growing Hardy Perennials

By Carl R. Hahn

Many of the choicest ornamental garden plants are hardy perennials – a large group of plants, either evergreen (woody) or herbaceous (non-woody) in which the above-ground portion dies to the ground at some point during the year, usually winter. They live, hopefully, for several years.

Some have been grown in gardens for centuries; others are recent arrivals. They can play a special role in the garden not achieved by any other group of plants. For those who seek in plants more than a dot of color, selected hardy perennials can provide aristocratic bearing, great character and elegance of foliage, fragrance and flowers.

The climate of the Washington area has proved to be hospitable to a vast number of hardy perennials. Those plants mentioned here are only a few of the many which can be grown successfully in this area. Our weather patterns, however, do preclude the growing of the more tender types native to areas with mild winters. Also, hybrid garden delphiniums, lupines and kindred plants requiring cool summers do not grow well here. Between the extremes there is a treasure house from which to select.

Perennials Earlier Here

Those who have not previously gardened in the Washington area – especially those from northern states – may be surprised to find that hardy perennials frequently start into growth here earlier and grow somewhat faster and taller than in cooler parts of the country.

Unlike annual plants which survive in nature by starting anew from seed each year, hardy perennials have an extra edge. In addition to developing seeds to produce future generations, perennials also have a living underground structure such as a rootstock, bulb, tuber or rhizome which lives on year after year.

The term "perennial" is not a synonym for "immortal"; the life spans of hardy perennials can vary greatly. *Gypsophila*, Baby's Breath, might be expected to live only three to four years locally, as it requires extremely well-drained soils, especially in winter, and prefers a somewhat alkaline soil. At the other end of the scale it would not be unreasonable to expect peonies and gas plants *(Dictamnus)* to survive for 30 to 50 years in their original location.

Plant Size Increases

The nature of many hardy perennials is such that the size of individual plants tends to increase over the years, resulting in weak, crowded growth with unproductive dead centers. It is thus necessary for the gardener to renew them periodically by division. Most perennials require division every three to five years, some almost never.

Division is necessary when: (1) growth is weak, flowers are smaller or fewer than normal; (2) the center of the clump is dead with all or most of growth forming an outside ring; and (3) plants are tangled and growing into one another.

Most perennials can be divided in the spring at about the time they start into growth. The strongest plants will be found on the outside of the clump. These may be lifted with a spade or garden fork. Select plants with three to five growing points, "eyes," or buds with as much of the root system intact as possible. A single clump can yield potentially hundreds of divisions. Select only the strongest, discard the rest, and replant immediately.

Perennials tend to be reasonably adaptable; but they are a large and diverse group with varying requirements as to moisture, light and soil. The successful gardener takes the time to match plants to the sites where they are to grow. Most perennials grow best in sun to semi-shade in reasonably rich, well-drained soil which is not excessively acidic.

Have Soil Test First

Before planting or replanting it is always wise to have a soil test to determine soil fertility and acidity levels, and to prepare the site accordingly.

As a general rule, soils for planting can be improved by incorporating to a depth of eight to 12 inches a two-inch thick layer of organic matter (compost, rotted sawdust, rotted leaves, peat moss) and the quantity of fertilizer and pulverized limestone recommended by a soil test.

After setting the plants, apply an organic mulch to a depth of two to three inches up to but not covering or touching plants. Water well. After planting, water during periods of dryness, take appropriate disease and insect control measures, and remove spent flowers and old flowering stalks to encourage reflowering later in the season.

Perennial Border

The classical approach to growing perennials is the perennial border. This style, which reached its highest development in England, is characterized by planting in stair-step fashion a bank of perennials against a wall or fence. Gardens of this type are not seen much any more because they are expensive and difficult to maintain. Plants tended to be crowded together causing them to stretch and require staking. Additionally, air circulation was poor, promoting disease problems.

The British perennials specialist Alan Bloom in recent years has advocated the planting of perennials in "island beds." Basically, these are free-form beds surrounded by a lawn area or paths. Bloom selects the tallest plants for the center of the bed. Progressively shorter plants lead to the edges. This allows better light penetration, improved air circulation and considerably easier maintenance. In addition, plants can be viewed from all sides.

Perennials are such versatile plants that they may be used in any manner that strikes the gardener's fancy. They may be introduced into plantings of trees and shrubs, bulbs, annuals, rock gardens or woodland gardens. The possibilities are endless.

Thirty Best Perennials for Washington Gardens

1. *Achillea* spp and cvs – **Yarrow.** Attractive fern-like foliage and yellow flowers combine in dense convex heads. Require full sun and grow best in well-drained soil of low fertility. Spent flowers be removed for continuous bloom. Cultivars: 'Coronation Gold' (yellow, June-July, 3 feet), 'Gold Plate' (bright yellow flowers 6 inches across, to 4 feet), and 'Moonshine' (light yellow, grey-green foliage, 1½ to 2 feet).

2. *Aconitum Carmichaelii* (syn. *A. Fischeri*). Late-flowering, erect, attractive divided foliage. Hooded flowers borne on short spikes a violet blue. Flowering occurs in August-September when few other blue flowers available. To 3 feet, best in partial shade, rich soil.

3. *Aruncus dioicus* – **Goatsbeard.** Large, to 8 feet; hybrids 3 to 4 feet. Cream-colored flowers in summer. Grows anywhere if given extra water but needs space. Fern-like foliage, flowers last for months.

4. *Asclepias tuberosa* – **Butterfly weed.** Orange flowers, sometimes yellow in midsummer. Needs sun, best in poor, well-drained soil. Rarely requires division or fertilization.

5. *Astilbe* x *Arendsii* – **Astilbe.** Great plants, especially valued for moist waterside locations. Best in partial shade but grow well in full sun if not allowed to dry. Flower in summer, seed heads remain attractive into winter. Fertilize in early spring, divide every 3 to 5 years. Cultivars: 'Avalanche' (white, 18 inches), 'Deutschland' (white, 2 feet), 'Europe' (pale pink, 2 feet), 'Fanal' (deep crimson red, 2 feet), 'Red Sentinel' (rich crimson red, 3 feet, earlier than most).

6. *Baptisia australis* – **Wild Blue Indigo,**

False Indigo. Beautiful plant, virtually pest-free and trouble-free. Valued for spikes of indigo-blue, pea-like flowers in June atop 3-to-4-foot stems. Unusual, attractive black pods remain ornamental for months, set off well against blue-green foliage and grey-green stems. Foliage attractive throughout growing season. **False Indigo** will grow in full sun or partial shade. Requires no staking or frequent division.

7. *Bergenia cordifolia* 'Purpurea'. Valued more for its bold cabbage-like, evergreen foliage which becomes purplish in winter, magenta flowers on red stalks in spring. Grows to a foot tall, about as wide. Protect it with slug and snail bait.

8. *Brunnera macrophylla* – **Siberian Bugloss.** Valuable for large, heart-shaped leaves which become larger and more attractive as they develop, and for blue forget-me-not-like flowers in April and May. Requires semi-shade, moist soil. Plants grow to a foot and hold dainty flowers above foliage. Seeds itself generously.

9. *Cimicifuga racemosa* – **Black Snakeroot.** Regal plant combining lofty, spike-like white flowers (5 to 8 feet) and attractive divided foliage. Shade or part shade, best in rich, evenly moist soil. Rarely if ever needs dividing.

10. *Coreopsis* – **Tickseed.** Among the best are *C. verticillata* (Threadleaf coreopsis) and its popular cultivars: 'Golden Shower' (bright yellow, 2 to 3 feet), 'Moonbeam' (creamy-yellow blooms, 1½ to 2 feet), 'Zagreb' (yellow to 1 foot). Foliage of all three is ferny. Can't be beat for drought resistance, tolerance of poor soil, adaptability to full sun or light shade, and continuous bloom through summer. Another member of genus, *C. grandiflora*, tends to sprawl except for dwarf cultivar, 'Goldfink' (9 inches) which is good front-of-the-border plant.

11. *Dicentra* hybrids and species – **Bleeding-heart.** *D. eximia and D. spectabilis* are worthy plants but have been surpassed by superior hybrids which combine long spring-to-fall flowering period, fern-like foliage and compact growth habit. Recommended cultivars: 'Adrian Bloom' (greyish leaves, crimson flowers, 1 foot), 'Bountiful' (long flowering season, deep pink to crimson flowers, 15 to 18 inches), 'Silver Smith' (bluish foliage, white flowers). Partial shade to almost full sun, although in latter site foliage burns by late summer. Rich, moist soil.

12. *Echinops ritro* 'Taplow Blue' – **Globe**

Thistle. Steel blue, thistle-like flower heads on 4-foot stalks, elegant prickly foliage. Striking, unusual plant for full sun and well-drained soil. Flowers July to September.

13. *Epimedium* – **Barrenwort, Bishop's Hat.** Best is *E.* x *rubrum* with semi-evergreen foliage, reddish-brown in fall, red flowers in early spring. Often used as ground cover. With its smaller white relative, *E. Youngianum* 'Niveum' does well as edger or in rock garden. It is 9 to 12 inches by about as wide. Semi-shade to full sun. One of few plants to survive when planted under surface-rooted trees. *Epimedium* x *versicolor* 'Sulphureum' is choice plant with yellow flowers. Other cultivars have bi-colored blooms.

14. *Eryngium alpinum* – **Sea Holly.** Largest flowers, 2-inch, thistle-like, steel-blue flower heads. Perhaps best of sea hollies. Uppermost leaves also are often steel blue. Needs well-drained soil, tolerates a little shade.

15. *Helenium autumnale* – **Sneezeweed.** Big 3-to-5-foot clumps provide daisy-like flowers in strong colors from late August through September when not much else is blooming. The cultivar 'Riverton Beauty' (yellow with bronze-brown eye) is 5 footer for back of border. Other good hybrids are 'Bruno' (mahogany brown, 2 feet), 'Butterpat' (gold, 3 feet), and 'Gypsy' (bronze and gold, 3 feet). Flowers generally small but produced by hundreds. In full sun and moderately moist soil will sometimes outproduce fall-blooming chrysanthemums.

16. *Helleborus orientalis* – **Lenten Rose.** Valuable 18-inch plant for handsome evergreen foliage and unusual bloom season, February through April. Flowers vary from off-white to plum. Last for weeks despite winter storms and spring rains but fade quickly if cut for a warm house. Grow best in moisture-retentive soil in light shade under deciduous trees or shrubs.

17. *Hemerocallis* spp and cvs – **Daylily.** Very popular plants with thousands of cultivars. Each will bloom for several weeks, most in early summer. Some species and cultivars bloom in May, others in October. A few such as 'Stella de Oro' will bloom continuously from early summer to frost. Easy and rewarding plants with wide range of colors and flower form. Heights vary from 15 inches to 4 feet. Stay away from evergreen forms; otherwise it's difficult to make a poor choice.

18. *Hibiscus moscheutos* – **Hibiscus.** 'Southern Belle' is spectacular, with flowers to 10 inches, stalks to 7 feet that die down in late

fall. Cut them off at ground level; new growth appears in late spring. May need staking. Protect from Japanese beetles. 'Frisbee' is short, to 3 feet, but with same size flowers. Easy from seed. Named varieties available in white, pink, and shades of red.

19. *Hosta* spp and cvs – **Plantain Lily.** Aristocratic, elegant, more valued for bold foliage than flowers. Good in high shade to almost full sun. Moist but not wet conditions. Many cultivars, dwarfs to giants, and white to purple flowers from July through September. *H. Fortunei* var. *hyacinthina* has bold, gray-green leaves and lilac flowers, is 2½ feet tall and as broad. *H. Fortunei* 'Albo-marginata' is similar but with white-edged gray-green leaves. 'Honeybells' grows to 3 feet and as wide, has light green leaves with wavy margin; fragrant, pale lilac flowers with darker lilac veining. *H. Sieboldiana* var. *elegans* is the largest of the hostas with superb, striking blue-grey leaves, a foot or more across. The cultivar 'Frances Williams' is a gold-edged version.

20. *Iris sibirica* – **Siberian Iris.** Among the least demanding and most rewarding of iris groups. Virtually pest free, unlike the plagued German irises. Grows to 3 feet. Foliage attractive all season in vase-shaped clumps. Flowers in many colors in June. Rarely needs dividing but does need moisture. Cultivars: 'Anniversary' (white with yellow touch), 'Caesar's Brother' (deep purple), 'Dreaming Spires' (lavender and blue), 'Flight of Butterflies' (blue petals, pale blue to white between veins, slow to start), 'Sparkling Rose' (rose pink), 'Tealwood' (deep violet), 'White Swirl' (good long-flowering white).

21. *Kniphofia uvaria* – **Red Hot Poker, Torch Lily.** Species has red and yellow flowers in summer. Hybrids flower in early summer in colors from ivory through yellow to coral and scarlet. Height varies from 2 to 3½ feet, fat spikes of bloom well above sizable clumps of narrow, sometimes rigid foliage. Particularly attractive are 'Earliest of All' (coral rose, 2 to 2½ feet) and 'Primrose Beauty' (yellow to 2½ feet). Only requirements are plenty of sunlight, protection from strong winds, which is hard on spikes, and soil that drains well in winter.

22. *Liatris spicata* 'Kobold' – **Gayfeather.** Reliable and easy plant with shaving-brush-like flowers on tall spikes. Rich purple flowers start blooming from top of spike, proceed downward. Foliage narrow, much like grass. Grow 1½ to 2 feet, need no staking or other requirements except sun.

23. *Ligularia dentata* 'Desdemona.' Choice plant, 2 to 4 feet high and about 2½ feet wide, with bold foliage and leaves 12 inches across, green with purplish tinge. Best in partial shade where it never lacks water.

24. *Lythrum salicaria* – **Purple Loosestrife.** Seems to be comfortable in almost any location — sun, shade, wet or dry. Flowers an inch across produced densely on 12-inch spikes. Blooms July to September, height 3 to 5 feet. Cultivars: 'Dropmore Purple' (rich purple, 3 to 4 feet, June-September), 'Firecandle' (rosy red, 3 feet), 'Happy' (deep pink, compact 15 to 18 inches), 'Morden's Pink' (rose pink), 'Robert' (rose red, 2 feet).

25. *Paeonia* hybrids – **Chinese peonies.** Long-lived, 30 to 50 years, best left undisturbed after planting. Available in a number of colors and flower forms (single, double, anemone-type), many are fragrant. Height to 3 feet, flowers 3 to 6 inches across in May-June. Full sun to light shade. Hundreds of cultivars available.

26. *Platycodon grandiflorus* – **Chinese Balloon Flower.** Common name from balloon-shaped flowers in blue, white or pink, 2 to 3 inches across, blooms July to September. Height 2 to 3 feet. Sun or partial shade, well-drained soil. Cultivars and varieties: 'Albus' (tall, white flowers), 'Apoyama' (dwarf, 6 to 10 inches, violet-blue flowers all summer), *P. Mariesii* (bright blue flowers, 18 inches, no staking needed); a white cultivar, 'Albus' and rosy lilac one, 'Roseus', available.

27. *Pulmonaria saccharata* – **Bethlehem Sage.** Distant relative of native Virginia bluebell, valued for flowers and persistent foliage. Flowers pink in bud, opening blue; trumpet-shaped, half-inch long, produced in clusters. Deep green, attractive leaves heavily dappled in white or grey. Flowers April-May. Height 9 to 15 inches, needs partial shade, evenly moist, well-drained soil. 'Mrs. Moon' has flowers larger than species. 'Pink Dawn' buds and flowers pink.

28. *Rudbeckia fulgida* var. *sullivantii* 'Goldsturm' – **Coneflower.** Appears like Black-eyed Susan to casual observer but is better garden plant. Flowers, 3½ to 4 inches across, have yellow petals and black cone-shaped centers. Blooming begins in July, continues through September on plants 2½ feet high. Prolific bloomer and seedling producer, grows best in soil not excessively dry.

29. *Sedum* 'Stonecrop.' Of many species and cultivars, hybrid 'Autumn Joy' is attractive in bloom or out. Combines pink and copper-red flowers in large flat clusters and fleshy grey-

Oscars for Ornamentals

The only formal selection in the United States of exceptional garden merit is the Styer Award, based at Swarthmore College's Scott Arboretum. A committee of evaluators from Pennsylvania, New Jersey, Maryland and Delaware selects one plant a year that shows outstanding ornamental qualities in the middle Atlantic states. The following six are an instructive list for any gardener who wants to acquire some certified plant aristocrats:

English Ivy 'Buttercup' *(Hedera helix):* New leaves are chartreuse, later turning to butter yellow. Use as an ivy ground cover or as a climber that will clothe a wall with cheerful yellow foliage, winter as well as summer.

Holly 'Sparkleberry' *(Ilex serrata* x *I. verticillata):* A dazzling display of red berries on this deciduous holly lasts until March. It needs a male pollinator. A National Arboretum introduction.

Virginia Sweetspire 'Henry's Garnet' *(Itea virginica):* Deciduous shrub to 10 feet with fragrant, enduring white flowers in June; its chief glory is the red to purple fall foliage which lasts well into winter.

Magnolia 'Elizabeth' *(M. acuminata* x *M. heptapeta):* A color break in magnolias with soft lemon chiffon blossoms. Not for the very small garden, it grows vigorously to 25 to 35 feet and about half as broad.

Flowering Cherry 'Okame' *(Prunus incisa* x *P. campanulata):* One of the earliest cherries to flower – bright pink – and it flowers its second year from cuttings. Vase-shaped to 25 feet.

Zelkova 'Green Vase' *(Zelkova serrata):* This American cultivar of the oriental zelkova has a vase shape that is as close as we'll probably get to a substitute for the afflicted American elm. A vigorous grower, 40 feet in 18 years, it is a first-class shade, specimen and street tree. It withstands air pollution and adapts to heavy clay soils but not to sandy soils.

– John G. Shaffer

green leaves. Flowers in late summer or early fall, holds dried but handsome blooms into winter. Best in well-drained soil, full sun or very light shade.

30. *Solidago* cultivars – **Goldenrod.** Hybrid goldenrods are fine garden plants which suffer from erroneous reputation that they contribute to hay fever. All have yellow flowers produced in late summer and early fall. Trouble free, requiring only sun and reasonably well-drained soil. Cultivars: 'Cloth of Gold' (primrose yellow, large clusters, 20 inches), 'Golden Mosa' (dark yellow, 3 feet), 'Golden Shower' (bright yellow, 3 feet), 'Golden Thumb' (deep yellow, 1 foot).

References

Harper, Pamela and Frederick McGourty: *Perennials, How to Select, Grow and Enjoy.* HP Books, 1985.
Sinnes, A. Cort and Michael D. McKinley: *All About Perennials,* Ortho Books, 1981.
Taylor's Guide to Perennials. Houghton Mifflin, 1986. Based on *Taylor's Encyclopedia of Gardening,* 4th edition, 1961. Edited and brought up to date by Pamela Harper, Mary Ann McGourty, David Scheid and others.

_____

Do's and Don'ts

DO continue watering your plants in the fall as they prepare themselves for their dormancy. Don't neglect watering them in winter, especially if they are broad-leafed evergreens.

DON'T try to keep a cool-weather lawn perfect in summer's heat and humidity. Wait until the weather is suitable. Fertilizing a cool-weather lawn in fall is the best, summer the worst. Fertilize in spring only if you have to get new grass or sod going.

DON'T use sphagnum peat moss as a mulch. It is a valuable product but more valuable in the soil than on it.

PHOTO BY EDMUND C. FLYNN

An old mill wheel with a backdrop of nandina serves as a focal point at this garden fence. The plantings in front include liriope, hosta, bloodroot, variegated English ivy and the evergreen ground cover bearberry or kinnikinick *(arctostaphylos uva-ursi).*

Bulbs Throughout the Year

By Charles A. H. Thomson

Bulbs can do marvels for the Greater Washington gardener. With a little care – appropriate soil preparation, placement, and sequencing – bulbs will provide blooms, fragrance, and often attractive foliage from February into December. Outdoors, many will persist and increase through the years. Indoors, many can be forced to provide bloom and fragrance during winter – and several of these kinds can then be planted out. Many do well in containers to grace patio and porch.

Washington's climate governs what bulbs can be grown here easily and well. Washington's temperature range is less important than its changeability. We can expect warm spells in winter and early spring, alternating with sharp freezes. We can expect quick rises in late spring and early summer. Climatic summer may persist well into calendar fall.

These vagaries can throw off planning for succession of bloom, or arranging for companions to bloom at the same time. Hot summers mean short seasons for underplantings and for bulbs to get ready for the following season. Long cold spells followed by sharp warm-ups can bring early and mid-season varieties, or mid-season and late varieties, into bloom at the same time.

Our hot humid summers do not favor tuberous begonias, but many lilies, dahlias, gladioli and some tender tropical or semi-tropical bulbs (like Aztec lilies) do very well. Heat and winds can make the early fall crocuses and colchicums look sad. Our experience counsels us to select bulbs that do not break dormancy easily or that can stand weather changes once they are up.

Cultural requirements for most bulbs are uncompromising in one major respect; they *must have good drainage beneath them*. While most bulbs are relatively free of damage from pests and diseases, lilies, gladioli and tulips are not. Gardeners can avoid troubles by correct choice of varieties, placement and planting of bulbs, and by timely controls of pests, especially aphids, cucumber beetles, and thrips. Wise selection and preparation of the site; planting at the right time and depth, and assuring good spacing for air circulation; good care to blooming; judicious cutting of blooms and foliage; and simple after-care will favor repeated performance. The critical time of care for most bulbs is in the six to eight weeks after blooming when they are readying themselves for the next season.

Site Selection

In choosing sites for bulbs the gardener needs to consider not only how placement affects bulb performance but also how it satisfies his tastes in garden design, or how it meets other objectives. Early and small bulbs, like species crocus, should go where they can be seen easily (by walks or driveways) or can be allowed to spread for good mass effect (by the edge of a border or verge of trees or shrubs). Many early bulbs do well around or under deciduous trees if they can bloom and ripen before trees cast heavy shade. Most bulbs do best in good light, but many appreciate part shade, especially if they do not have to compete with the roots of perennials, shrubs or trees for food or moisture. In siting daffodils, tulips, and lilies the gardener should consider their height and potential for focal points. Most bulbs may make foliage but little if any bloom in heavy shade; for such areas, think ornamental foliage like that of caladiums.

If you have woodland or meadow, consider naturalizing daffodils. Slope can be important not only to favor drainage, but to assure a good garden display. Exposure to sun on a south-facing slope will bring on bloom sooner than the same time of exposure on a north-facing slope. Hence, planting the same variety of bulb in both such situations will extend season of bloom.

Site Preparation

Sites must be properly prepared. Soil should possess adequate fertility, good tilth, compatible pH, and freedom from undue erosion. Good drainage under bulbs may call for deep preparation. Twelve inches is not too much for big tulips, daffodils or lilies; six might do for smaller bulbs. Assuring good tilth is vital. In our clay soils, plenty of coarse, sharp builder's sand and enough organic material (peat moss or compost) to make the clay crumbly may be needed. A proportion of one-third each of clay, sand and humus is often recommended; but the gardener should work from the kind of soil he already has. Some soils may be so sandy that adding clay might help. Gypsum can improve clay without changing pH. (See "Soils - Fertilizers - Mulches - Compost.") Dolomitic limestone also can improve tilth while raising pH and adding magnesium. ComPro can improve friability.

If drainage is a problem, the gardener may resort to raised beds. As for fertility, if the site has been growing good weeds, it probably can grow good bulbs. The gardener can learn much about its fertility and pH by observing plants already growing there. In assuring fertility it is most important to supply phosphorus where most bulb roots grow – that is, *beneath* the bulb's base.

Whether preparing holes or beds, dig in superphosphate before the bulbs are planted, adding an inch of "clean" soil – that is, without chemical fertilizers or fresh organic material – as a pad for the bulbs to rest on. Bone meal or other organic fertilizers tend to promote disease when soil is warm and wet. Bone meal is expensive, slow reacting, and loath to move down in our heavy soils. Sewage sludge (ComPro or Milorganite) is sometimes recommended but it must be checked for presence of heavy metals. If processed with lime it is a powerful soil sweetener. Ordinary 5-10-5 or 5-10-10 may be better bets, along with a pelleted slow-release fertilizer.

Planting

Time and depth of planting strongly affect bulb performance. Bulbs planted too soon or too late may simply rot or not have enough time to make roots to support good development. But better late than never; daffodils unplanted will never bloom. Even set out here as late as February they can make flowers and go on for subsequent seasons. Bulbs planted too shallow are more susceptible to damage from weather or the depredations of squirrels. Those planted too deep without adequate drainage beneath them may never make it beyond the first season's flowering. Bulbs planted deeply are less likely to split up into smaller ones that won't bloom, or that must be dug after a season or so because they are too crowded to bloom well.

Time of planting should respect the life cycle of the bulbs. Most spring bloomers are best planted in early to mid-fall. Smaller bulbs such as winter aconites or snowdrops should be planted as soon as available in August or September. Narcissi are best planted in early fall as soon as the soil has cooled down a bit. Tulips can wait until late November or December.

Depth of planting. Bulbs should be planted deeply enough to avoid damage from annuals or perennials grown around or over them. Even some smaller ones, like crocuses, can go four inches deep to their tops. Having at least seven inches of settled soil over the tops of tulip bulbs helps perpetuate the planting. The old rule of planting at a depth of three or four times the largest measure of a bulb is useful in handling unfamiliar material.

After planting and watering in, bulbs appreciate a good mulch. Pine needles, oak leaves, wood chips, shredded bark and the like are all good for the larger bulbs, but avoid materials like peat moss or maple leaves that pack. In spring you can pull back mulch from planted areas to help the soil warm up. If you fear premature emergence in our chancy springtimes, leave it in place until you think the weather is going to stay favorable. The often-recommended scratching in of an all-purpose fertilizer in spring is not needed for the bulbs if they have been properly fertilized at planting or after blooming. And the mulch-pulling and fertilizer scratching is all too likely to break off tender growing tips not yet visible.

Adequate water is a must. If dry spells occur, what nature does not provide the gardener should. Staking should be done as soon as new growth shows where stakes can be inserted safely, and before stems are likely to fall over. Use stout stakes that will support stems up to the start of their flowering heads – usually about three-quarters of their height. Fasten ties tightly to the stakes and loosely to the plants. If insects or diseases threaten, take prompt measures. The best fertilizers for daffodils are low in nitrogen, higher in phosphorus, and even higher in potash. Chemical sources with slow release may be better than organic sources. Tulips, however, can use more nitrogen so a 9-9-6 or 10-6-4 formula is appropriate.

Subsequent Care

During and after blooming, be on the lookout for plant damagers (thrips, Japanese beetles) and disease vectors (aphids, cucumber beetles) and deal with them promptly. If signs of botrytis or virus appear, spray for the botrytis and rogue out any plants that show bad effects from virus or from soil-borne diseases, such as fusarium rots. In cutting flowers, leave enough leaves and stem to ripen bulbs for following seasons. Remove spent flowers so plants will not spend energy in making seeds. See that the bulbs get adequate water and fertilizer for several weeks after blooming or until the plant has lost leaves so it cannot absorb more food. After that dig up bulbs that are overcrowded or need to be moved. If, like tulips, they are going dormant, clean them, grade them and store them in open bags in airy places until time to replant. If, like lilies, they are never dormant, replant them as soon as you can.

Good Kinds and Cultivars

By appropriate selection, siting and timing, crocuses, narcissi, tulips, lilies

---

Will the Real King Alfred Please Show Up?

It's not generally known but some years ago the most popular of all daffodils, the yellow trumpet 'King Alfred,' started to run out. It was a favorite from its introduction in 1899 but first the stocks lost vigor and fields in Holland could no longer produce it in quantity. Then new fields in Oregon took over, assuring good bulbs for many years. But the true King Alfred dwindled even there. Yet the name is so valuable that growers and purveyors have been substituting 'Golden Harvest' (a 1927 introduction), 'Unsurpassable' (1929) and 'Dutch Master' (1948). Brent and Becky Heath, proprietors of the Daffodil Mart in Gloucester, Virginia, still keep a few of the old classic going, just to show visitors what it really was like. But do not rue the disappearance of the ancient King; the substitutes are as good or better flowers. Fanciers of heritage bulbs can find a few of the Old Original but the rest of us need not worry. If the current substitutes start to peter out we can trust the Dutch and other growers to come up with great look-alikes, full of vigor and survivability.

– **Charles A. H. Thomson**

and dahlias can serve almost all of a gardener's major purposes. Hence, whatever their size, I call them major bulbs. Species crocus can start the bulb year in February and end it the following December. The earliest daffodils and tulips are not far behind in spring. Lilies pick up the blooming season in May and can extend it into September. Bedding dahlias start in June and go until frost. The Evans begonias start up in late May, providing colorful leaves and pink blooms in part shade until frost.

Crocus. Crocuses can be divided into early species, later hybrids, and fall-blooming species. The first group, flowering here in February and March, are short, to four inches or so, and hence not good under taller ground covers such as pachysandra. Many are bunch-flowering, making good clumps of color although individual blooms are not spectacular. Some can make sheets of color in time. Hybrid crocuses, coming in March or early April, have larger and more striking individual blooms. Taller, to six inches and with larger flowers, they can go under lower-growing ground covers such as myrtle. The fall-blooming species start to flower in late September and may persist into December, making interesting companions for, say, chrysanthemums. Crocuses range in color from pure white, some with stripes and feathering, yellows, bronzes, lavender blues (no true blues) to dark purple, often with contrasting anthers and stamens.

Daffodils (Narcissi)

Almost all daffodils do well in our area. They tolerate considerable variation in pH, doing best in the 6.0 to 6.5 range. They usually can survive and bloom well despite viruses. Their worst enemy here is basal rot. In most of our area this is not serious. The best answer to this is never to plant a doubtful bulb. When dividing discard any iffy ones and do not think you can rehabilitate a sick one.

Planting, placement and care. Plant smaller daffodil bulbs with three inches of soil above their tips, and have four inches over the top of the larger ones. Smaller forms of daffodils go well on slopes or in protected places, in clumps of six or more. Larger daffodils are effective in groups of three or more, and useful as focal points, as well as in naturalized settings. Cut flower stems to the ground if you wish; the leaves are what is critical for next year's growth. Cut foliage as soon as the tips turn yellow. Dig when your clumps or stands are so thick that few or no good flowers are produced. Select the larger, blooming size bulbs. Fertilize the soil again and replant them immediately, or better for the bulbs, dry them and store them in mesh bags for fall replanting. To get a naturalized effect in grass or open woods, throw the bulbs on the ground and plant them where they fell, using a mattock. You either can use mixtures of vigorous varieties, or plant drifts of the same ones. Your choice.

Classes. Officially daffodils fall into twelve classes. The first three, mostly large-flower types, are classed by the relation between the length of their trumpets or cups and their perianth segments. Trumpet daffodils have trumpets as long as or longer than their perianth segments. Large-cups have cup segments from one third to as long as their perianth segments. Small cupped daffodils have shorter cups. The next class is doubles, in which either the whole flower or the cup alone is doubled into many petals. Then come five classes of hybrids of the most important species: *triandrus*, *cyclamineus*, *jonquilla*, *tazetta*, and *poeticus*. These classes include some of the most varied and interesting forms. Next come the species and wild forms; then the split-coronas, in which the corona or cup is split toward the center for at least one third of its length. A final class of little interest to the home gardener is everything else.

Trumpets and large cups. By and large, these two classes provide similar colors, forms, and performance, blooming around here mostly in April or early May. They are big and bold and vigorous. You can have all-yellows, white perianth combined with darker trumpets, all whites, and those in which the trumpet or cup first blooms yellow and then turns white as the flower ages. Trumpets always have a trumpet form. Large cups can have either a shorter trumpet or a cup flattened back against the perianth. All of them stand up well to rain and wind. They also have the height to grow through ground covers.

Small cups. Small-cupped narcissi are usually a little shorter, more delicate and later blooming than the first two classes. They have a similar color range, but also include several with orange to red cups against white or yellow perianths – in striking contrast. Since their cups tend to burn in the sun, they should have a semi-shady spot or be cut in bud. Also, the later all-whites that bloom in May risk hot weather and pay the price in some seasons.

Doubles. Doubles, for me, are the least interesting and attractive class. Worse, many of their buds do not open. One of these most sure to open is 'White Lion;' one of the most attractive is 'White Marvel' in which only the cup is doubled. They are of medium height and vigor.

Hybrids of Major Species. The *triandrus* hybrids include some of the earliest and latest bloomers. They usually have several flowers to a stem, are short and fragrant. Some *cyclamineus* hybrids bloom in late March; others in mid-April. They too are short, with sharply swept-back perianths. The *jonquilla* hybrids have slender rush-like foliage. They throw several perfumed yellow blooms per stem, but often hide their color among the long leaves. They bloom from mid-season to late. With medium to very tall growth, they are effective in clumps in part shade. The *tazetta* hybrids are most valuable for their multi-flowered fragrance, their hardiness and multiple uses. They are among the easiest to force for indoor bloom; and after blooming, all but the "paperwhites" can go outside. The *poeticus* hybrids are late and lovely, having large rounded white perianths with tiny colored "eyes."

Species. The earliest of all daffodils, *Narcissus minimus*, stretches to its full four inches with an inch-long trumpet in February or early March. The latest, to bloom in mid-May, are *N. poeticus* 'Actaea' and *N. paeticus recurvus*. They

are good naturalizers. The hoop-skirt narcissus *(N. bulbocodium)* often blooms late here, and is effective in front of a handsome rock.

Split-coronas. Split-coronas come mostly in April with all-white, all-yellow or mixed colors, sometimes with flecks of orange or red. They perform well here; you may like their odd shapes.

Tulips

Although tulips generally do not persist as well in our area as do daffodils, they offer jewel colors, interesting variations in form and height, and a wide range of uses in home and garden. The earliest species tulips appear here in mid-March; the latest bloom in mid-May. The big show starts in late March with the later species and Single and Double Early forms. The show tapers off in mid-May with the Single Lates, Parrots and Late Doubles.

Height varies from the early 'Water-lily' *(Kaufmanniana)* tulips with blooms close to the ground, to the two-foot Darwin hybrids topped with five-inch flowers. Flower forms include svelte goblets, the great cups of Red Emperors, fringed and laciniated petals ('Burgundy Lace' and 'Parrot Wonder'), hourglass lily-flowering blooms ('West Point'), and the twisted horned tulip, *Tulipa acuminata* with contorted leaves. *Greigii* and *Kaufmanniana*, and some *Fosterana* tulips have streaked or spotted leaves, attractive when the plants are not in bloom. There are early and late doubles, with flowers like peonies; bunch-flowered (bouquet) tulips, and broken-colored tulips ('Mickey Mouse'). Some small ones *(Tulipa batalinii, Bakeri,* and *pulchella violacaea)* are useful for the rock garden and for accents by walk or driveway. Garden uses include beds, edges, rows, and clumps for accent. Many tulips, especially the Single Earlies, the single later and some of the species can be easily forced.

Culture. Culture of tulips is like that for daffodils, although tulips can be planted later and deeper. Rules for planting so-called "perennial" tulips (Darwin hybrids) are useful general guides. In

PHOTO COURTESY OF FRED WARD

Springtime brings tulips into bloom throughout the area – in private and public gardens alike. Here red and yellow varieties adorn the west grounds of the Capitol.

October or November, prepare planting areas to a depth of 12 inches. Set aside the top nine inches, and assure good drainage. Put a good source of phosphorus in the remaining three inches. Superphosphate (0-20-0) or a balanced fertilizer such as 9-9-6 will do.

Work in the fertilizer and some sand and humus if needed to give the bulbs a good root-run. Then put down an inch of "clean" soil (i.e., without added chemical or fresh organic components). Plant the bulbs from eight to 12 inches apart (closer for a quicker effect), and backfill the top nine inches (together with whatever amendments are needed to make the soil crumbly) so there will be at least seven

inches of settled soil over the tops of the bulbs. Level the bed, water it well, and then mulch it. In spring, make sure the tulips do not lack water up to the time of blooming. In cutting flowers, leave plenty of stem and leaf. Deadhead any spent flowers. Dig up any that show signs of disease. Fertilize the healthy ones with 9-9-6 or 10-6-4 and keep the bed moist until the leaves start to die back. When the leaves are half-dead, remove the stalks at ground level. At this point the leaves are doing little or nothing to strengthen the bulbs, and they may attract aphids or other carriers of disease.

For tulips you are not treating as "perennial," should you dig them up? If they are doing all right, just leave them. But if you want the space, and you fear a hot, humid summer, digging, treating and storing choice tulips may be worth the effort. When stems are nearly gone but still visible, dig up the bulbs, discard those too small to bloom, dry off the larger ones, and store them in mesh bags in a cool, airy place. Replant them in mid-fall. You should not replant tulips for several years in any place where tulips have suffered serious soil-borne disease. The offending organisms must die out; drenching will not help. You can, however, plant other bulbs, say daffodils or gladioli. where the tulips were.

The Tulip Year. The tulip year begins with species or "botanical" tulips – *Tulipa tarda, T. pulchella,* and *T. chrysantha,* that come in March – and ends with *T. celsiana* in mid-May. The *Kaufmanniana, Fosterana,* and *Greigii* species and hybrids, come from late March on. The Single and Double Earlies come then too, followed by the Darwin hybrids, the Lily-flowering, Fringed and Bouquet tulips, in April. The heavy-headed Parrots come next. Last are the Single and Double Late tulips, classes that now include those listed in the trade as Darwins, and Cottages.

Lilies

True lilies (*Lilium* spp. and cultivars) start to flower in mid-May and carry on into September, with the big show from mid-June to mid-August. Granted they have more diseases and may not last so well as other bulbs, they more than justify their use by their form, fragrance and sheer beauty. Moreover, unlike daylilies *(Hemerocallis)* the individual blooms can last a week or more. Stretching from 15 inches to seven feet in height, they can be used in the front and middle of a bed in May and June, and as accents in the mid- to back-border later on. Their chief drawback as a garden flower in our climate is their tendency to die back after blooming. Use companion plants, such as cleome, to fill the gaps.

The Lily Year. The lily year starts and ends with species, with some of the toughest and prettiest blooming in mid-season. Some of the earliest species (*L. pumilum, L. cernuum,* etc.) are hard to keep going here. The martagons, however, persist and increase and are useful in the front border in late May and June. *L. superbum,* once settled, is valuable for naturalized settings. The regal lily *(L. regale)* produces handsome fragrant white trumpets in late June. *L. henryi* and its offspring 'White Henryi' come a little later, and are dependable. The true tiger lily *(L. lancifolium)* is toughest of all. It gives nodding fulvous turkscap flowers in July and August on plants of considerable height. Its progeny, now being sold in a variety of colors, may not be so hardy.

A most valuable class for the Washington gardener is the Asiatic group that

Why Did They Peter Out?

Maybe our weather got too hot too soon, so the foliage, especially of the late-blooming tulips, burned up before it had a chance to strengthen the bulbs for next year's performance. Maybe they grew too well, exhausted the available nutrients and split up into too many bulbs that were too small. You didn't dig them up, fertilize the soil, throw away those not likely to bloom and replant the big survivors. Maybe they got sick, became infested by a virus or a soil-borne disease. (A virus that causes color-breaking in tulips may also stunt the plants.) Maybe you didn't plant them deep enough or you put some hot fertilizer where it would burn roots or injure the bulb's base. Maybe they didn't have proper drainage or enough water at the right time. Maybe they were inherently weak cultivars. Or maybe the squirrels ate them . . .

– **Charles A. H. Thomson**

bloom in June and July. They vary in height from two to five feet. Some of them have up-facing, some out-facing, and some down-facing flowers. They range in color from near-white through yellow and orange to dark red, most with spots, some with brush marks in the florets. There are no true blues. Few if any are fragrant. Some, like 'Enchantment,' can be forced under cool conditions or grown as pot plants.

Also in June Madonna lilies *(L. candidum)* and the Easter lilies *(L. longiflorum)* appear. The Madonnas, liking sweet soils and shallow planting, do not always do well here, but when they do they are unique. The Easter lilies, grown and forced for the season, can be transferred easily to our gardens. But they are short in relation to flower size, and bloom well long after Paschaltide.

The Aurelian hybrids are tall and fragrant, and make the best garden plants. They not only have trumpet-shaped flowers, but also bowl-shaped and reflexed flower forms. The Oriental hybrids constitute the most exciting but most heartbreaking group. Most of them bloom in late July and August, with trumpet-shaped, bowl-shaped, flat-faced and recurved flowers of surpassing beauty and aroma. Only one of the available forms ('Black Beauty') is dependably resistant to lily diseases.

In September the lily year ends with *L. formosanum*, a species making long, elegant, fragrant white trumpets on plants of medium height. Although susceptible to diseases, the gardener can keep his stock going by growing them from seed.

Lily Culture. Lilies like deep friable soil with food where their roots can get it. Since most lilies make stem roots as well as basal roots, giving them some surface feeding with an all-purpose slow-release fertilizer during the growing season makes sense. Lily bulbs are never dormant and when in leaf are usually hungry. They make their best bulb growth in fall. Most of them like a pH of 6.0 to 6.5, although the Orientals prefer a more acid soil. The Madonnas must have a neutral to slightly alkaline soil (from 7.0 to 7.5 pH). Lilies grow well in full sun or part shade, with their roots shaded and their heads in the light. Since many lilies are susceptible to mosaic, botrytis, and basal rot, the gardener should control both diseases and their vectors (aphids and cucumber beetles especially). Snails and rodents can threaten, too. Boards and beer, metaldehyde or mesurol for the molluscs, and dogs, cats and traps for the rodents are all useful.

Plant most lilies with about four inches of settled soil over the tops of their bulbs, for Madonnas no more than one inch in well-prepared, well-draining soil, placing a short marker stake beside each bulb. The best bulbs are available in October and November. The gardener should prepare his planting sites while the soil is still workable and mulch them well. On arrival, the bulbs can be tucked in place and the mulch replaced. The next spring fertilize them with a half-cupful per plant of a balanced fertilizer and follow on later with a slow-release plant food. Organics are slow releasers but foster disease. Foliar feedings are quick and clean but transient. Pelleted fertilizers may be better.

As the stalks grow, replace the markers with stakes of appropriate height for the expected stem length, say a three-foot support for a four-foot plant. Maintain good moisture, especially prior to and during flowering. When cutting flowers, leave at least a third, preferably more stem and leaves. Rogue out plants showing serious disease lest vectors carry trouble to healthy plants.

The best time to plant lilies is when good fresh stock is available. This in the past has meant fall, but now many good suppliers are holding stock for spring planting. Lilies can survive our winters, and only need to be dug when they are over-crowded. The best time to divide and replant them is in late fall, but if they have lost their leaves earlier they can be dug and inspected. If the bulbs appear to be sound they should be treated with a systemic fungicide and replanted promptly. Lilies do not like to be out of the ground, but can be held for some time in moist peat moss or sawdust.

Lilies can be grown in pots, provided the pots are deep enough to allow two or

Flowering spring bulbs take over the White House rose garden outside the President's oval office. Behind a border of 8,000 grape hyacinths, several thousand tulips are in bloom.

three quarts of soil per bulb. They should not be allowed to dry out.

Less Prominent Bulbs

While the foregoing kinds of bulbs I call majors, because of their prime usefulness, there are many others that I call minors that are also most valuable. They can be used to enhance the main elements of garden design, complementing other bulbs or other plants (perennials, shrubs, trees). They provide a wide variety of blooms for cut flowers, too, throughout the season. They can range from inches-tall anemones to feet-tall gladioli.

Earliest to appear (in January in some years) are the snowdrops, winter aconites, Glory of the Snow *(Chionodoxa)*, and the netted iris. Snowdrops *(Galanthus)* come with the earliest crocus, as do the winter aconites with their yellow blooms and pinwheel leaves. The aconites *(Eranthis)* are best propagated by seeds, or by very early divisions; bulbs available in fall may have dried out, and lost vigor. Glory of the Snow will survive late snows to make sheets and spots of blue with white in beds or in the lawn. Netted iris

(I. reticulata) give low and early elegant blue to purple flowers with yellow markings. Early squills *(Scilla siberica)* appear suddenly with brilliant blue flowers on short stems. Later squills *(Endymion hispanica* or Spanish squills) show up in mid-May to grace the front border, surround trees, or perk up a woodland or meadow with white, pink, bluish or purple spikes to 15 inches.

Grape hyacinths *(Muscari)* do best in clumps or as edgers. The common blue forms are complemented by a less vigorous white and a later form called 'Blue Spike.' They put up foliage in fall; not to worry. Winter does not bother them and they bloom on schedule. They go well with early yellow daffodils and candytuft. Dutch hyacinths *(H. orientalis)* are good to force for winter color and scent in the house, and good to spot in the perennial border. Forced bulbs can go to the garden and will last for years.

The ornamental onions *(Allium* spp) merit more use in our gardens. Most of them are hardy. They vary from early, low and pleasantly fragrant white *A. neapolitanum* to the higher, taller Stars of Persia *(A. Christophii)* and lower, yellow, odoriferous Golden Garlic *(A. moly)* to four-foot *A. giganteum* in mid-summer. Chinese Chives *(A. tuberosum)* will fill in among daylilies in August and September.

In early summer, tender and semi-tender bulbs come into their own. Peruvian daffodils *(Hymenocallis narcissiflora* or *Ismene calathina)* and Aztec lilies *(Sprekelia formosissima)* can be set out in late May or early June to bloom in 10 days and then provide hippeastrum-like foliage until frost. Then gladioli can take over, blooming until hard frost.

Plant gladiolus corms and cormels (bulblets) in mid-to-late April, mulching them well, for bloom in late June or early July. Make succession plantings for sustained flowering. Time from planting to flowering varies with variety. Smaller forms may bloom in 60 days; larger, later ones may take as long as 90 days. Those planted in late spring and early summer bloom fastest; those planted later take longer, because they are maturing at times of shorter days and less intense sunlight. All, especially pale colored ones, need protection (via systemic insecticide) from thrips that disfigure blooms and may damage corms.

Most varieties do well here; some even survive our winters. But for best bloom and survivability they should be dug, dried, separated and stored in cool conditions. They can be dug six weeks after blooming. They are best separated several weeks after digging, taking off the old corm. Good air circulation during storage is a must, in temperatures ranging from 35 to 60 degrees. Clean culture and by not planting glads where illness has occurred can keep most diseases under control.

Glads come in all colors except true blue and in a variety of flower forms. They vary in height from 15 inches to six feet. Flower sizes range from three-quarters of an inch to five inches across. Because of their short flowering period per spike, they are not a prime decorative flower for the garden. The best of the newer varieties will open 10 blooms per spike, and hold them for several days.

That is when the lowest flower withers, as new buds (up to 20 total) open.

Many gardeners raise them in rows, digging trenches a foot deep, treating the soil with a balanced fertilizer for the bottom of the trench, assuring good drainage, backfilling the trench so in heavy soil the corms will rest with three inches of good soil on top of them. In light soil, corms can go six inches down. Staking rows is easy – stout stakes every six to eight feet with stout cord holding up the plants. Cormels can be planted like peas, from March on, assuring good corms for later years. No glads are really fragrant; for late-season perfume, plant the "Abyssinian gladiolus" *(Acidanthera murieliae).*

The magic lilies *(Lycoris squamigera)* once settled are hardy, throwing up pink flowers on bare stalks in late July. Other lycorises, like the spider lily *(Lycoris radiata)* are later and more beautiful, but less hardy here. A yellow autumn "crocus" *(Sternbergia lutea)* blooms in October with yellow goblets, doing well in part shade. The rain lilies *(Zephyranthes)* give white or yellow blooms in sunny but protected spots from mid-August on, with new blossoms after each rain.

Colchicums (another autumn "crocus") are useful for late summer and fall. They shoot up white, blue and lavender blooms, some bi-colored and beautifully netted, mostly single, a few double. They put up heavy foliage in early spring that dies in summer before the blooms appear; hence planting them near plants that will hide their foliage in its season is a good idea.

Companions and Successions

Many gardeners try to cope with bare spots while bulbs are waiting to come up by planting several sorts of bulbs together, with say crocus at the front, followed farther back by daffodils or tulips and then by some of the later, even taller summer and fall-flowering bulbs. Others interplant bulbs between clumps of daylilies or other perennials, so the perennial foliage will cover dying leaves and fill blanks when the bulbs are dormant. Still others use annuals and perennials to follow bulbs. For example, sweet alyssum can cover spent crocuses. Marigolds and zinnias are good successors for larger bulbs. Even better may be chrysanthemums for later summer and fall bloom. Best may be the Evans begonias (B. grandis variety evansiana) that can be planted on top of bulbs, putting their little tubercles about ground level, or setting in plants. They will not appear until late May and then give good leaf and pink bloom until frost. They are very hardy; they spread, but can be controlled easily. As for ground covers over bulbs, myrtle will do for the larger ones. Chinese forget-me-not, Cynoglossum amabile makes a carpet over bulbs, and lasts all season, although it languishes in summer's heat. Nevertheless its sheet of blue forget-me-not-style flowers are effective spring and fall. Pansies and wallflowers do not do as well here as they do in cooler climates.

A Note on Sources

Where can all these bulbs be procured? The best source is the experienced local gardener who often has surplus to share, and more, good local experience. Local plant societies also have knowledge along with periodic plant sales and exchanges. Local plant sources (garden centers, nurseries, as well as hardware stores) can also be good. In season they will have broad selections, and you can choose well-sized and sound bulbs. Commercial specialists are good sources, too, especially for the less familiar varieties. Their catalogs are valuable in many ways. A caution: catalog information about when a bulb will bloom here often varies widely from our experiences here. For that information consult your local sources. Horticultural magazines often have good articles – too many of them written from a nation-wide perspective – but more to the point, good advertisements. Do not neglect the classified sections.

References

Rockwell and Esther Grayson: The Complete Book of Bulbs. Rev. edition, Lippincott, 1977. Far and away the best single reference; particularly good on bulb cycles.

McNair: All About Bulbs. Ortho, 1981.

Rix and Phillips: The Bulb Book. Pan Books, London, 1981. Comprehensive, but the cultural information is for England.

How to Grow Glorious Gladiolus, North American Gladiolus Council, no date. Best overall introduction.

Howie: Let's Grow Lilies, an illustrated handbook of lily culture. The North American Lily Society, revised edition, 1978. Mad illustrations but sound information.

Scott, et al.: Taylor's Guide to Bulbs, Houghton Mifflin, Boston, 1986.

Good Bulbs for the Greater Washington Area

There are many good bulbs for our area. These are among the choice ones. Listed are their names, class, color description, height and bloom times. Height and bloom times vary with cultural conditions and the seasons. The information here reflects experience in the Washington area.

Crocus

Gypsy Girl – Species. Yellow, 3 inches, February - March.

Purity – Species. White, 3 inches, February - March.

Tomasinianus Whitewell Purple – Species. Purple, 3 inches, February - March.

Pickwick – Hybrid. Striped purple on white grounds, 4 inches, March.

Purpurea Grandiflora – Hybrid. Dark Purple, 4 inches, March.

Remembrance – Hybrid. Blue, 4 inches, March.

Speciosus – Species. Lavender and white, 4 inches, October.

Daffodils

General Patton – Trumpet. White perianth, yellow trumpet; 20 inches, April.

Mount Hood – Trumpet. White, 18 inches, April.

Spellbinder – Trumpet. Yellow perianth, white trumpet; 20 inches, April.

Unsurpassable – Trumpet. Yellow, 20 inches, April.

Ceylon – Large Cup. Yellow perianth, orange cup; 18 inches, April.

Ice Follies – Large Cup. White perianth, yellow cup fades to white; 18 inches, April.

Salome – Large Cup. White perianth, pink cup; 18 inches, April.

Birma – Small Cup. Yellow perianth, orange cup; 16 inches, April.

Chinese White – Small Cup. White, 14 inches, May.

Cheerfulness – Double. White, 12 inches, April - May.

White Lion – Double. White, yellow flecks; 18 inches, April - May.

Thalia – *Triandrus*. White, 10 inches, May.

February Gold – *Cyclamineus*. Yellow, 14 inches, March.

Tete-a-Tete – *Cyclamineus*. Yellow, 10 inches, March.

Suzy – *Jonquilla*. Yellow perianth, red cup; 14 inches, April - May.

Trevithian – Jonquilla. Yellow, 14 inches, April - May.

Cragford – *Tazetta*. White perianth, orange-red cup; 12 inches, April.

Actaea – Poeticus. White perianth, yellow-red "eye;" 14 inches, April - May.

Poeticus recurvus (**Pheasant's Eye**) – White perianth, yellow "eye;" 14 inches, May.

Narcissus minimus – Species. Yellow, 4 inches, February - March.

Hoopskirt – Species. Yellow, 4 inches, March - April.

Narcissus jonquilla – Species. Yellow, 8 to 10 inches, April.

Baccarat – Split Corona. Yellow, 14 inches, April.

Orangery – Split Corona. White perianth, yellow corona; 14 inches, April.

Tulips

Tulipa tarda – Species. Yellow, white; 5 inches, February - March.

Waterlily – *Kaufmanniana*. White, red center blush; 5 inches, February - March.

Cherry Orchard – *Kaufmanniana*. Red, 10 inches, March.

Red Emperor – *Fosterana*. Red, 12 inches, March.

Yellow Dawn – *Greigii*. Yellow, old rose; 12 inches, March.

Bellona – Single Early. Yellow, 15 inches, March.

White Hawk – Single Early. White, 14 inches, March.

Mickey Mouse – Single Early. Yellow, red;

14 inches, March - April.

Peach Blossom – Double Early. Deep rose, 11 inches, March.

Georgette – Bouquet. Yellow, red; 14 inches, April - May.

Queen of Sheba – Lily-flowering. Rusty

Forcing Bulbs

Many bulbs are suitable for forcing – daffodils and tulips generally, hyacinths and other hardy bulbs. Crocuses and many smaller bulbs can be forced but they must be kept cool (below 60°F.) until they bloom.

Most bulbs being forced need a period of root formation before the tops grow and the blooms appear. Plant them in a clean container in a sterile root medium so they do not touch and are buried to their necks. Water them thoroughly and put them in a cool dark place – a cold frame, a trench, or even a dark closet. Leave them there until the roots show through the holes in the bottom of the pot. This may take eight to 12 weeks for daffodils, maybe more for tulips.

Then bring them out into a cool shady place. As the tops grow and buds appear, give them more light in a sunny window or under lights. Once they bloom, display them in a sunny place during the day but keep them cool at night. The blooms will last longer.

If you want to keep the bulbs going after blooming: Maintain the moisture, feed with a balanced fertilizer and plant them outside after the weather was moderated. Paperwhite narcissus do not need time for root formation but they are not worth planting out later. Tazettas can be planted out and bloom for many years in the garden.

Tender bulbs, such as amaryllis (hippeastrums), must be brought inside again in the fall and started up after several weeks of rest. Water them once with warm water and put them where they will get bottom heat. When the blooms come, bring them into good light. When the leaves appear, start feeding.

– Charles A.H. Thomson

PHOTO COURTESY OF DUMBARTON OAKS RESEARCH LIBRARY AND COLLECTIONS

A visitor to Dumbarton Oaks is surprised to learn that this seemingly natural area with its winding brick walk – known as Melisande's Allee – was in fact painstakingly created by Landscape Architect Beatrix Farrand in the 1920s. Before that there was an old cow path here lined on one side with silver maples. The trees on the other side were planted, and, before the walk was laid out, its exact position and width were carefully studied and several alternatives tried. In April the area is filled with sheets of golden daffodils.

red, orange edge; 18 inches, April - May.

Burgundy Lace – Fringed. Dark red, 18 inches, April - May.

Jewel of Spring – Darwin Hybrid. Cream, red picotee; 24 inches, April.

Parade – Darwin Hybrid. Scarlet, 24 inches, April.

Apricot Beauty – Triumph. Salmon-rose, 16 inches, April.

Professor Einstein – Triumph. Clear red, gold edge; 18 inches, April.

Flaming Parrot – Parrot. Primrose, flamed crimson; 18 inches, April - May.

Ace of Spades – Single Late. Purple-black, 18 inches, May.

Kashmir – Single Late. Red, 18 inches, May.

Perry Como – Single Late. Salmon-pink, 16 inches, May.

Lilies

Dawn Star – Asiatic. Cream, 2½ feet, June.

Enchantment – Asiatic. Nasturtium-red, 3 feet, June.

Gold Lode – Asiatic. Yellow, 4 feet, June.

Black Dragon – Aurelian. White, dark reverse; 5 feet, July.

Gold Eagle – Aurelian. Yellow, 4 to 6 feet, July.

Sentinel – Aurelian. White, 5 feet, July.

Stargazer – Oriental. Red, 3 feet, June.

Imperial Silver strain – Oriental. White with spots, 5 feet, July - August.

Jamboree strain – Oriental. Red, 5 to 6 feet, July - August.

Black Beauty – Oriental. Dark red, 6 feet, August - September.

Martagon hybrids – Martagon. Various colors, 2 to 4 feet, May - June.

Lilium lancifolium and hybrids (**Tiger**) – Species. Orange, white, dark red; 3 to 4 feet, June - July.

Lilium regale – Species. White trumpet, 4 to 5 feet, July.

Dahlias As Garden Enhancers

By Charles A. H. Thomson and Allan E. Baker

Many people think of dahlias as huge brilliant flowers a foot or more across, useful chiefly for exhibition. Yet dwarf and medium height dahlias are of prime value in the landscape and as a cornucopia of cut flowers.

Set out in late May or early June, as soon as our weather is warm and settled, bedding dahlias will start to give masses of flowers in July, and keep up production until the first hard frosts. They range in color from white to dark red. Their flower forms vary from ray-flowered singles through semi-doubles and doubles featuring cactus type, anemone type, and even so-called peony type, some very shaggy, some very formal. They can be grown from roots, pot plants started from cuttings, and from seeds. This latter method is not only a must for the hybridist, but fun for the hobbyist interested in producing the unpredictable. Our season is long enough so seeds sown indoors in March will make plants to go outdoors in May. They will produce good flowers by summer's end; and if the gardener protects them against the first hit-and-run frost, they will persist well into fall.

Bedding Dahlias in Masses

Bedding dahlias can be grown in masses, and are also effective tucked in among evergreen shrubbery (often out of bloom in summer) or used to cover spaces where spring bulbs have finished. Lower growers – some not over 10 inches – can go to the front of a bed, and the taller ones to the mid- to back border. Not only the flowers, but the leaves can be showy.

The 'Bishop of Llandaff', having red flowers with gold centers, sports dark purple leaves. The 'Redskin' series has flowers of several colors, often on the same plant. The dwarf forms do not require pinching to stay low, and without disbudding produce flowers to three inches across on multiple stems that can form a bouquet in themselves. To keep them dwarf, however, the gardener must go easy on fertilizer. Nevertheless he must never let the plants be checked in their growth, either for lack of food or moisture, until they get to their proper dimensions.

If the gardener is trying for a particular blend of colors in a flower bed combining annuals and other perennials for long-season interest, bedding dahlias can be most useful. They go well with other long-season bloomers like petunias and alyssum, and can provide flowers after iris and peonies are through. They can also precede and at times accompany chrysanthemums, with bedding dahlias to the fore and taller mums to the back of a bed. After frost has done in the dahlias, the mums will carry on.

To get a known color, the gardener can either buy roots or started plants of named varieties, like 'Red Imp'. Or he can buy pot plants with a floret or so on them. Or he can raise plants from seeds until they bloom, arrange them in the desired combinations of color, and transplant them from pots to their proper places.

If a gardener has seedlings he likes, he can dig their tubers at season's end, store them in moist peat or vermiculite in a place where the temperature runs between 35°F and 55°F, check them for desiccation, moisten them if need be, and start them up by encouraging sprouting (in a warmer location) say in April. Once the sprouts are growing, the gardener can divide the clumps, being sure there is a piece of tuber to support the sprout. These can be set out as soon as the weather is favorable or held inside in pots.

Dahlias have their share of diseases and insect pests: stunts, viruses, mosaics and other insect-borne diseases, along with damage to stems from borers, or damage to leaves and flowers from other insects. Judicious and timely use of good pesticides can handle most difficulties, but a plant stunted by disease and not by cultural deficiency should be promptly discarded. Mildews can be avoided by assuring ample sun and air circulation, or cured by use of a mildewicide (Benomyl or Actidione PM).

Bedding dahlias now offer a wide choice of size, form and color. The lilliputs are only 10 inches high. Mignons and anemone-flowered dahlias go to one and a half feet. Good mignons include red 'Nelly Geerling'; rose 'Murillo'; and white 'Sneezy'. Good anemones are white 'Toto'; yellow and pink 'Frisbee'; and orange 'Brio'. The shortest of the strains is 'Figaro F1', to 12 inches; then comes 'Rigoletto' to 13 inches, early mixed strains to 18 inches, and Unwin's Dwarf Hybrid mixtures to 24 inches – all with a range of color.

Planting the Tubers

To plant a dahlia tuber dig a hole eight to 10 inches deep and stir a handful of superphosphate into the soil at the bottom of the hole and cover with clean soil for the tuber to rest on. If the soil is heavy a shallower hole is adequate. Place the tuber horizontally in the hole with its eye facing upward and covered with three inches of soil. As the shoot grows, the hole can be filled gradually. The tall dahlias should be planted three to four feet apart and a six-to-seven-foot stake should be firmly planted next to each tuber before it is covered. The tall dahlias must be tied to the stakes as they grow. When three sets of leaves have developed, the tall dahlias should be topped to encourage side branching. Watering usually is not needed in the early stages unless an unusual drouth occurs.

In mid-July the plants will benefit from a side dressing of 5-10-5 or 5-10-10 fertilizer. High nitrogen fertilizer promotes fast growth and weak stems and should not be used. As the flower buds begin to form on the larger dahlias, the removal of side buds on each stem will promote larger – if fewer – blooms. Dahlias require at lest one inch of water each week after the plants become established. Mulching the bed with leaves or other material will assist growth by keeping soil temperatures lower and retaining moisture.

In the fall after frost terminates the dahlia season, the tubers should be dug carefully and set aside in the shade for a few hours so the clumps become less brittle and easier to handle. The main stem must be cut off close to the crown to discourage rot during storage. The soil should be washed away. The tubers can be divided either in the fall or in the spring, but to be viable each division must contain an eye near the stem from which the new plant will sprout. Mark the tubers with an indelible pen and store in dry vermiculite in a cool location that will not freeze. Dahlias can be checked for disease before storing by cutting a tip off a root. If a reddish brown ring is present just under the skin, the root is diseased and should be discarded. In early spring the tubers can be started in flats indoors for an earlier start or they can be placed in the ground in mid-May after the danger of frost has passed.

Seedlings, rooted cuttings and potted plants should be set out once they are hardened off, so the top of the root ball is three inches deep. Bedding dahlias can be placed 12 to 24 inches apart, depending on ultimate size. Seedlings and rooted cuttings of tall varieties should be spaced three to four feet apart, and staked.

Whether for hedge or exhibition table, for cut flowers or for pot, patio or individual accent, the versatile dahlias should figure prominently in Washington's summer garden scheme.

References

Chapter 16 in Rockwell and Grayson: *The Complete Book of Bulbs* (rev. ed. 1977, Lippincott); or entries on Dahlias in such encyclopedias as Everett, Taylor, Time-Life or Wyman.

Growing Daylilies

By George Coffee

What is a daylily? It's just about the prettiest, easiest to grow, most versatile flower we have, but a lily it is not. The true botanical name is *Hemerocallis* and the name daylily refers to the fact that the flower is open for only one day plus its resemblance to the true lily in form.

The daylily is mentioned by the Chinese in a song prior to 500 B.C. so it is no johnny-come-lately. When you look at the daylily of today and then look back at the orange and yellow ones that grew in grandma's garden or in patches along the roadside you realize the great achievements that have been made both in flower form and color.

Picture in your mind's eye, if you will, an array of colors from yellows so pale they are nearly white through rich golds and oranges; the palest of pinks and lavenders to reds so dark as to be almost black, and purples the color of Concord grapes; melon colors, blends and bicolors, many having beautifully contrasting green and yellow throats.

This gives you some idea of the vast range of colors available. Dream further of flowers with ruffled or piecrust edging ranging in size from only one inch to more than eight inches in diameter and plants from only 10 inches high to more than five feet tall and you begin to realize the many places these lovelies will fit into your scheme of gardening.

Types of Gardens for Daylilies

Daylilies are divided into three size groups. Large flowers are four and a half inches and miniature flowers are less than three inches. Daylilies of all flower sizes grow in differing heights and therefore lend themselves to different types of plantings. Miniature flowers on low-growing plants do nicely in rock gardens and in border beds. Many of the older varieties both large and small had the undesirable habit of closing up about dinner time, but not so today. The better and newer ones remain open later, mostly until midnight. So they do well planted around a patio to be enjoyed in the cool of the evening.

Daylilies frequently are planted in massed beds using either a single variety or a number of different ones. Examples of this type of planting can be seen in several spots around the District of Columbia where the National Park Service has made plantings in small park areas and in median strips – MacArthur Boulevard, for instance.

Perhaps their best setting, however, is in perennial beds with companion flowers and small evergreens interspersed among them to enhance their beauty. In such beds they should be planted at least four feet and preferably six feet apart with the companion plants between.

Perennials with Daylilies

Such perennial plants as blue, pink or white veronica, blue salvia, lavender, blue flax, Shasta daisies, and white, pink, red and lavender garden phlox and a host of others that bloom along with the daylilies are recommended.

All but the garden phlox are relatively easy to grow with a minimum of insect and disease problems. Garden phlox is very susceptible to foliage mildew in our hot, humid area and should be planted so that it gets good air circulation (not crowded) to allow rapid drying of dew and rain. They should be sprayed every 10 days to two weeks with a fungicide

(Benomyl).

There are a number of excellent annuals such as low-growing, soft blue ageratum, and the intense blue lobelia used as border plantings, snapdragons and others, that are suitable in daylily beds. But being annuals, they must be replaced each year. Blue and white companion plants are especially recommended for their contrast since there are no daylilies in these colors.

Time to Plant

The best time to plant daylilies in the middle Atlantic and Northeast areas varies with their basic types – i.e., whether they are dormant, semi-evergreen or evergreen (usually indicated in catalog descriptions). The dormant ones are the most successful and hence recommended for this area. Semi-evergreens, unless they can be planted early (not later than August 15) are best planted in early spring. The evergreen varieties are not recommended in this area for the beginner or less experienced gardener. A good sturdy plant put in a well prepared hole in late August or early September should bloom the next summer.

Generally speaking daylilies prefer a sunny location, but some filtered shade for part of the day, preferably afternoon, is not undesirable particularly for most reds and purples. No daylilies do well in complete shade.

Planting

Few, if any, plants equal or surpass the daylily in the ease and minimum effort required to produce beautiful flowers in your garden year after year. However, the old adage of "a 10-dollar hole for a one-dollar plant" is important in planting daylilies. Remember that you are planting plants that will stay in one place for four to six years or even longer in some cases before they need to be lifted and divided, so plant them well. They are quite tolerant of soil types, growing in clay, loam or sandy soils that are slightly acid (pH 6.5-6.0).

Prepare the planting hole for each plant by deeply spading an area about six to eight inches larger in diameter than the spread of the roots to be planted. Work into the hole generous amounts of compost or if compost is not available, peat moss and decomposed or dehydrated cow manure (one-half water bucket full or more for each hole) plus a handful of bone meal or rock phosphate. Set the crown of the plant about one inch below the surface, spread out the roots and cover with soil. Water well after planting to settle the dirt around the roots and then mulch well. Do not water again for two or three weeks.

Mulches and Fertilizers

Daylilies like to be mulched. This helps to hold their favorite food, water, in the soil. Fine textured mulches such as grass clippings or finely ground leaves are preferred over the coarser wood chips and pine bark that tend to harbor slugs that in turn like to enjoy a midnight snack of daylilies.

Daylilies are modest in their nitrogen requirements. In fact, if you were amply generous with compost at planting time no fertilizer is needed. Otherwise a couple of tablespoonsful of a low nitrogen fertilizer such as a 5-10-10 can be applied around each plant in early spring. Or an occasional foliar feeding with one of the soluble fertilizers can be applied during the growing season. They prefer water to nitrogen when blooming.

Diseases and Insects

Daylilies are practically free of diseases. "Spring sickness" may occur in early spring when new growth begins with twisted leaves that turn yellow and become slimy. The plants nearly always overcome this problem without adversity, but good fall cleanup of all old dead foliage is recommended as a preventative measure.

Tiny insects called thrips will cause an occasional blemish on a flower. To control them three applications of diazinon (Spectracide) at seven-to-10-day intervals in late spring is recommended, although the damage resulting from these critters may not justify the effort unless you are a perfectionist.

Slugs will damage the foliage by eating

the edges of the leaves at night. They are controlled by using a commercial slug bait, or by placing shallow containers of stale beer around the plants, or even by going out at night with a flashlight and picking them off. Red spider mites also are bothersome and can be controlled by periodic spraying with Cygon. Do not use Kelthane or Sevin on daylilies.

Time and Length of Bloom

On the average, daylilies will begin blooming in this area about July 1 and continue blooming into August. There are some later and earlier blooming varieties that will extend the blooming season. Also, with a good season and plenty of water during the summer many plants will bloom again with a second set of bloom scapes – a scape is a stalk – and continue to bloom until frost. As has been pointed out each flower lasts only one day, but with many buds on a scape a bright new flower is ready to greet you nearly every day. Remember that a daylily plant is not at its best until the second blooming season.

Where to See Daylilies

The plantings in Washington by the National Park Service have been mentioned already. The National Arboretum has an excellent display. In the last few years they have rejuvenated their plantings by taking out many of the older, less desirable plants, redoing the beds and adding many new plants. Practically every award-winning daylily can be seen here. The display is almost a history of daylilies.

The American Horticultural Society in conjunction with the National Capital Daylily Club has put in a display garden at their River View Farm near Mount Vernon. This is the place to see some excellent newer and more expensive daylilies you can put in your garden after the "bug bites you."

Each year the National Capital Daylily Club has a bus tour early in July to visit some selected private gardens within their club and either the same weekend or the following one a flower show is held at which hundreds of blooms are displayed and judged. The tour is reasonably priced, the show is free and both events will be time well and enjoyably spent.

GOOD CULTIVARS FOR THE AREA

White

'So Lovely' – 5½ inch florets, near-white, blooms late, ruffled.

Pink

'Lullaby Baby' – 3½ inch florets, light pink.

'Mae Graham' – Large ruffled bright pink, green throat.

'Ruffled Apricot' – 7 inch florets, apricot, lavender/pink ribs, gold throat.

'Siloam Little Gem' – Small florets, shrimp pink, red eye, gold throat.

Red

'Ed Murray' – 4 inch florets, black red, distinctive.

'Jock Randall' – Large bright rosy red.

'Little Business' – Small plant, 3 inch floret, bright red.

'Red Rum' – 4 inch florets, rusty red/coral, creped and ruffled.

Yellow

'Butterpat' – 20 inch plant, small flowers, midseason, fragrant.

'Java Sea' – 4½ inch flowers, unusual.

'Kinda Neat' – Florets 3 inches or less, 24-inch plant.

'Kindly Light' – 9 inch florets, spider (narrow petals), early midseason.

'Stella de Oro' – 2½ inch florets on 11 inch plant. Fragrant, early, close to continuous flowering to frost.

Gold/Orange

'Bertie Ferris' – Small plant, 2½ inch blooms.

'Windjammer' – 5½ inch florets, good performer.

Blend

'Little Rainbow' – 2 inch florets, melon pink, cream, yellow, orchid blend. Unique coloration.

Purple

'Mountain Violet' – 5 inch florets, purple.

———

Sources

Frank (Bud) Bennett, 21621 Second Street, Laytonsville, MD 20879

Brian Lazarus, 1786 Generals Highway, Annapolis, MD 21401

Branham Farms Ltd., (Mrs. Lola S. Branham), 607 Woodhaven Drive, Richmond, VA 23224

Tranquil Lake Nursery, 45 River Street, Rohoboth, MA 02789

The Azalea: Washington's Favorite

By John G. Shaffer

If Washington gardeners were given the choice of growing only one plant they almost certainly would select azaleas – lush in bloom throughout a long spell of springtime glory, and handsomer than many another shrub during the drab winter months if the varieties have been chosen wisely for quality of leaf and form. Azaleas have the further merit of being fairly easy to grow.

Most azaleas will take full sun. All will take part shade. They look their best in dappled shade, preferably under high oaks, yet they will survive even in "foundation planting" in full sun and in the clayey subsoil left behind by builders. Fortunately soils can be improved.

Azaleas are profligate in their variety. We can choose from several thousand species and cultivated varieties or "cultivars." In the Washington area a careful selection of evergreen and deciduous cultivars will provide bloom from early April until August. Some will rebloom.

Foliage Not Always Distinguished

Blossoms on the best cultivars are absolutely faultless and gloriously abundant. But as landscape plants, neither the foliage nor the shrubby form of most cultivars is particularly distinguished. The foliage, which is what you look at 12 months a year, is only moderately attractive except on a few cultivars such as 'Debonaire,' 'Glacier,' 'Girard's Rose,' 'Garden State Glow' and many of the Kurume hybrids. But then there are some whose foliage is actively bad. The popular 'Delaware Valley White,' sumptuous in bloom, has foliage that for much of the year is often a sickly shade of yellow.

The form of most azaleas is rounded,

like most other shrubs. Pleasant enough by themselves, a solid planting of azaleas lacks the contrast needed to make a landscape interesting. Therefore you must relieve the tedium of azalea piled upon azalea by growing them with plants that will provide contrast in form and leaf.

For contrast of form, use the rigidly upright Irish yews (*Taxus baccata* 'Fastigiata'), or for one less stiffly vertical, Hatfield's yew *(Taxus x media* 'Hatfieldii'). For contrast of leaf texture use needled evergreens – pines, Japanese temple cedars *(Cryptomeria japonica)* or yews. Or use the smaller deciduous trees such as American dogwood *(Cornus florida)*, sourwood *(Oxydendrum arboreum)*, various magnolias (particularly *Magnolia virginiana)*, *Stewartia pseudocamellia*, or any of the bold-leaved evergreens, including aucuba, osmanthus, rhododendron, rohdea or holly (American, English or Chinese, but not the little-leaved Japanese holly). The point is to give azaleas zip by contrasting them with plants which have a much different form and texture.

Companion Plant Know-How

The late Frederic P. Lee, a prominent Washington attorney and horticulturist, and one of the founders of the Men's Garden Club, knew how to achieve contrast. In *The Azalea Book* he devoted a whole chapter to companion plants for azaleas in the shady garden, relying in large part on experience in his own garden in Bethesda. Lee used coarse-leaved aucubas and hollies, and needled conifers, to contrast with the fine-leaved azaleas. Isolated azalea plants he pulled into a coherent composition with carpets of bulbs, herbaceous perennials, ferns and other

In this quiet and inviting garden retreat, azaleas and tulips are companions in bloom, sharing the top billing as the star performers in a seasonal show of color.

ground covers. In his garden he grew 18 varieties of ferns, 28 cultivars of plantain lilies *(Hosta)*, broad patches of lily turf *(Liriope* and *Ophiopogon)*, and clumps of wildflowers (bloodroot, trilliums, and Jack-in-the pulpit). He used aucubas, hollies, and sweet-box *(Sarcococca hookeriana humilis)* for evergreen contrasts,

and bleeding-hearts *(Dicentra spectabilis)* for bright accents in late spring. All these plants have the same needs for acid soil, moisture, and good drainage.

Fred Galle's books similarly emphasize the value of contrasting plants. *Southern Living Azaleas* (1974) has fine pictures of some, along with a short list. Lee's *The*

Azalea Book (1958, 1987), has longer lists giving hardiness and adaptability.

EVERGREEN AZALEAS

Here is a "preferred" list of evergreen azaleas, developed from polls by two Washington area chapters of the Azalea Society of America, plus the personal choices of five very experienced growers in the area. Only cultivars which were the choice of at least three of these seven electors are included.

Ambrosia. Flowers are yellowish pink, becoming pale apricot with age. Plant habit is tall and open. Blooms early.

Balsaminaeflorum. Pale orange red, double. Flowers quite large for the size of the plant, which is very low. Late.

Buccaneer. Brilliant orange red, difficult to combine with other colors except clear pale pink or purple. Give it some overhead shade, such as is cast by tall trees, because it burns in full sun. Early.

Dayspring. White, shading to palest rose pink with a few chartreuse dots in the throat. Broader than tall. Early.

Debonaire. Flowers almost circular, colored a vivid pink on some planting sites, and pale pink tending toward apricot on others. Plant is dense and twiggy, about three feet tall and equally broad at age 10. The dark green persistent foliage is an additional asset. A good specimen plant. Late.

Delos. Flower buds are shaped like roses; they open to rose pink. A gracefully arching plant. Mid-season.

Dream. Deep rose pink and frilled. Very showy. Plant is big and spreading, eventually reaching eight feet. Early.

Elsie Lee. Large, frilled, delicate lavender-pink. Plant is compact and upright, but slow-growing. Mid-season.

Festive. White but freely sanded and occasionally striped a dull rose. From a distance the effect is flesh-white. Erect and spreading growth to six feet. Early. Some growers have found this to be bud-tender in hard winters.

Girard's Rose. Large bright rose flowers, waved and ruffled. Habit of growth is upright, to two and a half feet in five years. Like most of the Girard hybrids it has glossy deep green leaves. Mid-season.

Glacier. Large, shining white with a faint green tint. Growth vigorous up to 5 feet in height. Foliage is dark green and lustrous. Mid-season.

Gumpo. Some plants bloom white, some are rose pink with flecks of deeper pink, and some are pale pink with a white edge. All are low and dense in form, slow in growth, and very late in bloom. Flowers are very large for the size of the plant. To see a mass planting of Gumpos go to the LBJ Memorial Grove (in Virginia just off the George Washington Parkway) where they surround the great memorial plinth as a clipped ground cover about one foot high.

Herbert. Frilled, reddish violet with darker orchid purple shading. Arguably the best of the purples. Spreading, it will remain low without pruning. Early.

Indica alba *(A. mucronatum)* and its variant *Indica rosea*. Pure white or rose pink and delicately fragrant. Will reach 6 feet in height and eight feet in width in 20 years. Loses most of its foliage in a hard winter. This variety has been in cultivation in Japan for more than 300 years. Mid-season.

Madame Butterfly. Flowers are white with a lavender flush. Profuse. Plant is low and spreading. Mid-season.

Margaret Douglas. Strong pink with an orange border. In always dominates its planting site. An excellent landscape plant even when out of bloom. Its form is beautifully rounded and the foliage remains deep green all winter. Ten-year-old plants are some four feet tall and almost as broad. Mid-season.

Marian Lee. Flowers have white centers with a faint tint of pink, and borders of strong red. Foliage is a good dark green. Ten-year-old plants are four feet tall and equally broad. This cultivar was named for the late Marian (Mrs. Frederic P.) Lee of Bethesda. Mid-season.

Martha Hitchcock. Flowers are white and magenta, and they're large. The garden effect is striking, although strident. Ranks at or near the top of all popularity polls. Broad-spreading and fast-growing, it must be controlled by pruning unless given plenty of space. Mid-season.

Nancy of Robin Hill. Light pink double flowers occasionally blotched with light red. "Lush" is the best description. Plant is broader than tall – 20 inches tall by 3 feet broad in 17 years. Rabbits love to chew this one.

Refrain. White suffused with brilliant but pale pink, then blotched and irregularly striped with purplish rose. Happily, this looks a lot better than it sounds. Tall, up to seven feet. Early.

Rose Greeley. White with a chartreuse blotch; frilled and sweetly scented. Plant habit is dense and spreading. A good specimen plant which becomes even more effective when planted en masse. Early to mid-season.

Saint James. Large flowers are yellowish pink, bordered with a shade that lies between dark yellowish pink and reddish orange. The garden effect is pinkish orange. White centers often appear after the plant develops masses of twiggy branches. Height is four feet and breadth nearly as much in 10 years. Late.

Wakaebisu. Salmon pink. More spreading than upright. May not bloom every year in colder areas to the north and west of the Beltway. Late.

White Jade. Large single flowers with a pale green tint. Foliage is dark green and glossy. Plant habit is broad-spreading to four feet. Late.

Yuka. Funnel-shaped white blossoms occasionally flushed and streaked strong pink. A mounding habit of growth to 18 inches in height and two and a half feet in breadth. Late.

Beyond these there are many excellent and worthy varieties, for example, my own favorite, the old Ghent hybrid *Daviesii*, which I value for its quiet restraint. The quiet beauty of *Daviesii* can contribute more to the garden than the scene-stealing showiness of 'Martha Hitchcock.'

Other good deciduous azaleas for this area are 'Narcissiflora' (double-flowered, yellow), 'Mary Claire' (pink with yellow blotch), 'Persil' (white and pale yellow), 'Tunis' (red and burnt orange), 'Homebush' (red, semi-double) and 'Gibraltar' (orange).

The North American natives are also excellent, combining well with wildflowers and other naturalistic plantings. You can choose from *R. calendulaceum*, (Flame Azalea), *R. periclymenoides* (Pinxterbloom); *R. vaseyi* (Pinkshell azalea), *R. viscosum* (Swamp azalea) and *R. austrinum* (The Florida azalea). They all are hardy; some are fragrant.

Other azaleas are important because they serve some other landscape purpose: they are genetically dwarf, or they flower again in the fall, as do the varieties 'Opal' and 'Dorset' most years.

The Satsuki hybrids are coming into favor because (a) by blooming late they extend the azalea season and (b) their flowers are interestingly varied and are larger than most. Consequently, and because there seems to be a move toward Satsukis, here is a list of the Satsukis preferred by George Harding, who grows more than 1,000 varieties near Damascus, Maryland.

Beni Kirishima; Bunkwa; Chinzan; Eikan; Gumpo (syn. Gunpo); Issho no Haru; Jindai; Kanki; Matsu no Hikari; Miyono no Tsuki; Myogi; Seigetsu; Shinkigen; Shinnyo no Hikari; Shunrei; Tatsumi no Hikari; Yuka.

How to Grow Them

The ideal planting site has five characteristics: (1) It is on a hillside from which late spring frosts will drift to lower ground and will not freeze the flower buds. (2) It is protected from high winds. (3) It gets some protection from summer sun, preferably by high shade cast by tall trees. (4) It drains well. (5) It has woodsy soil that is porous, contains a maximum of humus and is moderately acid. Only the fourth and fifth conditions are critical, and deficiencies of porosity, organic material and acidity can be corrected. High shade can sometimes be provided by pruning lower branches and thinning out existing trees.

Begin by having the soil at your planting site tested for acidity. Contact the Cooperative Extension Service in your county, city, or in the District of Columbia for advice on how to have this test made. What you want is a soil with a pH between 4.5 and 6.0. The Extension Service will tell you how to bring your soil to the desired pH level, either by adding ground sulphur or ferrous sulphate if the soil is too alkaline, or lime if it is too acidic.

Whichever substance you need, spread it in the recommended amount over the area to be planted. Then spread at least several inches of sphagnum peat, finely-ground pine bark or fibrous compost. Next, if your soil is clayey, spread several inches of coarse yellow-brown builders' sand over the whole site and a generous handful of gypsum at each plant site. Finally rototill or hand-dig all this into the soil until it is thoroughly mixed to a depth of at least one foot.

Planting Above the Ground

Another method of planting on clay is to ignore it. Set the plant on the surface of the ground and firm up good woods soil around the root ball. Plants so set will require more artificial watering the first season, and maybe the second season as well if the summer is dry.

Plants grown in plastic pots may risk self-strangulation. Roots which wind around the inside of the pot will continue to wind, even when released from the

An old favorite azalea is 'Palestrina' (also known as 'Wilhelmina Vuyk'). It grows upright and has a white flower with a chartreuse blotch.

pot, unless that spiral pattern is broken. With a knife, slice the root ball from top to bottom, about a quarter-inch deep, on all four quarters. Then slice an "X" across the base of the root ball. These disruptions of the spiral pattern will induce the old roots to move outward into the new soil you have prepared.

As for mulching, do it as soon as you've finished planting, using almost any organic material except sphagnum peat moss. Leaf mold from woods, particularly an oak woods, is best. Pine needles, sawdust if it is weathered, compost or any of the bagged ground barks are good. Put on two to three inches, extending well beyond the root ball and not quite touching the woody base of the plant. Lawn grass clippings are not satisfactory because they pack down and shed water. Replenish the mulch as necessary to maintain the two-to-three inch depth before summer's heat and drought.

Nitrogen Can Be a Killer

As for fertilizing, most authorities counsel the amateur grower against any except that provided by the decaying mulch. Too much nitrogen can be a powerful destroyer, killing the plant or burning its roots to the extent that growth is retarded. However if your compulsion to fertilize is irresistible, use non-burning cottonseed meal applied at the rate of three pounds to 100 square feet soon after the flowering period. Alternatively, you can use any commercial fertilizer which is manufactured for acid soil plants. In the latter case do not exceed the application rate prescribed on the bag. And no matter what you use, apply fertilizer only in late winter or early to mid-spring in order to avoid soft late-season growth which will freeze.

Pruning? Yes, but only soon after blossoms have faded. Otherwise you will have no flowers next year.

Pests and Diseases

Many azaleas are free from serious pests and diseases. In others they can be controlled. The worst is azalea petal blight.

Azalea Lacebugs. These gauze-winged insects about ⅛ inch long suck sap from the underside of leaves. Infested leaves are speckled and blotched, eventually changing from green to yellow, and on the underside are spotted with tar-like excrement. Look for minute nymphs on the underside of the leaves, along the mid-rib, when the first hatching of lacebugs occurs in late April to early May. If you find them, spray the underside of the leaves with any of the following: Diazinon, Malathion, Dimethoate (Cygon) or Acephate (Orthene). The first two pesticides are effective only when they directly contact the nymphs, and must be repeated several times at 10-day intervals. The latter two are systemics; they remain effective for several weeks, usually throughout the hatch period.

If the infestation has been heavy look again for nymphs during the two other hatch periods, late May and again in July, and repeat the spraying.

Whiteflies. These are very small (1/16 inch long) wedge-shaped insects with two pairs of white wings. They too suck from the underside of leaves, which then become sticky and turn mottled yellow with a black and sooty mold. Dursban or Dimethoate (Cygon) will give control.

Azalea Petal Blight. This is a fungus which has moved into the Washington area within recent years. It destroys azalea blossoms by turning them into a soggy mess, particularly during warm wet weather. Spray with Bayleton. Remove all blighted flowers, and at the end of the flowering season remove all the old mulch and replace it with fresh.

For other pests and diseases consult your local Extension Service.

Where to See Azaleas

U.S. National Arboretum. Six areas within the Arboretum feature azaleas. They are: (1) The B.Y. Morrison Garden of hybrids which Morrison developed for the Washington area, and which make up the bulk of the list of preferred varieties recommended in this chapter. (2) The Frederic P. Lee Memorial Garden, which contains the late bloomers. (3) The Azalea Loop between these two gardens, where cultivars are grouped by color. (4) Azalea Hill above the B.Y. Morrison garden, where azaleas are planted only for mass color effect. (5) The forecourt to the Bonsai Pavilion, where dwarf azaleas are used in the style of a classical Japanese garden. And (6) The Asian Valley.

Brookside Gardens. The Montgomery County display garden in Wheaton Regional Park. The collection of azaleas and well-chosen companion plants covers more than seven acres.

McCrillis Garden, 6610 Greentree Road, Bethesda. This garden was donated to the Maryland-National Capital Park and Planning Commission by the late William McCrillis; it is managed as an adjunct to Brookside Gardens. It consists of five acres of azaleas, rhododendrons and other woodland plants, all now reaching maturity. A more recent planting is of 300 late-blooming Satsuki cultivars imported from Japan for evaluation.

The Perkins Azalea Garden at the Landon School, 6101 Wilson Lane, Bethesda. Fifteen thousand plants. Watch for announcement of the annual festival in early May. It includes a sale of azalea cultivars and wildflowers, plus the "Azalea Classics" show by the Brookside Gardens Chapter of the Azalea Society of America.

Note

An earlier version of this article appeared in the September 1985 issue of *The Washingtonian* magazine.

References

Galle, Fred C.: *Southern Living Azaleas.* Birmingham, Ala., 1974. An excellent short introduction, with clear cultural information.

Galle, Fred C.: *Azaleas.* Timber Press, Portland, OR., 1985, 1987. This is now the definitive work on azaleas, bringing Lee up to date.

Lee, Frederic P.: *The Azalea Book.* Van Nostrand, Princeton, NJ, 1958, 1965. Long the best book on azaleas, this is still the most useful for the novice grower.

Do's and Don'ts

DON'T prune azaleas or broad-leafed evergreens after mid-July.

DON'T treat your lawn with an insecticide for grubs after you've put down milky spore.

DO cut down on your weeding chores by cultivating no deeper than an inch and a half.

DO pull up your weeds in the fall. A clean garden in the fall means fewer problems in the spring.

DO mulch your azaleas with leaves. Oak leaves are especially good. As your azaleas grow larger and leaves fall, rake more of them under the plants. Do this each year and you'll build up a mulch that will stop most weeds, absorb moisture and protect the azaleas from freezing.

DON'T plant your azaleas too low. Instead dig a shallow hole 50 percent larger than the plant ball. Put two inches of a 50-50 mixture of top soil and humus at the bottom, lower the ball into the hole, and pack two inches more of the mixture around it. Then top it off with still more of the mix. The top of the ball should be at least two inches or more above the surrounding area.

Rhododendrons: Stunning Beauty

By George Ring and Jacob B. Engle

The average gardener, even the beginner, can grow rhododendrons in the Washington area. But to do it successfully, he will need to plant varieties most likely to survive our hot, humid summers and cold winters and give them the right growing conditions.

Best Planting Time. Rhododendrons may be planted or moved almost any time except when the ground is frozen. Risk of losing a plant is highest during the hottest summer days or unusually cold winters. Many growers prefer to plant or transplant in early spring. This gives plants time to become established before extremely hot or cold weather.

Acquiring Plants. Plants can be acquired from local nurseries, amateur specialists in the area or by catalog order. Truckers generally sell collected native species usually hardy in this area. These have good foliage but less spectacular flowers than those of selected hybrids and species.

Small plants usually are the best buy. They can adapt to your situation and be moved to other locations. If a plant dies, less investment is lost. If you are willing to pay more for a quicker show, you may prefer to buy plants in bud or bloom. Make your choices on the basis of foliage as well as flowers. Foliage is on view the year around, flowers for a much shorter period. Consider eventual size: rhododendrons vary from dwarfs with leaves measuring a fraction of an inch to tree types with leaves a foot or more long.

Planting Sites. Hillsides are ideal unless they are too steep. Level ground with good drainage will do. Avoid low areas as they may be frost pockets or soggy. Some shade is usually desirable although some rhododendrons do well in full sun in this area. Too much shade usually results in few flowers. Too much sun can shorten life of flowers and damage foliage. An ideal situation is sunlight filtered through tall oaks with lower limbs trimmed out. Dogwood, pines and other evergreens are good companions unless they shade the rhododendrons too much. Avoid maples, tulip poplars and other shallow-rooted plants. Where there are no trees, the east and north sides of a house are usually suitable if protected from wind.

Soil. Most soil in the Washington area is adequately acid for rhododendrons in the 4.5 to 6.0 pH range. Lime leaching from house foundations or construction debris may alter the pH in spots. Take soil samples to your county extension service for tests. If they show the soil is too alkaline, add ferrous sulphate at the rate of nine pounds to each 100 square feet for each unit of pH to be lowered (for example, from 6.0 to 5.0). Or use sulfur, two pounds per 100 square feet for each unit of pH to be lowered. If your soil is sandy, less of either material will be needed; if heavy clay, slightly more.

Planting. To prepare a planting bed, spread about six inches of humus (decomposed leaves or other vegetation), peat moss, or compost over the ground and mix it into the top 12 inches with power tiller or shovel. If your soil is heavy clay, also work in sharp builder's sand or perlite. Or dig holes for individual plants if the soil is well drained. Make them 50 percent larger than the plant balls. Fill in around the balls with a 50-50 mixture of soil and humus.

Set plants at the depth they grew previously, making allowance for settling. Do not put soil on top of the plant balls. In

PHOTO BY GEORGE TALOUMIS

On the recommended list of rhododendrons for the Washington area is the pink-flowered medium-sized 'Scintillation' which blooms in mid-May and has a 4/3 rating by the American Rhododendron Society. It is hardy to -10°F.

poorly drained areas, set plants on top of the ground and surround the balls with good soil. Space plants in relation to their eventual size unless you are willing to transplant some as they get crowded.

Add a good mulch several inches deep to help retain moisture and prevent most weed growth. Good mulching materials include shredded pine bark, wood chips, oak leaves, pine needles or other evergreen foliage that won't pack down, and permit air and water to pass through. Do not cultivate near rhododendrons as this may damage their shallow roots.

Fertilizing. Fertilizing is needed only in deficient areas or to offset nitrogen depletion by mulching materials not well rotted. Soil tests may indicate specific requirements. Otherwise, use commercial fertilizers prepared for acid-loving plants at or below the rate recommended on the bag; or cottonseed meal: one cupful around the base of a three-foot plant, more or less for larger or smaller plants. Apply in late winter or early spring so new growth will harden off early enough to avoid winter damage. Well-established rhododendrons usually need

PHOTO BY GEORGE TALOUMIS

The white-flowered, low-growing 'Boule de Neige' blooms early in May and has an ARS rating of 3/2. It is hardy to -25°F.

no fertilizer but in some areas low in nitrogen they do. Some growers say phosphates encourage flower budding.

Pruning. To reduce size or change the shape of a plant, up to one third of it may be removed in any one year. This should be done right after flowering by cutting back to the next rosette of leaves below the spent blooms, or to an intersection of two or more branches. An entire branch can be cut off to help shape a plant. Do not leave a stub with no leaves or buds. Dead or diseased branches should be cut back to sound wood. A few varieties will not develop new growth from old wood. Experiment a little.

Disbudding. If you want a more compact plant, terminal leaf buds should be carefully plucked out as growth begins in the spring. Branches will grow from side buds. Leaf buds are long; flower buds are round.

Deadheading. Some rhododendrons use much energy in producing seed. Plants will be more vigorous if trusses of flowers are picked as they fade. This prevents formation of seed.

Watering. Water when precipitation is insufficient and soil dries. Even in winter, avoid excessive watering, especially in the fall when it may encourage late season growth which may become winter-damaged. Drooping leaves on warm mornings sometimes signal mois-

ture deficiency. Drooping leaves in the late afternoon are not a definite sign that watering is needed. If leaves do not return to normal within four hours of watering the problem could be caused by wilt, a disease caused by a fungus which attacks rhododendron roots with usually fatal results. If that happens dig up the plant and dispose of it away from the garden.

Insects and Diseases. Insects and diseases are no great problem in the Washington area if plants have suitable sites and growing conditions. Occasionally, stem borers, lacewing flies, root weevils, petal blight and root-rot *(Phytophthora cinnamomi)* may become prevalent enough to justify treatment. Most of these problems can be prevented or controlled by these practices:

- Buy and plant healthy plants.
- Provide good drainage, planting high in well-drained sites.
- Mulch to conserve moisture and water only as needed.
- Plant cold- and heat-resistant varieties.
- Prune dead and dying stems and remove from plant vicinity.
- Protect from petal blight and root rot.

Petal blight is indicated by brown or watery spots on flowers which soon become brown and slimy. It is most prevalent in hot and humid weather. The most effective control is Bayleton sprayed directly on flower buds when they begin to show color, and repeated if needed two weeks later.

Root weevils normally do not survive in the heavy soils of the Washington area but may become a problem in exceptionally well-drained soils. Grubs feed on roots and adults chew notches on leaf edges at night. Drench soil and foliage with an Orthene spray for good results.

Root rot is caused by a fungus *(Phytophthora cinnamomi)* which becomes active in high temperatures in our wet soils. To control it, provide good drainage by planting on top of heavy soils and by mulching to keep soil cool. Do not plant in holes in heavy, poorly drained soils. Tru-

Recommended Rhododendrons for the Greater Washington Area

Plant Name: Cultivar or species	Rating	Hardiness degrees F	Plant Size	Blooming Season	Comments
REDS					
'America'	3/2	-20	Medium	Mid-May	
'Jean Marie de Montague'	3/4	0	Medium	Early May	Needs winter protection
'Mars'	4/3	-10	Medium	Late May	
'Nova Zembla'	3/3	-20	Medium	Early May	Requires excellent drainage
'Vulcan'	3/4	-5	Medium	Late May	
PINKS					
'Ben Mosely'	3/4	-20	Tall	Mid-May	
'Cadis'	4/4	-15	Tall	Late May	
'Conewago'	3/2	-25	Medium	Early April	Small leaves
'Mrs. Furnival'	5/5	-10	Medium	Late May	Eye catcher
'Pink Twins'	4/3	-15	Medium	Mid-May	Hose in hose
'P.J.M.'	3/4	-25	Medium	Late April	Smaller leaves
'Scintillation'	4/3	-10	Medium	Mid-May	
'Tom Everitt'	4/4	-15	Tall	Late May	
'Wheatley'	4/4	-15	Medium	Mid-May	
'Windbeam'	4/3	-25	Medium	Late April	Small leaves, slow grower
R. carolinianum	2/3	-25	Tall	Early May	Needs perfect drainage
R. mucronulatum	3/2	-25	Tall	Early April	Pink form best
R. racemosum	3/3	-5	Semi-dwarf	Late April	Small flowers and leaves
WHITES					
'Boule de Neige'	3/2	-25	Low	Early May	
'County of York'	3/3	-15	Tall	May	
'Catawbiense album'	2/3	-20	Tall	Late May	
'Janet Blair'	3/3	-20	Tall	Mid-May	
R. Maximum	2/4	-25	Tall	June	Some shade, superior foliage
R. yakusimanum	3/4	-10	Semi-dwarf	Early May	Slow growing
R. yakusimanum 'Mist Maiden'	4/5	-20	Low	Mid-May	Faster growing than species
LAVENDERS AND PURPLES					
'A. Bedford'	4/3	-5	Tall	Late May	
'Caroline'	3/3	-15	Tall	Mid-May	Root rot resistant
'Everestianum'	3/3	-15	Tall	Late May	
'Roseum Elegans'	2/4	-25	Tall	Late May	Old standby, needs sun
YELLOWS AND BLENDS					
'Goldfort'	4/3	-10	Tall	Early May	Cream
'Mary Belle'	4/4	-15	Medium	Late May	Peach
'Mary Fleming'	4/3	-25	Semi-dwarf	Late April	Bisque yellow, salmon streaks
R. Keiskei	3/3	-10	Semi-dwarf	Late April	Small leaves

Rhododendron Care

For more flowers and better plant form, deadhead, disbud and trim your plants. Deadheading is picking off the trusses after the flowers wilt. Disbudding is pinching off the growth (pointed) buds in early fall or early spring. The fat buds produce the flowers. In trimming, prune branches back to the next rosette or leaves or intersection of two or more branches. An entire branch can be pruned to shape the plant. Don't leave stubs. Prune any dead or diseased branches back to sound wood. Some varieties will not develop new growth or flowers from the old wood. Shaping your plants is important in their early years. Experiment.

– Jacob B. Engle

---

ban as a soil drench is a preventive treatment.

Stem borers may cause an occasional problem indicated by dead or dying new growth tips in the summer. The following year, grubs bore down the stem to the crown and may kill the plant. To control them cut out and destroy dead and dying growth. If grubs have bored into the crown, pour melted paraffin over the plant base.

Lacewing fly is seldom a problem. Some rhododendrons in bright sun may show a mottled leaf surface with tissue removed between leaf veins. Control is dimethoate (Cygon), a systemic insecticide applied as a spray in early June. One spraying may be effective for a year or more.

About Plant Recommendations: Some good hybrids and species are suggested both for beginners and more advanced growers. They have been selected from the hundreds available because experience has shown them to be good performers in the Washington area. A few may be available only from specialist nurseries; others often are available from local nurseries. There are many others equally good, or better, among the thousands of varieties and species.

Ratings, hardiness and other details are mainly those provided by the American Rhododendron Society (ARS). Quality ratings, expressed in fractions, refer to flower quality (numerator) and plant quality denominator.

There are five ratings: 5, superior; 4, **above average; 3, average; 2, below average, and 1, poor. A 5/4 plant thus has superior flowers and above-average foliage.**

Size terms: dwarf, under 1½ feet at maturity; semi-dwarf, under 3 feet; low, under 4 feet; medium, under 6 feet, and tall, over 6 feet.

References

Antonelli, A.L. and others: *How to Identify Rhododendron and Azalea Problems.* Pullman, Wash., Washington State University Cooperative Extension, 1984.

Leach, David G.: *Rhododendrons of the World.* New York, Scribner's, 1961.

Livingston, Philip A. and Franklin B. West, editors: *Hybrids and Hybridizers.* Newtown Square, PA, Harrowood Brooks, 1978. Excellent sections on varieties for Middle Atlantic and Virginia regions.

Do's and Don'ts

DO buy small or medium-sized rhododendrons (six feet at maturity) unless you have a large garden. The large ones will grow up to 10 feet or more in a few years. Select your plants on the basis of foliage as well as flowers. You'll see the leaves the year round, the flowers only for a few days.

DON'T leave dead trusses on the ground when you trim your rhododendrons after the flowers wilt. Put them in the trash to prevent any possible spreading of diseases.

Rose Growing Simplified

By Frederick John Rosenthal

Growing roses in the Greater Washington area really isn't difficult, and you can have beautiful blooms from mid-May through late October. For elegance as well as frequent blooming, Hybrid Teas will be your best bet while Floribundas can't be beat for massed beds of color the summer through. Many are delightfully fragrant. Grandifloras make excellent hedges or back of the border specimens. Don't overlook Miniatures for edging and for the small yard. For accent plantings, you can't do better than Tree Roses, Pillar Roses, or Climbers. Some of the Shrub Roses and Old Roses boast unbeatable fragrance, hardiness and ease of care.

Roses need plenty of sun (six to eight hours if possible), preferably with some afternoon shade. Keep bushes away from the competing roots of trees or large shrubs. Provide good drainage and a well-prepared soil. Roses thrive best in a slightly acid soil, with a pH between 5.5 and 6.8. Check your drainage by digging a hole one to one and a half feet deep and filling it with water. If after 24 hours the water has disappeared, fine; if not, either choose another location or raise the planting site somewhat above the surrounding ground.

Digging the Hole

Having chosen your spot, dig your hole or bed from 18 inches to two feet deep, removing all rocks and debris, and then add a double handful of superphosphate (0-20-0) per bush or twice that amount of bonemeal (4-12-0 or 0-11-0). Next, for every two shovelfuls of soil that you return to the hole or bed, add a shovelful of damp peat moss or well-rotted compost or manure. Mix the whole mess well together for the full depth of the bed or hole, and let it settle for several weeks in advance of planting time.

You can plant bare-root roses either in fall or spring in the Washington area. Potted roses are available in early May. Buy only the very best from a reliable nursery, garden center, or mail order source and stay away from so-called bargain sales. When your bare-root roses arrive, soak them in water for about eight hours, then plant them right away. If you cannot do so, follow the instructions enclosed with the package until you are ready to plant.

Now open up the hole wide and deep enough to accommodate the roots without crowding or winding them around. Leave a cone of soil in the center of the hole. Now bring your bush to the garden immersed in a pail of water, for the roots should never be exposed to sun or wind. Spread the roots out over the cone in a slightly downward and outward direction. Plant the bush so that the bud union is one inch below ground level. Now backfill the hole, tamping the loose soil gently around the roots with your fingers or a blunt stick, then more firmly, until the hole is about two-thirds full. Then fill it to the top with water. This helps to settle soil around the roots and to eliminate air pockets. It is safer than tromping the loose soil with your feet which can break roots and compact the soil.

Protect Against Wind and Sun

Fall-planted bushes must be protected against desiccating winter winds and sun. Spring-planted bushes also require protection against sun and wind for two to three weeks. The customary procedure is to mound soil – from another part

Our National Flower

It's official. Public Law 99-449 decrees that "the flower commonly known as the rose is our national flower." The rose takes its place beside the bald eagle as a national symbol. It happened quietly in 1986. In the past proposals for a national flower always stirred noisy debates in Congress: standoffs between backers of the rose and the marigold, with no end of support for other contenders, some of it serious, much of it playful – for the carnation, corn tassel, daisy, mistletoe, and columbine, among others. One wag proposed the "cement cloverleaf."

The rosarians, after losing many battles, finally won the war. The American Rose Society, mindful of earlier strategies that failed, organized a low-key campaign at the local level. Action in Congress took the route of a joint resolution, co-sponsored by majorities in both Senate and House, and approved in both by voice votes. With a similar lack of fanfare, the President signed the legislation into law.　　　　– J.E.

of the garden – eight to 10 inches high over the bud union, and around the exposed canes. Leave it there until an overcast day in spring, when forsythia is in bloom and danger of killing frosts is past. Then remove the soil very carefully from the canes so as not to injure any newly-emerging shoots.

A good way to do this is by washing it away gradually with the garden hose. You can protect a spring-planted bush by inverting a bean or bushel basket over the canes, and weighting it down with a brick. No muss, no fuss, no bother! And clean! Others have had success using a tan-colored small trash-can liner over the newly-planted bush.

Spring is the preferred season to plant potted bushes. Prepare the soil and hole as for bare-root roses. Then cut and remove the container carefully, so as not to disturb the rootball. Plant the bush, making sure that the bud union is one inch below the soil level. Because potted roses are already in growth with developed foliage, and the season is more advanced, they need no mounding or baskets, although a light mulch is helpful to prevent drying out.

Spacing of Plants

If you are planting more than one bush, space Hybrid Teas, Floribundas, and Grandifloras 30 to 36 inches apart on centers. Some roses may require somewhat more or less, depending upon the variety and vigor of the plants. Miniatures need about 12 inches, while Climbers need at least 6 feet between them for best results.

Basic care consists of feeding, watering, mulching, and spraying. Newly-planted bushes should require no feeding until after their second flush of bloom. Then you may give them a small handful of granular 5-10-5 or a special rose food once a month, with the last application no later than mid-August. This is to avoid the stimulation of new growth that will not harden before winter.

Established bushes get the same feeding, except that you start in March. Fertilizer should be gently scratched into the top inch to an inch and a half of the soil in order not to disturb the feeding roots which grow close to the surface, and then thoroughly watered in. Many of our area rose growers now make a one-time spring application of a slow-release all-season fertilizer (such as Osmocote). While it may cost a little more, it saves much time and labor.

Beginning in early June, when the soil begins to heat up, spread a good mulch, such as tanbark, pine bark, hardwood bark, woodchips, cocoa shells, or a similar material round your bushes to a depth of one and a half to two and a half inches. This will keep down weeds, reduce the need to cultivate and water, minimize rain-splash spreading of blackspot, facilitate the absorption of water in the soil, and generally keep the soil around the roots cooler than the surrounding air, thus encouraging root spread of the plant.

Roses Need Water

Talking of water, it will pay you and your roses to keep an eye on the daily weather reports in the paper, or better yet, to install a rain gauge. Roses are thirsty plants and unless the weekly rainfall adds up to one inch, you should make up the deficiency. Two gallons of water are equivalent to one inch. And when you water, soak the soil, not the leaves, for it is the roots that need it. And I don't mean sprinkle; I mean soak!

Spraying, which is primarily a preventive rather than a curative procedure, should be done religiously from early spring until after the first killing frost. It is easier to prevent diseases and insects from harming, or even killing your roses than it is to combat them after they have taken hold.

The best all-around pesticide combination in this area has proved to be one tablespoon of Isotox (a systemic insecticide), plus a half tablespoon of Benlate (Benomyl) and three-quarters of a tablespoon of Phaltan (both fungicides effective against blackspot and mildew) per gallon of water. A good substitute for Isotix is Orthene, while Funginex, a liquid fungicide, can replace both Benlate and Phaltan. Actually, it is best to alternate the appropriate pesticides so that neither insects nor fungi can build up resistance to them.

An All-America Rose selection, the popular hybrid tea, 'Touch of Class,' has high-centered coral blooms and an attractive petal shape. It has been a winner of many awards.

Growers Agree on Fungicide Use

Many rose growers have reduced the frequency of spraying insecticides. They use a strong jet of water from a hose or water wand to combat harmful insects and do not resort to stronger measures until an infestation becomes intolerable. All of them agree, however, that regular use of fungicides is essential. To protect your roses, apply spray material once a week in the early morning or late afternoon but never in the heat of mid-day once temperatures go above 85°F. During hot summer days, you may space your spraying program 10 to 14 days apart. Spray from the bottom of the plant upward, hitting the underside of the leaves, where most insects hide and many fungal spores alight, and then give a final light flourish over the top of the bush. Spray a light mist and do not drench the plants, for too much spray material will as surely hurt and defoliate them as the pests you are trying to save them from. Never spray on a windy day, and obey all instructions on the labels.

You should be able to harvest some fine blooms during the first year after you have planted your bushes. I must warn you, though, not to cut any long-stemmed beauties as yet. In their first year, your bushes will require all the foliage they make to get properly established in their new home. So cut only very short stems until the last crop of the year, when you may cut longer ones, as the bushes are about to enter dormancy.

The following year, you will have a larger and stronger bush and then you can cut longer stems, if you desire. And by no means judge your new bush by the blooms it produces during its first year. Give it at least two years to prove itself.

Then, if you do not like it, replace it with another.

Pruning a Necessity

Pruning is a vitally necessary part of rose culture. Proper pruning rejuvenates a bush, shapes it to pleasing form, keeps it in good health, and will produce larger and better quality blooms than an unpruned, straggly bush. There is no mystery about pruning, once you know the reasons for it and how to go about it. There is no better way to learn about pruning than to attend a free springtime pruning demonstration given by the Potomac Rose Society, where you can observe experts at work and ask questions. Watch for radio, television, or newspaper announcements in late February and early March for details of dates and locations.

As you prepare your roses for their winter sleep, you need only prune the tops of the very tall bushes to keep them from whipping in the rough winter winds and loosening the roots. Then take out any crossing branches or diseased wood. That is all. You save the real pruning for spring.

Spring Pruning Time

In this area, we generally prune from mid-March to early April. You will need heavy leather gloves; sharp, clean pruning shears, preferably those with curved blades; lopping shears for heavier canes or climbers; a small saw for the heaviest canes; and a pruning paint or sealer (such as Elmer's Glue-All) to cover the cut ends of canes to prevent entry of boring insects.

On the basis of hard-learned experience we recommend moderate pruning in the Washington area. This is because the healthy, green wood contains some of the reserve food made by the leaves during the previous season and stored to provide nourishment for the new shoots of the coming season. Remember, continued low pruning will only lead to weak, short-lived plants.

First, cut out all dead and diseased canes; those that are dark brown or black. Next, prune out any unwanted growth, and this includes crossing canes that rub against each other, those that grow into the center of the bush, and the small, twiggy lateral growths that will not produce any worthwhile blooms. Cut these latter off flush with the main stem. Try to avoid scratching or hurting the green bark on healthy canes as this will leave them open to infection. What you have left now is a sturdy framework for the coming season's growth.

Pruning Determines Shape and Vigor

How you prune the remaining canes will determine the shape and vigor of the bush, so proceed by slow stages to cut these strong, healthy canes back to green-centered wood. For Hybrid Teas, this may be anywhere from 18 to 36 inches above ground; and for Grandifloras from 30 to 36 inches. For Floribundas we try for similar heights, depending upon the growth habit and natural height of the variety. Some Floribundas are naturally low and spreading; others grow tall and willowy.

Always cut just a quarter-inch above a bud (or eye), slanting the cut at 45-degree angle to the rear of the bud. By making your cuts above an outward pointing bud, you encourage an open, vase-shaped bush. Such a bush will admit sun and air into its center, encouraging new canes to break from the bud union; also it will make it easier to spray and combat pests during the growing season.

Seal all cut ends, and you are done. Winter damage to the canes may occasionally dictate more rigorous pruning, and the end result may look lopsided and lower than you had hoped. Do not be dismayed. While no bush should suffer such treatment year after year, an occasional end result such as this may set it back briefly, but by summer a strong plant with a good root system should be back to normal.

Climbers Are Different

Miniature roses are pruned exactly like their big sisters. Climbers, on the other hand, require a different technique. In the spring, you remove dead and diseased canes as for bush roses. Make several cuts along the cane, and then carefully remove the small sections, so as not to injure the remaining healthy canes.

If the climber has grown dense, you can also remove about a third of the oldest canes. Train the remaining canes horizontally, if possible. This will encourage the emergence of lateral shoots from the main canes: these will produce most of your blooms. After the first spring bloom, cut these lateral shoots back to three or four buds from the main cane, and also remove additional older ones that did not produce any worthwhile blooms.

Your final tasks should be to remove all debris, to administer the year's first feeding, and then to give all bushes a double-strength clean-up spray of your regular pesticides to kill any over-wintering pests.

When You Cut You Also Prune

By the way, every time you cut a bloom during the growing season, you also are pruning the bush. Thus you can continue

The hybrid tea, 'Pascali,' is an All-America Rose selection. Its flowers are white, not large but well shaped.

to shape the bush into a pleasing form. When you cut fresh blooms, and "dead-head" wilted ones, make your cut so as to leave as much foliage as possible. This provides the plant with its food factory. Make your cut a quarter-inch above a five-leaflet leaf, leaving at least two such five-leaflet leaves on the stem between the cut and the main cane. The bud or eye between the cane and the leaf will produce a new shoot for you with more blooms. In this area, you may have as many as three to four crops from one bush if you follow this practice.

While for many years good rose growers in our area had to do little or nothing to ensure that their bushes would survive our winters, the occurrence of much colder and severer weather since the mid-seventies has forced them to provide winter protection.

To do this, you can obtain empty bean or peach baskets from roadside fruit and vegetable stands or some supermarkets. Line them with newspapers and stuff them with oak leaves. Cut back the canes and tie them together to accommodate them under the baskets. Invert the baskets over the bushes and weight them down. You can also make 12-inch-high newspaper or hardware-cloth collars to put around the roses and stuff them with oak leaves.

And, you can always mound soil into and over the crown to a height of eight or so inches. Planting the bush with the bud union an inch below the ground also helps winter survival. The main concern should be to protect the bud union – the living heart of the rose – from harm.

Try Older Varieties

Whether or not you winter-protect your roses is entirely up to you. But there is another alternative: that is to grow some of the older, hardier garden rose varieties. The Rugosas, Hybrid Rugosas, Autumn Damasks, Damasks, and Gallicas, to mention only a few, have stood the test of time against any degree of winter coldness that we are likely to encounter in this area. They require no pampering.

Possibly the hardiest of the lot are the

Rugosas and their hybrids. Numerous varieties are now available. Rugosas (so-called because of their deeply ribbed, crinkly leaves) are so tough and adaptable that they can take the salt spray of the seashore, will grow in almost any soil, will thrive among tree roots so long as they are in full sun, and have even been used as traffic barriers on highway median strips. While their blooms generally do not last too long, either as cut flowers or on the bush, they repeat rapidly and bloom all season long. The single forms (five petals) have the added attraction of forming brightly-colored scarlet or orange hips which are rich in vitamins and are enjoyed by birds and people alike.

No less hardy are the Gallicas, the oldest of the garden roses, which appear in the ancestry of most of the others. Seldom more than three to four feet high, they are ideal for small gardens; also they thrive with a minimum of attention on most soils. While they bloom only in spring (beginning with the second year after planting), they more than make up for this with gorgeous blooms ranging in color from pink through mauves and purples to maroons.

Damasks are historically important, their fragrance having been transmitted through the centuries to many contemporary varieties of modern roses. Centifolia roses and their mutants, the Moss Roses, are often called Cabbage roses because of the huge number of their petals. Most bloom only in spring though a few will repeat.

If you are interested in pursuing this facet of rose growing, send away for a catalog to *Roses of Yesterday and Today*, 802 Brown's Valley Road, Watsonville, CA 95076-0398. It will provide you with many hours of fascinating reading for only $2.

The Author's Recommendations
Of Good Roses for the Area

Rugosas
 'Belle Poitevine' (pink)
 'Blanc Double de Coubert' (white)
 'Frau Dagmar Hastrup' (pale pink)
 'Delicata' (pink)
 'Snow Dwarf' of 'Schneezwerg'
(white)

Gallicas
 'Charles de Mills' (dark crimson
and purple)
 'Tuscany Superb' (purplish-mauve)

Damasks
 'Madame Hardy' (1983; white with
green button center)
 'Rose de Rescht' (fragrant, red)

Hybrid Teas
 'Fragrant Cloud' (fragrant,
orange-coral-red)
 'Mister Lincoln' (tall, dark red)
 'First Prize' (pink, not fragrant)
 'Garden Party' (ivory-white, stately)

 'Century Two' (clear pink)
 'Swarthmore' (cerise, towering)
 'Confidence' (fragrant, light pink to
yellow blend)
 'Tiffany' (fragrant, rose to pink)
 'Double Delight' (red-ivory bicolor,
fragrant)
 'John Waterer' (deep red)
 'Red Lion' (red)
 'Wini Edmunds' (strawberry red with
creamy reverse)

Grandiflora
 'Queen Elizabeth' (carmine, rose,
pale-pink; a first and only)

Floribundas
 'Europeana' (dark red huge trusses)
 'Sunsprite' (light yellow)
 'First Edition' (orange)
 'French Lace' (ivory)
 'Faberge' (peach-pink, reverse
tinted yellow, elegant!)

More Preferred Roses
for the Area

John Rosenthal is one of the most skilled rose growers in the country and his list of preferred roses is an excellent one. Here are some of the newer roses I would recommend. I've restricted the list to the best of those I've raised in my own garden.

Hybrid Teas
'Dolly Parton' (fragrant, full-bodied orange/red blooms)
'Pristine' (white with blush of pink, very vigorous)
'Touch of Class' (coral, high-centered blooms, attractive petal shape; has taken over first place as top U.S. award winner)
'Pascali' (white, not large but well-shaped flowers)

Grandifloras
'Aquarius' (good producer of excellent pink blooms)

Floribundas
'Margaret Merrill' (white, excellent foliage, very fragrant)

Polyanthas
'The Fairy' (clusters of pink blooms, vigorous)

Climbers
'America' (coral pink, almost hybrid tea size blooms)
'Dublin Bay' (by far the best red climber, blooms fade gracefully with minimum of color change)
'Spectra' (multi-color yellow/orange/pink blooms on long stems)

Old Roses
'Four Seasons Damask' (pink blooms throughout growing season, fragrant)

Landscape Roses
'Carefree Beauty' (pink blooms throughout growing season, fragrant)

Miniatures
'Starina' (orange-red; highest rating in any class)
'Cupcake' (medium pink, vigorous)

— **Robert Alde**

Roses Like Water

Roses like water assuming the soil is well drained. The minimum for good growth is one inch of rain a week or the equivalent from irrigation. Three to four inches a week will give you better results. (One inch of rain is equal to two gallons of water.) And, as John Rosenthal emphasizes: When you water them, soak them. Don't sprinkle. Roses also like sunlight. Bloom production in garden sites with less than six hours of direct sunlight will be less than in sites with more than six hours. Less than four hours will result in generally unsatisfactory performance.

– **Robert Alde**

Books

Time-Life Encyclopedia volume on roses.
Ray, Richard and Michael MacCaskey: *Roses, How to Select, Grow, and Enjoy.* HP Books, Tucson Ariz., 1981.
Wolf, Rex and James McNair: *All About Roses.* Ortho Books, San Francisco, CA, 1983. Endorsed by the American Rose Society.

_____

Do's and Don'ts

DO give your plants plenty of space. They need light to develop. If they are crowded they can be in stress and may even suffer physical injury if a neighboring plant with sharp spines punctures their leaves.

Chrysanthemum: Queen of Autumn

By Emerson P. Slacum

In autumn no other flower can surpass the versatile chrysanthemum. Masses of mum blooms of every color and hue (except blue) predominate in the fall landscape. There are at least 13 different bloom forms, sizes, and forms of culture for many purposes.

Mums are available from tiny "button" size to massive 12-inch show types, like the well-known "football mum." There are cultivars not only for garden use, such as the low-growing cushions and taller garden types, but also those adapted to bonsai culture, cascades, trees, and hanging baskets. For all of their versatility, mums are comparatively easy to grow.

Site Selection, Soil Preparation

Choose a site that gets at least six hours of sun a day, with good air circulation. If drainage is a problem, prepare a raised bed. If pH and fertility are problems, take care of these by appropriate adjustments (see "Soils - Fertilizers - Mulches - Compost"). Get a soil test and follow directions to achieve a pH between 6.0 and 7.0 and adequate fertility. Good tilth is important too, so that air, water and nutrients are available to plants and roots can grow easily.

Preparation of the planting area can begin as early as it is comfortable to work outside and the soil is not too wet. Prepare a planting medium, spread it over the site being prepared, spade it in deeply and mix it with the existing soil. Enough for an eight-by-10-foot site can be made up by thoroughly mixing: one wheelbarrow of manure or compost (approximately two bushels), four pounds of superphosphate (0-20-0), one bushel of peat moss, four pounds of ground lime-stone (dolomitic or agricultural, not hydrated lime), and four pounds of 5-10-5 fertilizer. This mixture also can be used for pots, or used to amend smaller sites such as a perennial bed. Adding this or a similar mixture will raise a bed, promoting good drainage.

Planting and Culture

The best and cheapest way to get new plants is to acquire rooted cuttings in late spring. These are available from local chrysanthemum societies and growers, or from commercial sources. Or the gardener can root his own, taking short tip cuttings emerging in spring from established plants, and rooting them either in water or in a suitable (preferably sterile) soil mix. Once well rooted, the cuttings should be kept moist but not wet, and then transplanted into peat or plastic pots, and grown in good light indoors or in a cold frame to make a good root system. Once that is done, those grown inside can be hardened off and, as soon as the weather is settled, planted in their desired locations in the garden or in well-drained pots.

New plants should be planted about 12 inches apart and each plant given a cup of "starter solution" (a quarter-cup of 5-10-5 fertilizer to a gallon of water). Also, other soluble fertilizers like Miracle-Gro can be used as directed on the label. After planting, beds should be well mulched with pine bark, pine needles, straw, or any other material that does not compact, to retain moisture, keep down weeds, and to prevent fungus diseases.

Mums are vigorous feeders and for best results they need to be fed every two weeks, using liquid or other fertilizer in the recommended proportions on the label of the product. Discontinue feeding when the buds show color.

Caution: Chrysanthemums are most sensitive to amounts of sunlight and darkness. They begin to form bloom buds as the hours of daylight diminish, beginning in the latter part of July. However, if artificial light – even in very small amounts – falls on the plants, they will delay bud-set and keep on with vegetative growth. Therefore, never plant mums under a "picture window with the traditional lamp," street light, lamp post, nor a floodlighted area.

Decorative

Most garden varieties reach their peak of flowering in October and extend their colorful display until the first killing frost. Some cultivars are frost-tolerant; other late-bloomers must be protected. Clumps of mums left in the ground for a second season may start blooming in mid-July, but such clumps may not be as vigorous or attractive as those from cuttings or divisions.

Spoon

Pinching, Disbudding

When the new plants are six inches tall, usually several weeks after transplanting, make the first pinch by removing the top half-inch of the plant with your thumbnail. This causes side branches to develop and the plant to become fuller. When the branches of the cushion-types and garden-hardy varieties are four to six inches long, pinch them again and continue to pinch each new shoot until July 15, which is the last date for pinching. This will produce a compact plant with a multitude of blooms. Some cushion varieties will achieve this on their own; but for best plants, pinch!

Spider

For the large-flowering mums, such as the incurves ("football mums"), reflexes, spoons, quills, and spiders, disbudding is a must to achieve larger flowers. After the first pinch, only two or three top branches are allowed to grow. All lower branches are removed.

When the flower buds form, no further work is required on garden varieties, but for those on which you plan to grow large blooms, permit only the center bud to develop on each remaining stem. When

Exhibition

The simple act of "pinching" a chrysanthe-mum begins when it is about six inches tall. Place the terminal branch between the forefinger and thumbnail and remove the top half-inch. This encourages branching. As branches for the cushion types and garden-hardy varieties reach four to six inches, pinch again and continue to pinch each new shoot until July 15, the last date for pinching. This will produce a bushy plant with many blooms.

this center bud is about the size of a small pea, remove the cluster of smaller buds surrounding it by "rolling" them off with your thumb. New axillary branches which may develop in leaf axils should be pruned out. Some growers end up with only one stem and only one flower to pro-duce the largest and best mum.

Insect Pests and Diseases

Like most other growing plants, mums have their insect enemies and are sus-ceptible to certain fungus diseases. Aphids as well as leafhoppers and other sucking and chewing insects prey on mums. A continuous schedule of spraying at least every two weeks, and after rains, will help to ensure healthy plants. Use a mixture of Malathion and Captan together, mixed according to directions on the producers' labels. Spraying needs to be started as soon as the rooted cut-tings are transplanted. Damage by slugs is evidenced by holes in leaves or frayed foliage and should be checked by Bug-Geta or a similar product.

SUMMARY

New mum growers should keep the following "musts" firmly in mind:

1. Mums do best in full sun; six or more hours of sunlight is enough. All types of plants grown in the ground or in containers in full sun may be moved, for decorative purposes, to a more shaded location when color shows in buds.

Good Chrysanthemums for the Greater Washington Area

"Cushion" Cultivars: Low growing, compact plants (up to 16 inches), requiring no disbudding or staking, and a minimum of care:
   'Jackpot' – vivid yellow decorative, prolific blooms, frost-tolerant.
   'Yellow Cloud 9' – large flowers, pale yellow, semi-incurve.
   'Baby Tears' – white, small button, low, prolific bloomer.
   'Grandchild' – very hardy, lavender-orchid (or white) formal pompon.
   'Pancho' – best bright orange pompon.

Taller Garden Varieties (17 to 36 inches):
   'French Vanilla' – 3-to-4-inch white blooms, lives over winter, multiplies profusely.
   'Indian Summer' – popular "Harvest Giant" variety, early bloomer, scarlet-bronze decorative.
   'Carrousel' – 4-inch aster purple, spider-spoon quill bloom.
   'Red Headliner' – 3½-inch velvety oxblood-ruby decorative.
   'Statesman' – 1½-inch brilliant yellow, makes a good spray.

2. Locate beds away from encroaching tree or shrubbery roots which may rob nutrients and moisture.
3. Locate beds in areas of good water drainage. Mums will not tolerate low areas with poor drainage. Raised beds of well-prepared soil are ideal.
4. Locate beds away from artificial night light.
5. Space plants properly for good air circulation. Consult your handbooks before starting your soil preparation.

Reference

Washington gardeners are fortunate in having two of the largest chapters of the National Chrysanthemum Society, Inc., located here: the Potomac Chrysanthemum Society and the Old Dominion Chrysanthemum Society, plus a new third group, the Chesapeake Chrysanthemum Society. The national society publishes numerous handbooks for the amateur grower. *The Beginner's Handbook for New Growers of Chrysanthemums* is included in the membership fee, and is available from local societies.

Fall Garden Color

For fall color in the garden try any of these in addition to the better known shrubs and trees such as American dogwood, sourwood, most of the viburnums, and some of the azaleas:

Chinese Pistachio *(Pistacia chinensis.)* Eventually a small tree which turns flaming crimson in fall.

Smoke Tree *(Cotinus Coggyria)*, particularly in its high colored cultivars such as 'Foliis purpureis,' ('Purpureus' or, best of all, 'Royal Purple'.) Leaves turn light red to wine purple, contrasted with the fawn to purplish gray flower panicles which persist into late fall.

Disanthus cercidifolius, which has no common name. This 10- by 12-foot shrub has an interesting criss-cross twiggy habit and in fall turns red, purple, orange and yellow. That's when it's stunning.

Enkianthus campanulatus and *E. perulatus*. The first is brilliant red, the second turns scarlet. The major difference is that *E. campanulatus* is bigger, growing slowly to 30 feet, while *E. perulatus* won't grow much above six feet. Both require acid soil.

– John G. Shaffer

New Camellias

Camellias flourished here until the onset of cold and wind in 1977, 1978 and 1982. Now it is risky to grow them outside without special placement and protection from dessication. You must put them where they will not get winter sun or drying winds. Plants in the ground can be heavily mulched and protected from wind and sun by burlap barriers or hedges. They can be grown in pots. Small pots can be overwintered in sun porches or garages, big pots protected by thermal blankets. New cultivars are being bred that are bush-hardy and have good flowers. 'Frost Prince' and 'Frost Princess' are already in nurseries. Better ones are on the way. Meanwhile, the best bets to be grown with special tactics are 'Kumasaka' (pink), 'Frost Queen' (white), 'Mathotiana' (red), 'Governor Mouton' (red) and 'Leucantha' (white).

– Charles A. H. Thomson

Do's and Don'ts

DON'T pull up the onions in your lawn. Dig them up. Better yet, give them the "cotton glove" treatment. Wearing a rubber or latex glove under your cotton glove, dip your fingers and thumb in a strong weed-killer such as 2,4-D and stroke the onion. Or use a half-and-half mixture of undiluted 2,4-D and used engine oil.

DO check your soil pH from time to time. No matter how well you feed them, plants can't get a square meal if the soil pH is wrong.

DON'T be afraid to experiment with hardiness. Many gladioli will winter over here; so will some of the chrysanthemums. Providing for the right microclimates may allow you to stretch the season, and grow plants that otherwise would succumb to heat or cold.

Iris for Your Garden

By Charles A. H. Thomson

For Washington area gardens, iris offer beauty and versatility. They bloom from spring into fall and provide striking spiky foliage for the balance of the season.

The bearded iris are best known. They offer a magnificent range of flower color, ranging from white to deep purple-red. Some have contrasting, some self or complementing colors in their upreaching petals (standards) and their out- or down-reaching petals (falls). Many are fragrant. Most of them bloom through April and May. Some will bloom again in summer and fall.

Dwarfs, 15 inches or less, are suitable for edging, the front of a bed, or for cut flowers. They bloom here in early April. Medians, 28 inches or less, bloom a little later. Tall ones, rising to 40 inches or more, start blooming in late April and come into full beauty in mid-May. Modern varieties may be in bloom for a week or so. Fans of gray-green leaves remain after that.

Culture is easy. Plant the rhizomes – thickened stem roots – 12 to 15 inches apart so their necks are at ground level and their roots spread down naturally from each side. Iris grow best in full sun and in well-worked neutral to slightly acid soil with plenty or organic material. They will grow in part shade but refuse to bloom in full shade. They welcome balanced fertilizer applied in early spring and again in mid- to late summer. Most of them like moisture but not wet places.

Borers, Soft Rot, and Leaf Spot

The three main enemies are borers, soft rot, and leaf spot. A systemic insecticide applied when the fans are several inches tall in spring takes care of the borers before they burrow into the rhizomes and ream them out.

Soft rot occurs when the rhizomes are cut or damaged; it can attack in spring and summer. High planting and good drainage help; but if soft rot is noticed (it smells, and the fans come away easily) dig up the affected parts of the clump, cut off any diseased tissue, expose the healthy remainder to strong sun for several days, and replant in soil not previously contaminated. A soil drench of streptomycin can help sterilize infected soil, but it also can burn the person using it. So wear protective gloves and clothing and follow directions on the bag.

Leaf spot is chiefly disfiguring, not slowing the plants down much. It can be controlled by cutting off and disposing of dead and diseased foliage and applying a fungicide.

Bearded iris give little bloom their first season but afterwards make up for this. Later, when the rhizomes have died in the center of the clump or the bloom is reduced, dig them up, cut off any dead, weak or diseased parts, trim them to strong new divisions and replant.

I like to put them in one-foot triangles, facing the way I want to look at the new planting. The best time to dig and replant is mid-summer while summer and early fall are best for new planting. Set the rhizomes out as soon as good stock is available. Iris can be lightly mulched their first winter but not after that.

PHOTO BY GEORGE TALOUMIS

◀ **Tall bearded iris start blooming in late April and come into full beauty in mid-May. Like the dwarfs and medians they provide a magnificent range of flower color. This lovely cultivar is the white 'Wedding Bouquet.'**

Bearded iris that don't re-bloom need some companions from June on. Many annuals or perennials are suitable: marigolds, zinnias, daylilies, chrysanthemums, even portulaca. Look for plants that have not only good flowers but also interesting contrasts in leaf and plant form and texture. Be sure they do not crowd the irises.

Iris Without Beards Desirable

Iris without beards should be used more in our gardens. They offer wider ranges of shape and bloom color, foliage, and plant habit. They also are not as subject to diseases and pests as their bearded cousins.

Siberian iris *(Iris sibirica)* bloom with tall bearded iris. Improved varieties now have a longer season of bloom and a wider range in stature, form and color than the old standbys. Japanese iris (*I. kaempferi* cvs) also are being improved. Dr. William L. Ackerman at the National Arboretum has produced cultivars that combine longer bloom season with beauty comparable to that of many old standards. They must have an acid soil and plenty of moisture, especially before blooming. They make large clumps that rarely need dividing, sending up great plate-sized single, semi-double and double blooms in solid and contrasting colors, many interestingly netted and flecked. Japanese iris flower here from early June into July.

There are other excellent non-bearded iris. The crested ones *(I. cristata)*, only a few inches tall, bloom in late spring and spread by rhizomes with fans of six-inch leaves. Good for edging or circling trees, they also can enhance the semi-shade border and the wild garden. The roof iris *(I. tectorum)* are larger and have similar values. Blue and white forms are around. Louisiana iris bloom at the same time with larger clumps and taller stems – to 20 inches. The very tall, to seven-foot, water flags *(I. pseudacorus)*, come later. They grow best in wet places and may seed themselves wildly.

Varieties of Bearded Forms

As for varieties, among the bearded forms they are legion, and most do well in Washington gardens. Proved local favorites include 'Cup Race' (white), 'Pink Taffeta' (pink), 'Launching Pad' (yellow and white), 'Blue Sapphire' (blue), and 'Dusky Dancer' (purple-black). Good inexpensive rebloomers include 'English Cottage' (blue and white), 'Corn Harvest' (yellow), 'Summer Holidays' (blue), 'Red Grapes' (red), and 'Violet Classic' (violet). 'Baby Blossom' is a lovely dwarf. Among the older, taller bearded iris, don't miss such classics as 'Stepping Out.' The latest and most expensive may not be the most suitable iris for the general gardener.

Two words of caution: First, don't try the Pacific Coast iris as they have great difficulty with our hot-wet summers. Second, don't let the quicksands of the world of iris engulf you. There is more to gardening than iris . . .

Sources

Good local information is available from the Chesapeake and Potomac Iris Society. They have annual auctions at which the best, sometimes the latest, and surely the most suitable for our gardens are available at far less than commercial prices.

The best references are *Basic Iris Culture* and *The World of Iris*, both available from the American Iris Society, 7414 East 60th Street, Tulsa, Oklahoma 74145.

Do's and Don'ts

DON'T fertilize your roses after August 15, thus avoiding growth that is easily winter killed.

DON'T expect to grow flowers just like the ones in the seed catalogs. Yours may be smaller and paler. Remember that when the catalog description says "up to two feet," that doesn't mean at least two feet. Of course, in our area it could mean even more.

DON'T expect flowers (with rare exceptions) on plants unless they get the prescribed amount of direct sunlight. Some plants will not even grow leaves without direct sunlight.

Successful Gardening in the Shade

By Els Benjamin

One of the great myths in gardening is that nothing can be grown in the shade. This is poppycock. True, the desire for growing luscious vegetables, scads of annuals or summer-flowering bulbs must be given up as hopeless. This still leaves us, however, with a wide selection of desirable plants that should satisfy any gardener.

Broad-leaved evergreens thrive in shady gardens: azaleas, mountain laurels, pieris and a host of others are among the cream of the cream of ornamental display. Almost all of the hardy early-spring flowering bulbs, such as daffodils, crocus, winter aconites or squills put on a colorful display year after year under deciduous shade with little care on the part of the gardener.

The selection of perennials is also large, including such beauties as bleeding hearts, astilbes and hostas, not to mention dozens of ferns and wildflowers.

Year-Round Beauty

In general, the shade garden is at its best from early spring through early summer. It can be a place of beauty year round, however, with judicious planning and careful siting of plants. Because the use of annuals with their bright flowers is so restricted, an appreciation for leaf forms and variegation, plant textures and bark patterns is awakened in the shade gardener. Also such garden features as small ponds, paths of wood rounds or slate, or a bench or gazebo enhance the intimacy of the shade garden, while offering a sense of fresh perspective and discovery.

When first planning a shade garden, careful stock should be taken of the kind of shade that is cast on the ground. Dense shade is defined as three to four hours of sunlight per day during the growing season or shade cast by permanent structures, such as enclosing walls, or by evergreens, or Norway maples when in leaf. Medium shade is three to six hours of sunlight, or very bright skylight on the north side of a house. Light shade means six to eight hours of sunlight, or filtered sunlight all day.

To Get More Light

Not much can be done to lessen shade where permanent structures are the culprits, but large canopy trees, such as tulip trees *(Liriodendron),* oaks and especially maples can have their lower branches removed. Lower branches of spruces, southern magnolias or similarly shaped trees should never be removed; it would spoil their beautiful form. Scrub pines can be pruned up ruthlessly.

To get even more light, remove dying trees or undesirable trees such as weeping willows, silver maples, Siberian elms or wild cherry trees. Even so it should be remembered that shade usually will get worse with time because of the growth of the canopy.

Once the degree of shade has been assessed, the next order of business is to evaluate the soil. The right soil is fully as important to the good growth of plants as mother's milk is to babies. Most plants in the shade prefer a soil that has about 50 percent clay, 35 percent organic matter such as compost or peat moss, and 15 percent sharp sand for drainage. Soil preparation is often tedious in a shade garden, because of interfering roots from trees and large shrubs. Rototilling is often not possible. The gardener must use hand tools, working around the worst

PHOTO BY GEORGE TALOUMIS

Gardening in the shade increases an awareness and appreciation for leaf forms and plant textures. Here are viburnums, ferns, *smilacina* (false Solomon's-seal), a rhododendron and *zebrina* (wandering jew) plus a touch of foreground color in impatiens and wax begonias.

obstacles and cutting through small roots.

Where roots are so pervasive that holes are hard to dig, lay down a 12 inch layer of wood chips, dig a hole in the mulch and the soil underneath and place the plant with plenty of topsoil in this mulch. It is not the ideal way of planting, but with time the mulch will break down and provide a suitable growing medium. Be careful not to smother shallow-rooted trees such as dogwoods, but keep the mulch outside the drip line.

As soon as shade has been evaluated and the availability of suitable locations for plants have been determined, and before any planting starts, it is essential to have a good landscape plan. This will avoid costly mistakes and allows gradual implementation, a plus in a shade garden, where trial and error are more common than in a sunny garden.

The framework or skeleton of any landscape design is the woody plants: trees, shrubs and ground covers. In a shade garden there usually exist four layers of plants: a canopy of large trees, such as oaks and maples; a layer of understory trees such as dogwoods, redbuds or other trees that grow to about 25 feet; a layer of shrubs such as azaleas, rhododendrons and viburnums, and a layer of low-growing plants like the many ground covers. Most herbaceous plants also fall in this layer. The right amount of plants in each layer will make for a harmonious and natural looking shade garden.

Avoid straight lines and take advantage of plants with green-white leaf variegation or with white flowers. Light colors show up better in the shade, while dark colors recede. Variegation also relieves the tedium of too much green in the summer. Do not count on much fall color. The bright reds and yellows of fall are a result of intense sunlight and cool nights. However, white and green variegation is excellent in reduced sunlight.

Leafy Plants are Welcome

Herbaceous plants are the meat on the skeleton. They quickly fill up all those empty spaces between the woody plants, especially welcome in a new garden with many small woody plants. They come in an infinite variety of flower colors, leaf shapes and heights, from the three-inch-high species crocus to the six-foot-tall bugbane *(Cimicifuga)*.

Avoid those quick-growing plants that become infernal nuisances, such as the charming violets and the pretty goutweed *(Aegopodium)*. They are impossible to eradicate without spraying with an herbicide.

The leaves of some herbaceous plants die down after flowering, not to be seen until next spring – most hardy spring flowering bulbs and such perennials as the bleeding heart *(Dicentra spectabilis)*, *Doronicum* and many wildflowers. Do not despair over the empty spot, but mark the disappeared plant with a label and plant next to it the one annual guaranteed to bloom in the shade: the impatiens. It actually does not like sun.

A few other annuals tolerate light shade: caladiums, ageratums, salvias, coleus, begonias and the New Guinea impatiens. All others require full sun. Experiment also with some tropical plants, such as *Achimenes* or *Streptocarpus* (both in the African violet family), elephant's-ears, calla lilies, or *Pachys-*

tachys, a shrub with scarlet or yellow flowers. All should be available from local sources. Granted they may look a little out of place but so what? The juxtaposition of an "accepted" plant with an offbeat one gives a garden that delicious sense of surprise.

Criteria to Apply

When shopping for woody plants consider not only looks and price, but apply the following criteria: Will it survive Washington area winters? What is its ultimate height? Does it have year-round interest? Is there a cultivar or variety that has superior flowers, leaves, fruit or bark? Is it prone to diseases and pests? Does it need a lot of maintenance due to messy fruit or brittle branches? And, most of all, will it grow in the shade?

After the fun of designing and planting, the gardener soon finds that shade gardening's biggest chore is leaf removal. Leaves must be raked from all grassy areas to avoid smothering the turf. Leaves can stay on planted beds – a good winter mulch – but must be removed before new leaves appear on herbaceous and woody plants. The best time is mid-March.

Less Water Need a Misconception

The second task is watering. The idea that shade gardens need less water than sunny gardens is a misconception. A thick layer of mulch will keep moisture in, but tree roots are heavy water consumers, against which newly-planted small shrubs, ground covers and herbaceous plants cannot compete. Water thoroughly for a couple of hours if rain has not provided an inch or two of water recently.

The third essential task in a shade garden is branch removal. Remove fallen branches from the ground to avoid creating sites for over-wintering pathogens and weed seeds. Prune shrubs to avoid legginess and keep larger plants in check to keep that sunlight coming in.

And what does the shade garden give in return? It gives coolness in the summer and restfulness from a harried world.

A Basic List of Plants
Suitable for the Shade

L	= light shade, 6 to 8 hours sun
M	= medium shade, 3 to 6 hours sun
D	= dense shade, less than 3 hours sun
1	= noted for flowers
2	= noted for fruit
3	= noted for bark

UNDERSTORY TREES

Amelanchier canadensis – **Shadbush:** L, 1, 2.

Cercis canadensis – **Redbud:** L-M, 1.

Cornus florida and cultivars – **Flowering Dogwood:** L-M, 1, 2.

Cornus Kousa – **Chinese Dogwood:** L-M, 1, 2, 3.

Cornus mas – **Cornelian Cherry:** L, 1, 2.

Halesia monticola – **Silverbell:** L, 1.

Stewartia species – **Stewartia:** L, 1, 3.

Styrax japonica – **Japanese Snowbell:** L, 1, 2.

Styrax obassia – **Fragrant Snowbell:** L, 1, 2.

DECIDUOUS SHRUBS

Clethra alnifolia – **Summersweet:** L-M, 1 (fragrant).

Corylopsis spp – **Winter Hazel:** L-M, 1.

Enkianthus campanulatus – **Redvein Enkianthus:** L-M, 1.

Hamamelis – **Witch Hazel:** L-M, 1. 'Arnold Promise' (yellow), 'Diane' (red).

Hydrangea arborescens – **Hills-of-Snow:** L-M-D, 1, 2.

Lonicera Maackii – **Amur Honeysuckle:** L-M, 1, 2.

Viburnum spp and cvs – **Viburnum:** L, 1, 2 (one evergreen).

BROAD-LEAVED EVERGREEN SHRUBS

Aucuba japonica and cvs – **Aucuba:** L-M-D, 2 (on female only).

Azalea, more than 500 cultivars – **Azalea:** L-M, 1.

Camellia japonica and cvs – **Camellia:** L, 1 (semi-hardy).

Daphne odora and cvs – **Sweet Daphne:** L-M, 1 (fragrant).

Ilex spp and cvs – **Holly:** L-M-D, 2 (on female only).

Kalmia latifolia and cvs – **Mountain Laurel:** L-M, 1.

Pieris japonica – **Japanese Andromeda:** L-M, 1.

Sarcococca Hookerana var. *humilis* – **Sweet Box:** L-M-D, 1 (fragrant).

Skimmia japonica and cvs – **Skimmia:** L-M-D, 1, 2 (on female only).

NEEDLED EVERGREENS

Tsuga canadensis and cvs – **Hemlock:** L-M-D, 2.

Cephalotaxus Harringtonia – **Plum Yew:** L-M-D.

Taxus spp and cvs – **Yew:** L-M-D, 2 (on female only).

GROUND COVERS

Hedera helix and cvs – **English Ivy:** L-M-D, evergreen.

Pachysandra terminalis – **Japanese Spurge:** L-M-D, 1, evergreen.

Vinca minor and cvs – **Periwinkle:** L-M-D, 1, evergreen.

PERENNIALS
(Genus name and major species)

Anemone japonica cvs – **Windflower:** flowers white, pink, late August/September.

Astilbe – **Goatsherd:** flowers white, pink or red in May.

Begonia grandis – **Hardy Begonia:** flowers pink in late summer.

Convallaria – **Lily-of-the-Valley:** flowers white, fragrant in May.

Corydalis – **Fumitory:** flowers yellow all summer.

Dicentra spectabilis – **Bleeding Heart:** flowers pink or white in April.

Doronicum – **Leopard's Bane:** flowers yellow, March/April.

Epimedium – **Barrenwort:** flowers yellow, pink, red, white in March.

Eupatorium – **Hardy Ageratum:** flowers blue, late August/September.

Helleborus – **Hellebore:** flowers pink, cream, as early as January/February.

Hosta – **Plantain Lily:** grown for the leaves, tolerates dense shade.

Ligularia: flowers yellow in June/July.

Myosotis – **Forget-me-not:** flowers blue in spring.

Primula – **Primrose:** all colors in spring.

Pulmonaria – **Lungwort:** flowers pink changing to blue, early spring.

Stylophorum – **Celandine Poppy:** flowers yellow in May.

Trillium: flowers white, pink, maroon, yellow in April.

PHOTO BY EDMUND C. FLYNN

A swimming pool is a focal point – and a mirror. To achieve this effect concrete for the walls was mixed with black paint during construction. Behind the gazebo is a bank of large pink dogwoods. Left is a shagbark maple, azaleas and rhododendrons. Right is a plum yew *(cephalotaxus)* and a group of cherry laurels.

References

Brooklyn Botanic Garden: *Gardening in the Shade.* Brooklyn, N.Y.
Schenck, George: *The Complete Shade Gardener.* Boston, Houghton Mifflin, 1984.
Wilson, Helen van Pelt: *Successful Gardening in the Shade.* New York, Doubleday, 1975.
Allen, Oliver E.: *Shade Gardens.* Alexandria, VA, Time-Life Books, 1979.
Jekyll, Gertrude: *Wood and Garden.* Suffolk, Eng., Baron, 1899. (A classic.)

Do's and Don'ts

DON'T prune your shrubs and trees on impulse. There is a right way and wrong way and a right time and wrong time, and it varies with the species. Inept and untimely pruning can earn you cutting remarks from other gardeners. Check your Extension Service bulletins for information.

Do's and Don'ts

DON'T always blame poor drainage for mossy spots in your lawn. Dig down a bit. You may find that rocks or stones are impeding the grass growth.

DON'T let spring-flowering bulbs stay in the sun for long when you dig them up for storage. And do clean them well before storing.

The Wildflower Garden

By Diane Lewis

For me a wildflower garden is a pleasure to contemplate. I have walked through glades of unforgettable beauty and wished to recreate these delightful scenes when I returned home. To a beginning gardener this may seem an impossible goal to attain. Indeed, it can be as difficult as you want to make it. All home garden areas, however, naturally furnish a range of mini-environments which can be used to advantage in creating a wildflower garden.

Study your home grounds objectively. You may find shady nooks, low, damp locations, or dry hot banks. These areas, enhanced somewhat, can furnish the habitats for your garden. Two factors, your specific environment, coupled with correctly-chosen plant material, are the essential ingredients for success.

Various spring woodland species require differing degrees of light, soil acidity, and moisture; but there are many that fall within an easy-to-achieve range of culture. For these plants shade is necessary for protection from the hot summer sun; yet light is required for good bloom. You may need to thin out the trees in a wooded location or remove some lower branches. Shaded areas of northern exposures also may be utilized.

Organic material such as sphagnum peat moss, compost of oak leaves, or cottonseed meal must be incorporated into the soil to furnish an acidic situation. This also conditions the soil for easy root penetration and allows for the circulation of water and air. If the area worked is not a natural woodland it would be advantageous to add some soil from a nearby wooded area. This introduces the necessary bacteria and fungi tolerant of acid soils. Acidity can also be adjusted chemically. Various sulphates of iron or ammonia, may be added carefully but are not always necessary if sufficient natural materials are provided.

A top dressing of light-weight mulch two to three inches deep should be maintained. This protects the soil from sudden temperature changes and aids in the conservation of moisture. With moisture, the organic materials decay and nutrients become available. Fertilizer is usually not necessary. Water may be needed during dry spells.

Plants requiring good drainage should be placed on slopes, in raised beds, or in soil pockets among rocks. Species needing more moisture can be planted in natural drainage areas, in low spots that never quite dry out; or you can create an artificial bog with plastic sheeting laid 12 inches under the soil, with its edges slanted upward to ground level.

The summer field flowers require less exacting conditions. A good garden loam, mulch, and plenty of sun is usually sufficient for their success. Meadow plants are generally larger. They give great abundance of bloom and have a longer blooming period. These wildlings are grown less often than the delicate woodland species, but they can be used in garden borders in the same way that cultivars are enjoyed. They may self-sow or spread more readily, however, and this should be considered when placing them.

◄ **Queen Anne's-lace *(Daucus carota)* is a European biennial that is now quite at home and a delight to see in our fields and along roadsides. It is a wild form of the cultivated carrot. The root is not edible.**

Methods of propagation change with the many plants available. Growing from seed is ecologically sound but sometimes difficult to achieve, especially for some of the woodland species. It is easier to harvest and to propagate seed from the stronger field flowers.

Division is best for quickest results but get your plants from conservation-minded sources such as those that sell container-grown seedlings. Since many nurseries gather their plants from the wild, I recommend that you buy only those in no danger of extinction. Don't convince yourself you are saving the endangered ones. You will be aiding in fact in their demise. Keep a step ahead of the bulldozers to acquire these beauties and transplant them with great care.

Plants transplant or divide easily when not actively growing, in fall or early spring. The next best time is after flowering. Place your divisions in a previously-prepared bed. I suggest you shade these plants from bright light for about 10 days to overcome shock of transplanting. I use one of the slatted flats I receive when buying annuals for each plant or small group. This gives light shade and makes for a ready reminder that these plants need observation and maybe watering.

When making divisions, grit your teeth and pinch the plant back; remove all flowering parts and seeds. You want to establish a good root system; the flowers have to wait. The second year of growth, expect a bit of bloom. The third year should see a strong plant with an abundance of flowers if the habitat is properly selected. In many cases it will self-sow. If this happens, I know the plant is "mine" for I have provided the necessary environment not only for a mature plant but for the more fragile seedlings.

Concepts of landscape design also should be considered even if your garden is naturalistic. Contrasts of color and form give added value to individual plants which by themselves may not be apparent. Succession of bloom is important when using plants that become dormant after flowering. Many ferns, evergreen or deciduous, blend well with wildflowers and are useful for additional interest.

Selection of plants must be based on knowledge of growth habits. If possible observe in the wild those that interest you, or use the books available on gardening with wildflowers. Since "wildflower" is a relative term, any plant not a hybrid or a cultivar could be considered for your wild garden. Those most widely grown are of special beauty or not invasive.

Favorite Wild Flowers Of Easy Culture

These are wildflowers of open, deciduous woodlands or light shade, moist but well-drained, humus-rich and with moderately acid soil. Exceptions will be noted. They are listed in their approximate order of bloom.

Round-lobed Liverleaf – *Hepatica americana*, March: Early blooming. Delicate blue, occasional pink flowers, 2-to-4-inch stems; leathery leaves evergreen, wine-colored on undersides after flowering. Favors rocky outcroppings. Good drainage a must. Divide in fall.

Bloodroot – *Sanguinaria canadensis*, March-April: Starry, 2-inch white flower, yellow stamens, 6-inch stem clasped by blue-green leaf divided into irregular lobes. Leaves expand, then vanish for a year. Set red rhizomes horizontally a half-inch deep. Plant among later-blooming perennials. The double cultivar 'Multiplex' is special.

Spring Beauty – *Claytonia virginica*, April: Fragrant clusters of white star-like flowers, pink veining; long lasting bloom among narrow, succulent leaves. Prostrate plants disappear after flowering. Plant tubers 2 to 3 inches deep. Interplant with small ferns. Excellent for low, moist spots under trees. Not fussy.

Eastern Trout Lily – *Erythronium americanum*, April: Yellow, bell-shaped flower nods over 5-to-8-inch leafless stem; speckled leaves make attractive ground cover. Blooms when bulbs work down to correct depth. Prefers damp woods. Set bulb-like roots 8 inches deep; spreads by offshoots. Interplant with Wild Phlox for cover during dormancy.

Rue Anemone – *Anemonella thalictroides*, April: White or pink blossoms appear above a whorl of lacy, bronzed foliage that greens later. Long-lasting flowers on wiry 6-inch stems. Plant tubers an inch deep in colonies among small rocks. Self sows. Nurseries sell 'Schouf's Double Pink.'

Wild Ginger – *Asarum canadense*, April: Heart-shaped, 4-inch leaves cover maroon, bottle-shaped flowers at ground level. Blooms long-lived, spicy. Fleshy rootstocks creep below soil to form large colonies in deep shade. Plant rhizomes horizontally an inch deep. Evergreen species available.

Dutchman's-breeches – *Dicentra cucullaria*, April: White flowers like pantaloons on arching stems to 10 inches, grey-green dense foliage. Requires rich soil for good blooms. Plant tooth-like tubers an inch deep when dormant in fall. Interplant with crocus and small hostas for succession of interest.

Twinleaf – *Jeffersonia diphylla*, April: White, one-inch flowers on 10-inch stems above cleft leaves resembling green butterflies. Foliage good contrast to other plants. Seedcases interesting as they lower to one side to spill seeds. Space 8 inches apart.

Wild Phlox, Sweet William Phlox – *Phlox divaricata*, April-May: Fragrant flowers with notched petals show variation in shades of blue, some pure white; evergreen leaves on 12-inch stems. Creeping rootstocks form colonies. In planting set one-inch deeper. Covered nodes send up extra flowering stalks. Remove spent blossoms.

Virginia Bluebells – *Mertensia virginica*, April-May: Drooping pink buds become blue flowers atop 18-inch succulent stems. New leaves, 2 to 5 inches, purplish green, oval. Large colonies flourish in damp areas, will tolerate drier locations if soil is organic and shaded. Set top of rootstock an inch below soil. Rare white form available.

Bluets – *Hedyotis caerulea*, April-May: Tiny, sky-blue, 4-petalled flowers with yellow eyes form drifts of hundreds of blossoms; 3-inch plants self sow easily in moist, humusy soil in open shade to full sun.

Foamflower – *Tiarella cordifolia*, April-June: Flowers tiny, fuzzy stamens on 8-inch spikes; maple-like evergreen leaves spread with rooting runners, forming ground cover that may bronze in fall. Needs cool shade, moist conditions. Easily multiplied by division.

Trilliums (three easy-to-grow members of this desirable group), May: **Great White Trillium** – *T. grandiflorum:* white flowers lasting a month, turning rose with age; yellow anthers on 12-to-18-inch stems. **Stinking Benjamin** – *T. erectum:* 8 to 12 inches, dark red flowers contrast to others. **Toadshade** – *T. sessile* var. *luteum:* mottled leaves, small chartreuse flowers. All need filtered sunlight, well-

drained locations, extra water when spring is dry. Never pick flowers.

Merrybells – *Uvularia grandiflora*, May: Deep yellow flowers on forked stems to 12 inches; neat, crisp ovate leaves; 3-sided seed capsule lasts to frost. Stringy white rhizomes form good-sized clumps. *U. perfoliata* is lighter yellow, fast spreading.

Greek Valerian – *Polemonium reptans*, May: Many clusters of blue bells on 12-inch plant, ladder-like leaves. Fibrous rooted. Shade needed for healthy foliage. Propagate by division. Will self sow.

Crested Iris – *Iris cristata*, May: Blue-violet petals with yellow fuzzy crest form 2-inch flowers above fan-shaped clumps of 6-inch sword-like leaves. Keep mulch from covering slender mat-forming rhizomes. Needs occasional resetting, good light. *I. verna:* flowers darker, orange crest, needs more acid soil. Divide after blooming.

Dwarf Larkspur – *Delphinium tricorne*, May: Deep-violet flowers, 12-inch stems with finely-divided leaves. Plants have tuberous roots, need neutral to moderate acid soil. Remove spent blooms. Mulch with marble chips. Plant with Maidenhair Spleenwort, edge of woodland.

Yellow Lady's-slipper – *Cypripedium Calceolus*, May-June: Striking yellow pouches with twisting green or brown petals on 10-inch stems, deeply-veined leaves, fragrant flowers large (var. *pubescens*) or small (var. *parviflorum*). Woods soil with fungi beneficial. Plant when dormant; rhizome works down to 2 inches.

Shooting-star – *Dodecatheon Meadia*, May-June: Deep pink dart-shaped flowers atop 10-inch hollow stems, leaves form rosettes similar to primrose. Fragrant rootstock needs spring moisture, tolerates dryness when dormant. Avoid rich soil. Mulch well.

Jack-in-the-pulpit – *Arisaema triphyllum*, May-June: Interesting compound flower in green- or brown-striped hood on 12-to-30-inch stems, large leaves divided into 3 leaflets; after flowering red fruit cluster persists. Prefers lots of moisture but tolerates many conditions. Set large corms 5 to 8 inches deep, smaller ones 2 to 4 inches.

Wild Columbine – *Aquilegia canadensis*, May-June: Complex red/yellow flowers with nectar-filled spurs over finely-divided foliage, 1- to 2-foot stems. Roots deeply, tolerates drought but doesn't move easily unless small. Needs good drainage, some sun. Short-lived in rich soil. Easily grown from seed.

Fringed Bleeding-heart – *Dicentra eximia*, May-September: Dusty rose hearts on 12-inch stems bloom for long periods, prolonged by extra mid-summer watering and fertilization. Succulent ferny foliage. Heavy rootstocks form dense clumps. Provide good light but shade from sun. Mix with strong plants. Self sows, divide every third year.

Spotted Cranesbill – *Geranium maculatum*, June: Clusters of 5-petaled magenta-pink flowers, deeply-cut leaves, 1-to-2-foot stems. Thick clumps in open shade if moderately moist. Oblong capsule fruit. Propagate by division.

Butterfly Weed – *Asclepias tuberosa*, June-August: Pretty milkweed without milk. Bright orange blooms, oval leaves, 2-inch velvet-soft stems. Flowers attract butterflies. Pods contain silk-plumed seeds. Brittle aromatic taproots reach great depths. Plant when dormant. Tolerates poor soil but needs sun.

Pot-of-gold – *Coreopsis verticillata*, June-September: Yellow, fragrant, daisy-like flowers on wiry 18-inch stems that bear whorls of delicate linear leaves. Creeping aggressive roots fill difficult, dry sunny spots with lengthy bloom. Shear occasionally to promote flowering. Becoming uncommon in wild. Divide in spring.

Cardinal Flower – *Lobelia Cardinalis*, July-September: Brilliant red tubular flowers on 2-foot spikes rise above rosettes of evergreen foliage. Fibrous root system depends on abundant moisture, high fertility. Open shade needed for color brightness. Remove spent flowers, divide at this time. **Great Lobelia** – *L. siphilitica:* Can take more sun.

Turk's-Cap Lily – *Lilium superbum*, July-August: Dozens of large orange flowers with black spots, prominent stamens on 8-foot stems; leaves in whorls up stalk. Plants long-lived, bloom for long periods. Plant bulbs a foot apart, 5 inches deep in damp, well-drained edge of woodland. Will reproduce from offsets, or lift bulb, remove and plant outer scales, replant bulb.

Purple Coneflower – *Echinacea purpurea*, July-August: Striking purple-pink ray florets to 3 inches surround high cone of brown disk florets; "petals" bend backward with age, bloom over long period. Strong 2-to-4-foot stems bear rough ovate leaves. Needs full sun. Transplants easily, self sows.

Sundrop – *Oenothera fruticosa*, July-August: A day-blooming evening-primrose. Notched 4-petaled, 2-inch sunny blooms on 12-inch stems; lance-shaped leaves form evergreen rosettes. Spreads readily but shallow roots make control easy. Tolerates thin, dry soil in sun to light shade. Divide in spring.

Bee Balm, Oswego Tea – *Monarda didyma*, July-September: Flaming-red multiple flowers top sturdy 3-foot stems, leaves blushed with red, all parts aromatic. Spreads rapidly. Lasting blooms and attraction for hummingbirds make it desirable. Prefers moisture, some sun; tolerates range of conditions. Named varieties offer a range of color from white to dark red.

New England Aster – *Aster novae-angliae*, August-October: Many rosy-pink or purple 1-inch flowers on tall stiff stems to 5 feet, leaves long and narrow. To reduce height pinch stem tips in June, again July. Grows edge of woods to full sun. Tolerates ordinary garden soil, benefits from division every 3 years.

Fairy Candles, Bugbane – *Cimicifuga americana*, August-October: Slender wands of 2-to-4-foot white flowers above bold compound leaves. Similar to *C. racemosa* (**Black Cohosh**) but lacking rank odor and not as tall. Blooms when few other plants are in flower. Requires moist soil, rich in humus, high shade for best bloom. Divide plants when dormant, an inch below soil, 2 inches apart.

References

Bell, C. Ritchie and Ken Moore (edited Harry R. Phillips): *Growing and Propagating Wildflowers*. University of North Carolina Press, 1985.

Bruce, Hal: *How to Grow Wildflowers and Wild Shrubs and Trees in Your Own Garden*. New York, Alfred A. Knopf, 1976.

Miles, Bebe: *Wildflower Perennials for Your Garden*. New York, Hawthorn Books, Inc., 1976.

Sperka, Marie: *Growing Wildflowers*. New York, Harper & Row, 1973.

Local Sources for Wildflowers

Great Falls Greenhouses, 10106 Georgetown Pike, Great Falls, VA 22066.

Jan Midgley, 6 Oaklyn Court, Potomac, MD 20854.

Potomac Nursery and Garden Center, 9545 River Road, Potomac, MD 20854.

Mail Order Sources

Mary Painter, Virginia Natives, the Wildflower Nursery, Wildside, P.O. Box 18, Hume, VA 22639.

Woodlanders, 1128 Colleton Avenue, Aiken, SC 29801.

Vegetables in the Home Garden

By Henry E. Allen

Urban sprawl has given us less space in which to garden. As a result new gardening practices and techniques, and the improved skills of the plant breeders, have brought about dramatic changes in the last decade.

When I was growing up in Montgomery County every family had its "kitchen garden." Ours was more than a quarter of an acre. Today, with new techniques and improved cultivars, I can produce as much as we did then in a fifth of the land. Space was not a problem then and we made no effort to conserve it. Today we try to make every square foot productive.

As the price of fresh vegetables increases, you may find it pays to grow your own. The varieties you can grow usually are far superior in flavor and nutritional value to those in the supermarket, and they are later and better varieties than you can buy.

Where is the best place to locate your garden? Good soil, good drainage, freedom from erosion, availability of water, and proximity to the kitchen are important. So is ample sunlight and lack of competition from the shade and roots of trees and shrubs. The plot should be large enough to grow all the produce you and your family want throughout the year but not so large that care of it becomes a burden.

Single Plot Not Necessary

It doesn't have to be a single plot. You can have four or five separate beds in different places. You can plant vegetables among your flowers, too, provided your pesticides do not contaminate your edibles. Radishes can be tucked in among other plants, and lettuce makes a great edging for both spring and fall. Even growing vegetables in containers on a patio can provide the makings of a good salad.

If your space gets eight hours a day of sunlight, you will have enough light to grow almost any vegetable in season. All the leafy vegetables and some root crops such as beets and carrots can be grown in half that light, provided they get filtered shade from deciduous trees and not dense shade from solid structures. Remember that in February the amount of sunlight will not be as great as in summer when the sun nears its zenith and trees are in full leaf. Avoid the root zone of trees and shrubs; they compete for moisture and nutrients. And remember, too, that young trees and shrubs grow each year and expand their root zones and shade patterns. Keep in mind nearness to a source of water and ease of access from the kitchen and service area.

PLANNING THE GARDEN

Plan your garden to get the maximum return from your efforts and space. Where space is limited, grow vertically for the greatest yield. Pole beans outproduce bush types. Vining cucumbers grown on a trellis yield more fruits than bush types in the same space. Squash and melons can be trained on an A-frame. Tomatoes grown in wire cages or staked give more usable fruit than those sprawling on the ground.

Whether you grow a one-, two- or three-season garden, space efficiency is important. Some vegetables, and some cultivars of vegetables, are more space efficient than others. Several years ago the National Garden Bureau, a seed-industry group, did a nationwide survey

PHOTO BY ANDREW JOHNSON, COURTESY OF PEGGY NEWCOMB
(Thomas Jefferson Memorial Foundation)

The serious vegetable gardener can learn much from a trip to Charlottesville, 90 miles south of Washington, to inspect the recent restoration of Thomas Jefferson's kitchen garden at Monticello. The 1,000-foot-long garden is on a plateau carved from the side of his "little mountain" with eight acres of fruit groves below. Jefferson was a practical and innovative gardener who kept meticulous records, practiced crop rotation, experimented in developing hybrids, and ingeniously extended his growing season by several months. In 50 years of gardening at Monticello he raised 250 different vegetable varieties. He grew tomatoes and eggplant that others scorned and cauliflower and broccoli that few others knew about.

to determine which vegetables gave the most yield per square foot, the best average value per pound harvested, and the least seed-to-harvest time.

They found that the tomato was not only the most space efficient but also the most popular. Next in order were bunching onions, leaf lettuce, turnips for greens and roots, summer squash, edible podded peas, onions for storage, pole beans, beets, bush snap beans, carrots, and cucumbers grown on supports. At the bottom of the list of 36 vegetables surveyed were pumpkins, all types of melons, sweet corn, eggplant, okra and all peas except edible podded. In-

cidentally, indeterminate tomatoes will out-yield determinates and vining watermelons will out-perform the bush types in both yield and flavor.

Your Preferences Most Important

More important than space efficiency are your own preferences in vegetables. There is no point in planting onions or turnips if you don't like them. And the rare taste of fresh corn from the garden can override its low rating in space efficiency. Corn from the garden cannot be matched even by picked-the-same-day corn from roadside stands. And no frozen or canned peas compare with fresh peas from the garden. Grow what you want.

When you have decided on what you want and how much you want to plant, decide on how you are going to plant – in single rows, wide rows or broad bands, or in blocks. Single-row planting is desirable for tomatoes, okra and other larger plants. Corn needs at least triple rows to assure good pollination. Much usable space is lost, however, if bush beans, root crops and leafy vegetables are planted in single rows. A wide row can be any width you want – 12 to 18 inches works well for most crops. You can plant bush beans three or four rows on six-inch centers, nine-inch centers if they are bush lima beans.

Block planting is an adaptation of broad-band planting. The area to be planted can be measured off in square feet or yards and each plot planted to a single crop. This is especially well suited for gardening in raised beds. They should be no wider than twice the reach of your arm – usually no more than four feet – to permit easy weeding and harvesting from either side. Length should be determined by ease of access; eight to 10 feet is about average. Raised beds provide greater root space for growing plants, better drainage and quicker warming of the soil in spring, permitting earlier planting. Be sure they get enough water.

Succession Planting, Inter-Cropping

When you plan for the most production throughout the growing season, consider the possibilities of succession planting and inter-cropping. In succession planting in the same row, band or block, you can start the season with a short-season crop such as lettuce. When the lettuce is finished – in late June in our area – you can plant a root or fruit crop, such as carrots or bush beans. Then, in late August, when bean production is declining, put in a fall crop such as kale or spinach; both will go through the winter in our area, providing an early spring harvest. Cauliflower, broccoli, Brussels sprouts, savoy cabbage and Chinese cabbage are all good for fall planting and will produce into mid-December. Brussels sprouts

will stand hard freezing and can be harvested into early spring. Carrots or turnips will provide winter harvests if mulched well after the soil freezes.

In planning your garden for successions in the first year, and in later plantings, observe the old rule: Don't follow the same type of crop in the same place. Start with leaf, follow with fruit, end up with root crops.

Intercropping – planting some plants between other plants – can be achieved either by planting both early and later maturing vegetables at the same time in the same row, or by planting rows or bands of early maturing vegetables between rows where later ones will go.

For example, radishes and lettuce can be planted in the same row. The radishes will mature before the lettuce plants have grown to full size. Once the lettuce is gone put in a root or fruit crop. For me, growing a band of spinach or spring onions where I will set out my tomato plants has worked well. Also, radishes or lettuce can be planted between rows of onions grown for storage. Cauliflower or kale can be planted for fall or winter use where early peas were raised. Bush beans can follow spring cabbage or broccoli. There are many possibilities.

Importance of Timing

Timing is vital in succession planting. You need to know when a particular crop will have given its best and should be replaced. You can determine this from "the first dates to harvest" dates in Table 2, or in the catalogues or on the seed packets. Table 2 is the better guide since information in catalogues or on packets can vary from our experience in this area. You also need to know how long a vegetable will continue to produce. With peas, for example, if a cultivar is listed as taking 69 days to first harvest, you should pick your first peas 10 weeks after they were planted. In an average season they should bear well for three or four weeks after that. Remember that a vegetable planted in the spring is likely to mature more quickly than the same one planted in the fall. Spring-planted vegetables get increased warmth and day length while fall-planted ones get the opposite. Both days to harvest and length of harvest vary considerably in our area because of our changeable climate. Local experience is your best guide.

A Trick in Pest Management

A trick in the gardener's bag in Integrated Pest Management (see below and in "Pest Control in Your Landscape") is to time your crops to grow when their pests are less prevalent or diseases less likely. Thus you might time your squash to grow when the moth responsible for the squash vine borer is not active – after late June or early July in our area.

Quality and quantity of product are important, too. Especially for quick-maturing vegetables, succession planting assures continued quality and avoids glut and famine. Planting several small sowings of radishes at 10-day intervals is better than a single larger planting. Plant two 25-foot rows of bush snap beans three or four weeks apart rather than a single 50-foot row. Prompt and sustained harvesting of fruit crops will prolong their productive season.

Think about your available light. If possible, lay out your rows or bands in a north-south direction to assure the most light for all your vegetables. Place the taller growing ones such as corn, pole beans and trellised vegetables to the north so they will not shade the lower growing ones to the south. In some instances, however, you may want to take advantage of shade from the taller crops to get leafy vegetables started despite the heat of summer. They will be growing in good light when the taller crops are removed.

Plan to plant any permanent or semi-permanent crops such as asparagus, rhubarb or berries in separate beds or to one side of your garden so they will not interfere with annual tillage.

Correct Spacing Necessary

Spacing is critical. Table 2 gives you the needed information. The first figures in the column under distances between plants in a row are the minimal distances after thinning between plants, however

planted. The first column under distances between rows is for hand cultivation, the second allows for some type of mechanical cultivation.

Now you are ready to draw a plan of your garden to scale. It is easier to change your mind or correct errors on paper than to change things around once the garden is planted.

PREPARING THE SOIL

If your soil is typical of most in this area, generally classified as "clay loam," it is more clay than loam and probably on the acid side. (See "Soils.") Don't despair. Clay soils can be made quite productive by adding large quantities of organic matter – compost, rotted manure, peat moss, aged sawdust, spent hay and straw, and grass clippings. In many cases coarse sand can be added. If sand is added, spread two or three inches over the entire bed along with five to six inches of organic matter. Work the whole mix thoroughly into the top eight inches. That should give you a soil of excellent tilth.

Two other soil factors are important: acidity and availability of nutrients. Most vegetables do well in a soil ranging from pH 6.2 to 6.8 and some tolerate even a slightly more acid soil. If you have reason to believe your soil is too acid have it tested. Your Cooperative Extension Service can tell you how to do this in your particular county or city or in the District of Columbia. Based on test results, you will be advised on how to adjust both pH and fertility. If lime is suggested, use dolomitic lime. It contains 20 percent magnesium, an element in which many of our soils are deficient. It helps tomatoes fend off blossom end rot while the calcium helps curtail early blight. You can apply lime in spring or fall. Since it moves slowly in the soil, work it in to the full depth of your tillage to make it available to the root zone. Be patient. It takes time for limestone to provide the alkalinity necessary to get your pH to the point where your plants can make an effective use of plant food.

Do not try to alter your pH by more than one point in a year. A comforting word: If the soil in your bed is growing

PHOTO BY EDMUND C. FLYNN

Shown here are two techniques that improve yields for the home gardener: the use of raised beds and floating row covers. The featherweight fiber covers not only help to extend the growing season – they let in light and water and keep out cold – but also protect plants from many garden pests. You can leave them in place right through your harvest.

good weeds, it has good fertility and should grow good vegetables.

Don't Work Soil Too Wet

Do not work the soil when it is wet. You can compact it and not get the thorough mixture of all the soil amendments. And you can damage its structure for at least a season. To test for wetness, dig down five or six inches and squeeze a ball of the soil in your hand. If it crumbles it is dry enough to work. If it doesn't, wait.

If it is still early spring with a chance of more freezing, thawing and heaving, you can turn over the soil in big "bites" (or spits), leave it for weather to mellow it and dry it out to the point where you can spread your amendments and prepare a fine bed.

In using a spade or fork, drive the tool straight down and not at an angle. If the soil is heavy take small "bites." In spring, lift each "bite" and place it on top of the preceding row. Knock the organic material and any weeds from the top of the "bite" into the furrow. Then break up the rest of the "bite" with your tool as you continue to fill in the furrow. After turn-

ing a strip three or four feet wide, use a rake to break up clay clods and then to smooth them out. In this way, you avoid trampling and compacting freshly turned soil. If you are preparing raised beds for broad-band or block planting, you can work from the sides of the bed, so you never need step on the prepared area. Later, in sowing seed, you can make your soil fine enough to allow good germination of the seed.

Consider Double Digging

If your soil drains poorly, consider double digging to loosen the layer below the topsoil. This may be hardpan or just heavily compacted clay. Take out a row of "bites" at the edge of the bed and lay it aside. Work in organic matter, appropriate fertilizer (superphosphate in particular) and limestone with a spade, fork, pick or mattock. Then cover this row with surface soil from the next row of "bites" and prepare the exposed subsoil as before. Repeat this for the full extent of the bed. Then pick up the first layer and use it to cover the last exposed row.

If the top layer needs more organic

matter, fertilizer or lime, add it and mix it thoroughly to a depth of eight inches. This will give you a raised bed because of the materials you have added and because you will have created more air space. If you don't trample it during your garden operations, it will stay raised until the organic material in it breaks down. You will have improved the drainage, tilth and fertility. If double digging is not feasible – it is hard work and you may have a layer of rock underneath your topsoil – you can create a raised bed, either standing by itself or surrounded by timbers, bricks or cement blocks.

Gardening on a Slope

Gardening on a slope can pose problems: in controlling erosion and runoff, conserving topsoil, preventing washout of plants, and allowing deep watering of your vegetables as they need it. The solution depends on several factors: whether the garden is at the top, middle or bottom of the slope, and the grade and direction of the slope.

If the grade is slight, running rows on a contour across the slope may be all that is necessary. If the grade is greater, terracing may be needed. In my garden I have created terraces with cement blocks. They provide level beds easy to water, cultivate and maintain, and the soil is deep enough to grow any root crops. Drainage ditches on the side of terraces can control runoff and prevent erosion.

If your soil is heavy, it may be less likely to erode. If it is in good tilth, it may be more subject to erosion. A cover crop sown in the fall can aid in preventing erosion, especially in early spring when the ground underneath is still frozen. Cover crops do wonders for improving the tilth of the soil, too.

SEEDS AND PLANTS

What vegetables will you plant? And where will you get your seeds and plants? Selecting the proper cultivars is almost as important as properly preparing the soil.

In the last 10 years the plant breeders have given us the greatest selection of superior vegetables ever offered. They have improved flavor, increased yields, a built-in resistance to pests and diseases, and a greater tolerance of cold and heat. They take less time from planting to harvest, thus allowing a longer period of production and, sometimes, two or more crops a season. We have more compact plants that take less space without reducing yields, although some of the newer bush cultivars do gain compactness at the expense of productivity. There are cultivars that have been miniaturized for container culture.

Where do you get them? The better ones will not appear in the seed racks. Go to the catalogues for the best selection. (Some of the best cultivars that are favorites in the Men's Garden Club are listed in Table 1.)

Not all cultivars are suitable for the greater Washington area. The catalogue recommendations are not always valid for us. Recognizing this, some years ago I compiled, in collaboration with some members of the Men's Garden Club, a list of vegetable cultivars best suited to our home gardens. The latest list appears as Table 1. It is revised every two years. Our main criterion is proven performance here. We include cultivars with longer seasons of productivity, acceptable hardiness, tolerance of pests and ease of culture. We choose hybrids when available.

Most hybrids out-perform the open-pollinated cultivars and are worth the additional cost of seeds or plants. The listing is not in any order of preference nor is it all-inclusive. All are good ones but there also are cultivars not listed that are very good indeed.

Buy seed packaged for the current year, preferably with information on the packet about the germination rate. Don't get carried away by the pictures and glowing descriptions in the catalogues. Buy only what you reasonably can expect to use. If you have seeds left over in the spring, save them for use in the fall or next year. Most seed, except for onions and parsnips, will remain viable for at least two years and even longer if properly stored.

To store seeds, keep the packets in a

tightly-sealed container. Place a couple of tablespoons of powdered milk wrapped in a tissue in the container to absorb excess moisture. Keep the container in the refrigerator or in the coolest or driest place in the basement or other inside storage area.

Choose Transplants With Care

If you buy transplants, choose them with care. Buy only named cultivars that are suitable for this area. Don't accept plants that are spindly, have spots on the leaves, lesions on the stems, or knots on the roots. Above all, don't accept plants infested with whitefly. Buy stocky plants with a good green color that are not root bound or overcrowded in flats. These will transplant to your garden with minimal root shock and adapt quickly to your environment. If they have not been outside, harden them off before putting them in the ground.

Even good suppliers may offer transplants not true to name if their own suppliers have made mistakes. Why not buy your own seed and start your own transplants? (See "Grow Your Own Transplants.")

When should you plant? Table 2 is the best guide. The average dates given there are just that – averages to guide you to dependable times to sow or transplant. In some years we may be able to sow earlier than in others. There are many devices today to permit earlier outside planting than the dates shown. Such devices include tunnels, cloches and floating row covers. In summer we may be able to plant at dates later than those indicated if we use cultivars with a short time to harvest and if we want to take a chance of a prolonged Indian summer.

PLANTING THE GARDEN

With your garden plan in hand, decide whether you need more soil amendments or fertilizer than you provided when you prepared the soil. If so, add this now, keeping in mind the requirements of each vegetable during its growing season and the advice you get from your soil test results.

If tilth is poor, work in more sand or compost or both. If you did not provide fertilizer earlier, add a pound (one pint) for each 15 feet of single row or for eight square feet of bed or band. If no recommendation was made from your soil test, you can use a balanced fertilizer such as 5-10-5 or 5-10-10 on most crops. I use 10-6-4 on all leafy vegetables, onions and corn and 5-10-10 on other crops. Mix all these amendments well into the top layer of the bed.

You are now ready to begin planting. Make furrows or prepare your band or block, and plant your seed at the depth indicated in Table 2 or on the packet. If the soil is dry, water the furrow before planting the seed. If the soil is likely to dry out and form a crust after you fill in and tamp the furrow, cover the planting area with burlap or boards or other commercial products available for this purpose to keep the soil moist until germination commences. Do not let the soil dry out. Remove the cover when germination starts.

Avoid Crowding of Plants

Don't plant seeds too thickly. If you have top quality seeds the germination rate should be good even if it is not shown on the package. When plants come up too crowded they compete for sunlight, moisture and nutrients. Unless they are thinned when small those that remain can be weak and spindly.

In following the average planting time shown in Table 2, start your cool weather crops (those with planting dates from February through April) as soon as the soil can be worked. In some years this turns out to be late but it is better to have a good late garden than a poor early one. Garden peas are the exception; they are a cold-weather crop and when planted later than the end of March seldom produce good harvests. They cannot tolerate high temperatures; the mid-June heat will wilt them down in a few days.

Sets are fine for "spring onions" but, if you are growing for winter storage, those grown from seed are preferred. The choice of varieties in sets is limited. Onions from sets, especially if they are more than a half-inch in diameter, are prone to splitting and developing seed heads. Thin-necked onions are the best for winter storage. Varieties such as 'Sweet Sandwich' and 'Spartan Sleeper,' when properly cured, will keep up to 10 months without sprouting. To develop good-sized bulbs, seeds should be started indoors in late February and transplanted to the garden in mid-April.

If the onion maggot is a problem, treat the soil with diazinon before planting. Prepare a drench as directed on the container and water it in well. Or work diazinon granules into the soil about 10 days before planting. This also will control maggots on other root crops. If your onions begin to show whitish blotches and distorted leaf tips, followed by withering and browning off, you probably have thrips, a serious pest of onions. They can be controlled by spraying with diazinon at three-week intervals during the growing season.

Getting a Jump on the Season

While warm weather crops such as sweet corn, all types of beans, southern peas, squash, cucumbers and melons should not be planted until the soil has warmed – at least to 68°F – there are ways to get a jump on the season. To hasten warming of the soil, cover it with plastic. Clear plastic is more effective than black for this purpose but it will not inhibit weed growth. However, a light cultivation when the plastic is removed before planting will take care of the weeds.

You can start your cucumbers, squash and melons in individual peat pots or Jiffy-7 pellets two to three weeks before the normal planting dates and move them to the garden in mid-May when the soil has warmed enough to promote rapid growth. I have, on occasion, handled pole lima beans in this manner.

Growing under plastic tunnels or floating row covers is another technique to hasten early crops. Also, the plant breeders have developed some new corn varieties with increased cold tolerance and improved flavor. Some of them will germinate at soil temperatures as low as

52°F. They can be planted two to three weeks earlier than the mid-season and late varieties that should not go in until around mid-May.

Lima beans, with the exception of 'Fordhook 242,' which was developed specifically for this area, will not set pods when night-time temperatures remain above 72°F. If you can't plant them by June 1, wait until the first week in July. Thus they will not blossom in the hottest part of the summer and drop their pods.

Cucumbers may be planted in a row and trained on a trellis. This conserves space and the plants produce better fruit, free of sunscald. To support cucumbers – and beans, too – use wood or polyvinyl chloride pipe for framing and nylon netting or poly cord for support. Wire can be hot enough in the summer sun to burn young tendrils trying to cling to it.

Setting Out Transplants

The best time to set out transplants is in the late afternoon or early evening, or on a cloudy day. Be sure they are well watered before setting them out. Prepare the planting holes before you take the transplants from the flats or pots. Set the plants slightly lower in the ground than they were growing in the flat or container, add enough soil to cover the roots, and water with a fertilizer high in phosphorus – a "starter solution." Then fill in the hole to level with dry soil.

If your transplants are in peat pots, break out the bottom of the pot even though it may come with a hole, and be sure that the tops are covered. If exposed, capillary action will draw moisture from the soil and plant roots. If the transplants are in Jiffy-7s or similar netted blocks, cut away the nylon netting which can inhibit root growth. Be sure to provide protection from the hot sun and wind for a few days until they become established.

CARE OF THE GARDEN

Our enthusiasm for our garden runs high in spring and we often plant more than we can care for. So, start small and expand as you need to. The important

Which Tomato Should You Grow?

More than 300 tomato cultivars are available to the gardener with fruits of all shapes, sizes and colors and vines of differing growth habits and varying degrees of disease resistance.

For the Washington area it is essential that you choose cultivars with resistance to at least Verticillium and Fusarium wilts (designated VF) for a sustained yield of quality fruit.

Determinate plants produce fruit on the terminal buds and stop growing when the fruit is set. Growth habit is compact and well adapted to container culture. There is a concentrated set of fruit in a short period of time, an advantage if your crop is to be canned.

Indeterminate plants continue to grow and bear fruit until frost, reaching heights of six feet or more if staked or trellised. For table use indeterminate red cultivars are the most popular among home gardeners.

Tomato cultivars developed for commercial use usually have thick walls and skins. While they are good for processing, they are less flavorful than the juicier types.

The acidity of all tomatoes is about the same – regardless of color, size or flavor – according to an analysis of 356 cultivars made by the U.S. Department of Agriculture. Pink, orange, yellow and white types, frequently described as "low acid," are no less acid than standard red types, despite their milder flavor.

– Henry E. Allen

tasks ahead will be weeding, mulching, watering, staking, pruning and harvesting.

Weeds rob your plants of moisture and nutrients and may harbor insects and diseases that will come back to infest crops in succeeding years. They are controlled most easily when they are small, just emerging from the soil. Shallow cultivation at this time will eliminate most of them without damage to the tender roots of your crops. Weed seeds live for years in the soil, however, and only need to be brought near the surface to germinate. Each time you cultivate you will turn up a new weed seed. Never let a weed go to seed.

Mulches will help control weeds as well as conserve soil moisture and maintain an even soil temperature. Black plastic is used for this purpose by many gardeners but I prefer organic mulches applied after the soil has warmed up around mid-June. They protect the surface soil from hard rains, permit the free passage of air and moisture into the soil and inhibit weed germination. When turned under they provide additional humus to the soil.

Among materials that can be used for this purpose are straw, half-rotted compost, leaves, grass clippings (if the lawn hasn't been treated with an herbicide), shredded fodder, spent hay, ground corn cobs, and fine wood chips and shavings. Fresh organic materials, except grass clippings, will draw nitrogen from the soil as they decompose. To assure sufficient nitrogen for your crops, increase the application of your fertilizer by about one fourth, or provide a small amount of straight nitrogen such as sodium nitrate.

One Inch of Water a Week

Adequate moisture is one of the most important items in garden care. A good garden soil requires about one inch of water per week, either from rain or irrigation. During hot, dry spells in midsummer, when transpiration is great, adequate water is most important. A good soaking to a depth of five or six inches once a week is far better than frequent light sprinklings. When only the soil surface is wet, the roots will turn up to seek moisture and never develop a deep structure. This results in weak plants that are less able to withstand insect or disease damage. Also, deep roots

The tomato cultivar 'Big Girl' and such standbys as 'Supersonic,' 'Jet Star,' 'Better Boy,' 'Park's Whopper' and 'Pole King,' among others, have disease resistance and are favorites in the Men's Garden Club.

help a plant withstand drought better.

Garden care also includes the proper thinning of crops, the pruning and tying of tomato plants if they are staked, training beans and cucumbers on their supports, keeping crops harvested, and inspecting plants carefully for signs of insects or diseases, and then taking measures to control them.

MANAGING GARDEN PESTS

A gardener at times can be his own worst enemy. He is prone to rush out with a spray or dust at the first sign of a "bug" without knowing what the "bug" is and what, if any, damage it is causing.

If damage from pests appears in your garden – and in our area one or more of them are sure to strike – the vital first step is to determine what is causing the damage and whether it is or will be excessive. Then and only then take steps to correct it, using chemical controls **only when necessary** as a last resort. (See "Pests in the Home Landscape.")

If you believe the damage is serious and might get worse, and know what pest or pests are causing the problem, find out what you need to do to control them. You may not need to do anything if natural

controls are allowed free rein. While many gardeners are aware that toads, terrapins, praying mantids, and many birds eat insects, many do not recognize that the major natural enemies of an insect are other insects.

Predators and Parasites

The enemies of harmful insects can be divided into two groups – predators and parasites. Predators usually eat a number of species and consume a lot at one feeding. Predators include mantids, ladybird beetles and their larvae, most ground beetles, syrphid (hover) flies and lacewings. Parasites live on or in another insect, lay eggs inside them and in most cases cause the host to die. Most parasites are so small that most gardeners are hardly aware of their presence. They have no common names. Many are small wasps that lay their eggs on aphids, mealybugs and other soft-bodied insects or in the larvae of moths, butterflies and beetles.

Parasitic insects are extremely "host specific." The wasp that attacks the cabbage aphid ignores the rose aphid; another wasp does that one in. Knowing the predators and the parasites and their life cycles is one of the keys to Integrated Pest Management.

The average gardener doesn't have to be an expert in this difficult field but you should realize that there is an interaction between the populations of controlling insects and their prey.

As the prey population increases, the food for the controllers increases and so do their numbers. But as the controllers become successful they diminish their food supply and their populations decrease. You should not interfere seriously with this balance of nature so long as the damage is acceptable.

We can credit the explosion of spider mite populations to the use of insecticides that controlled them imperfectly while destroying their natural enemies. The experts have had to find new controls that are target specific, that kill the target insect without killing off its enemies. It means that the gardener, and the farmer, have had to give up old hopes of exterminating a pest population and settle instead for reasonable control.

Important to Keep Them There

Keep in mind that the predators and parasites are "out there" and that it is important that they stay there. It is only because they are there that we can grow anything at all. Without them our plants would be devoured by herbivorous insects.

The success of any Integrated Pest Management program depends on knowing the most vulnerable period in the life cycle of the target insect and applying the most effective control at that time. Many of today's insecticides and fungicides are designed to biodegrade quickly. If they are applied too soon or too late they will not work.

Most of the new bio-insecticides are most effective if applied when the insects are immature. We are fortunate in this area to be able to turn to our extension services and their plant clinics and master gardeners, supported by our universities, to find out when pests are coming on the scene, are active, and how best to cope with them.

A great deal can be accomplished by good cultural practices. Keep your garden and its surrounding areas free from weeds and debris where insects breed and over-winter. Remove "clean" spent plant material to your compost heap. Consign insect-infested or diseased plants to the trash. Rotate your crops. By changing plant locations you sometimes can starve out or reduce the pest populations to a tolerable level. Make sure any plants you bring into the garden are disease free. Cultivation, especially in spring or early summer, destroys some insects. Fall or winter tillage exposes many more to freezing.

Try Physical Means First

Once your pest targets are identified, see whether damage can be prevented or held to a minimum by physical means. For instance, aphids can be "washed off" vegetable plants with a strong stream of water. This damages their mouth parts so they cannot feed again; it does not harm their natural enemies. If you hand-pick tomato hornworms and crush the eggs, larvae and adults of Mexican bean beetles, it usually is enough to keep these pests at acceptable levels.

You can use a paper or foil collar around transplants to thwart cutworms. You can place a six-to-eight-inch piece of tarpaper, plastic, old rug or other barrier on the soil around the stems of cole crops to prevent damage from root maggots. Radishes grown under screening will be free of maggot damage. Screening or other floating row covers also will protect spinach and chard from leaf miners and cole crops and lettuce from cabbage worms and loopers. Floating row covers not only prevent insect damage but discourage cats from digging, keep out rabbits, and prevent crows from pulling up corn and beans.

Three Problem Groupings

There are three groupings of insects basically that cause problems. One group spends all or part of their lives in or on the soil. This includes grubs (the larvae of beetles), maggots (the larvae of flies), cutworms (the larvae of moths), and sow-

PHOTO BY HARRIS SEEDS

'Lady Bell' is a choice hybrid bell pepper with superior disease resistance. Other cultivars of equal quality – 'Bell Boy,' 'Pro Bell II' and 'Park's Whopper' among others – also are recommended for home gardens here and new ones are introduced each year. The old-time 'California Wonder,' an ancestor in their development, is now "old hat."

bugs and billbugs. Most of them feed on roots or underground parts of plants or the tender young foliage of emerging plants.

A second group comprises chewing insects, including a number of caterpillars (larvae of moths, skippers and butterflies), some often referred to as worms: the imported cabbage worm, parsley worm, corn earworm, and tomato hornworm; and borers (the squash vine borer and corn borer.) These, along with a number of beetles, chew on foliage, stems or fruit. Some are vectors of disease. Both spotted and striped cucumber beetles spread bacterial wilt to cucurbits, and once a plant is infected there is no cure; survival depends on the built-in resistance of the plant. Potato flea beetles attack a variety of plants, especially tomatoes, peppers and eggplant and also spread viral diseases. Both flea and cucumber beetles lay eggs on the ground; their larvae burrow into the soil and feed on roots, thus weakening and killing their host plants.

The third group is made up of sucking insects. They not only suck juices from plants but also spread viral and other diseases. The most common are aphids, leaf hoppers, bean and onion thrips, greenhouse whiteflies, and spittlebugs.

Three Kinds of Controls

To control these groups, and some others as well, the gardener can make use of three kinds of materials and techniques for using them: (1) natural controls and cultural practices, (2) non-toxic substances, and (3) chemicals of varying degree of toxicity.

Natural controls are your first line of defense. Always try relying on them at the outset. You may not have to do anything. Then, if your pests are getting out of hand, use the second line: non-toxic controls, such as streams of water, handpicking, and correct timing of crops. Your final line of defense is chemicals. One of the most valuable biological controls is *Bacillus thuringiensis*, known as BT – its trade names include Thuricide and Dipel. If applied early when caterpillars are small, BT will take care of most if not all the insects that affect cole crops, tomatoes and corn. A new BT strain, effective in the control of the Colorado potato beetle, will be available to the home gardener in 1989 under the brand name M-One.

Insecticidal soaps help to control aphids, mealybugs, and soft-bodied insects as well as mites. One of the most promising bio-insecticides is Margosan-O, a seed oil extract from the exotic neem tree of India which has proven effective in the control of 131 pests including cutworms, leafminers, Colorado potato beetles, flea beetles, thrips and whiteflies. It is not toxic to people or pets, or to bees or earthworms. It can be used as a soil drench or foliar spray and works in several ways depending upon the insect. It repels some, disrupts feeding in others, and alters the growth pattern in a few. It is registered now for use on ornamentals and greenhouse plants but should be approved by EPA for use on food crops in 1989.

Some old-time "natural" insecticides such as pyrethrum or rotenone are effective against insects but are toxic to fish. They are not toxic to people or pets.

Target-Specific Chemicals

All too often the situation arises when the gardener must turn to chemicals. The ones he chooses should be as target-specific as possible and biodegrade quickly so as not to build up residues in the soil, or prevent the gardener from eating his own produce when it is at its peak.

You need not be confused by the wide array of insecticides displayed in the garden centers. Three of them are enough to take care of most of your needs. These are diazinon (Spectracide) for the control of grubs, maggots and other ground insects; carbaryl (Sevin) for the chewing insects, and malathion for the sucking insects, other than the greenhouse whitefly. Whiteflies have developed an immunity to several chemical controls used on food crops. Most insecticides, especially Sevin, are toxic to bees and other pollinators, so apply them either early or late in the day when the bees are less active.

Mites are not true insects. They thrive

in hot, dry weather. If sprays of water or insecticidal soaps, or even summer oils, are not effective, you can control them by using dicofol (Kelthane), a miticide that is not injurious to predator or parasitic insects. For slugs and snails, which are molluscs, try a bait that contains metaldehyde. The pelleted form seems to hold up better in the garden. When placed in protected places – inside a box or can with access holes too small for pets – it poses no hazard to birds or pets.

VIRUSES, FUNGI AND BACTERIA

Other pests in the garden are not as evident as insects but their devastation can be more serious. These are diseases caused by viruses (weakness, decline, death), by fungi (molds, mildew, rusts), and by bacteria (wilts, rots, slimes). Unfortunately, they are seldom noticed until a plant begins to decline, and then it is too late for prevention. There are no controls for viral diseases. Infected plants should be rogued out and destroyed immediately to prevent further spread.

Some fungicides have curative properties but most of those that are registered for use on food crops do not. Fungicides will not eradicate a disease but can help to control it and prevent its spread. Early detection and prompt treatment are important.

Three Major Disease Controls

Three fungicides may control most fungal and bacterial diseases in the garden. They are: chlorothalanil (Daconil 2787), Maneb, and fixed copper (Kocide 101).

Chlorothalanil, long used by commercial growers, is now available for home gardeners as an agent in various liquids or wettable powders. It is effective in the control of rust on beans, alternaria leaf spot on cole crops, anthracnose on tomatoes and cucumbers, downy mildew on cole crops, powdery mildew on cucumbers, early and late blights of tomatoes and potatoes, black rot on squash and pumpkins, and leaf blights and spots on other vegetables.

Maneb, a compound based on manganese, will control many of the above

---

AAS Winners

When you see a flower or vegetable in a seed catalog designated as an All America Selections (AAS) winner it means this: That professional horticulturists and plant breeders in more than 50 trial gardens across North America have found it to be the best in its class for the home gardener.

AAS is a seed-industry cooperative. Each year seed breeders from all over the world send seed samples, descriptions and photographs of their competing new cultivars to AAS. From these about 60 new flowers and 40 new vegetables are entered for trials the second year. The eventual AAS winners are selected from these trials.

Not all AAS winners adapt to our local growing conditions. Because of rigorous testing under varying conditions, however, the chances of success with an AAS winner are greater than with a cultivar picked at random.
– Henry E. Allen

---

diseases as well as rust on asparagus, anthracnose on beans, cucurbits, peppers and tomatoes, and downy mildew on lettuce, onions and spinach.

Fixed copper is the most effective control for bacterial blights and may be used on beans, peppers, tomatoes and potatoes. It also controls angular leafspot on cucumbers. Always check the labels of each fungicide for specific diseases controlled and crops for which it is labelled.

It is worth pointing out that many a good garden has been raised without the use of any of these fungicides. This can be done by the selection of resistant vegetable varieties, by proper cultural practices, and by the timing of crops. No cucumber has yet been bred to resist bacterial wilt but many are now available that are resistant to most of the fungal diseases mentioned. Mildews can be avoided by spacing plants to assure good air circulation and the evaporation of excess moisture. Early and late blight on tomatoes can be avoided by keeping the plants evenly moist and assuring proper fertilization. Choosing the hardiest varieties helps.

Always Read Labels

Insecticides and fungicides differ in their degree of hazard to users. Some require special precautions in handling. It is imperative that you read and follow precisely the instructions on the labels for safe handling and proper use, and the safe interval between application and harvest.

Before you buy any pesticide, read the label carefully to determine whether it is registered for the use you have in mind. Read it again before you prepare your spray. Then, before you use it, ask yourself: "Is this application really necessary? Is this the proper dosage? Is this the right time?"

Another bit of advice on pesticides: Don't buy the large economy size unless you can use it all in one season. Most chemical products tend to break down after a period of time and lose their effectiveness. It is a waste of time and effort to use such a pesticide. Some manufacturers list the "bench life" of their products. Your supplier probably can advise you if that information is not on the container. Don't store your pesticides in a tool shed in the hot sun; heat and light tend to break down compounds rapidly. Above all, do store them in a locked cabinet if there are children around.

If you have difficulty in diagnosing insect or disease problems, consult your Cooperative Extension Service for help.

CONCLUSION

There are no fixed rules for gardening and no precise formulas for the planting, care and feeding of each type of vegetable. Techniques continue to change. New product development is making gardening easier. Pesticide research, both chemical and biological, is making insect and disease control safer and more effective. And plant breeders are bringing us hardier plants with increased insect and disease resistance as well as improved flavor and nutritional value.

Gardening can be an adventure in exploration. Try one or two of the new cultivars coming out each year. Gardening also should be an adventure in adaptation, a challenge to see what you can do with the resources at your disposal. Be innovative. Apply your own ideas and techniques. Let your garden be a place for relaxation and enjoyment where you are in control and the growth of each plant becomes an experiment instead of a routine performance.

I hope your garden provides you with delicious vegetables. More than that, I hope it provides you with excitement and satisfaction.

References

Ortho editorial staff: *All About Vegetables*, Ortho Books, 1980. San Francisco, CA 94104.

Ortho editorial staff: *When the Good Cook Gardens*, Ortho Books 1974. San Francisco, CA 94104.

Faust, Joan Lee: *Book of Vegetable Gardening*. Quadrangle/New York Times Book Co., 1975. New York, NY, 10022.

Raymond, Dick: *Joy of Gardening*. Garden Way Publishing Co., 1983. Charlotte, VT 05445.

Patent, Dorothy Hinshaw and Diane E. Bilderback: *Garden Secrets*. Rodale Press, 1982. Emmaus, PA. 18049.

Westcott, Cynthia: *The Gardener's Bug Book*. Doubleday and Company, 1973. Garden City, NY.

Westcott's Plant Disease Handbook, 4th edition, revised by R. Kenneth Horst. Van Nostrand Reinhold Co., 1979. New York, NY.

Gardening for Food and Fun, Yearbook of Agriculture, 1977, U.S. Department of Agriculture.

Control of Insects and Diseases in Home Vegetable Gardens. Extension Bulletin 252, Cooperative Extension Service, University of Maryland, College Park, MD.

Do's and Don'ts

DON'T let your azaleas or rhododendrons get wet feet because of poor drainage. Plant high. You can even set your plants on top of the ground and surround the root ball with a mix of top soil and humus.

Table 1. Recommended Cultivars of Vegetables for the Home Garden
(AAS denotes All-America Selection)

ASPARAGUS Mary Washington (rust-resistant strains), Jersey Centennial.

BEANS, BUSH
Green Snap Blue Lake 274, Topcrop (AAS), Tenderpod (AAS), Greencrop (AAS), Tendercrop, Slenderette (French type), Gourmet (French type)
Yellow Snap Goldcrop (AAS), Sungold, Slender Wax, Majestic, Golden Rod
Broad Roma II, Jumbo
Lima Fordhook 242

BEANS, POLE
Green Snap Blue Lake, Kentucky Wonder
Broad Romano, Burpee's Golden
Lima King of the Garden

BEETS Pacemaker III, Warrior, Avenger, Red Ace, Burpee's Golden, Cylindra, Long Season (Winter Keeper)

BROCCOLI
Heading Green Comet (AAS), Goliath, Green Valiant, Bonanza
Sprouting Italian Green Sprouting (Calabria), Raab (Rapine)

BRUSSELS SPROUTS Jade Cross E, Prince Marvel, Captain Marvel

CABBAGE
Early Stonehead (AAS), Emerald Cross (AAS), Market Victor
Late Burpee's Surehead, Danish Ballhead, Penn State Ballhead
Savoy Savoy Ace (AAS), Savoy King (AAS), Savoy Princess
Red Ruby Ball (AAS), Red Acre, Ruby Perfection (late)
Chinese Tropical Delight (spring), Early Hybrid G (spring), Jade Pagoda (fall), Monument (fall), Michihili (fall)

CARROTS Pioneer, Spartan Winner, Royal Chantenay, A-Plus

CAULIFLOWER Snow Crown (AAS), Snow King (AAS), Alert, Snowball

CELERY Green Giant, Utah 52-70, Summer Pascal

CHARD, SWISS Lucullus, Perpetual, Fordhook Giant, Rhubarb (red)

CORN Three types are available: 1) *Standard* with original sugary gene (Su), 2) *Sugar Enhanced* in which 15 to 25 percent of the kernels carry extra sugar genes of the Eternal Heritage (EH) or Sugar Enhancer (SE) types, and 3) *Super Sweet* with the Shrumlan 2 (Sh_2) sugar genes in every kernel. When planting isolate the latter from all other types.

	Standard (Su)	*Sugar Enhanced (EH/SE)*	*Super Sweet (Sh₂)*
White	Chalice	Platinum Lady	How Sweet It Is (AAS)
	Quicksilver	Silverado	Summer Sweet 8601
	Silver Queen	White Lightning	
Yellow	Golden Queen	Kandy Korn	Early Xtra Sweet (AAS)
	Seneca Horizon	Miracle	Illini Gold
		Tendertreat	Summer Sweet 7200
Bi-color	Butter & Sugar	Honey & Cream	Honey & Pearl (AAS)
	Sweet Sal	Gold 'n' Pearl	Milk & Honey

CUCUMBERS
Slicing Sweet Success (AAS), Gemini, Victory (AAS), Slicemaster, Raider, Sweet Slice, Dasher II
Pickling Saladin (AAS), Liberty (AAS), Calypso, County Fair 83

EGGPLANT Dusky, Black Nite, Black Bell, Black Magic, Classic, Tycoon (oriental type), Imperial (European type)

ENDIVE   Green Curled Ruffec, Florida Deep Heart, Full Heart Batavian

KALE   Blue Knight, Vates Dwarf Blue Curled

KOHLRABI   Grand Duke (AAS), Purple Danube, Early White Vienna

LEEKS   Broad London, Giant Musselburgh, Alaska, Unique

LETTUCE
  Head   Great Lakes 659, Frosty, Ithaca, Mission (spring)
  Butterhead   Buttercrunch (AAS), Summer Bibb, Tania
  Looseleaf   Green Ice, Salad Bowl, Black Seeded Simpson, Slobolt, Grand Rapids, Ruby (AAS), Red Sails (AAS), Tango
  Cos (Romaine)   Valmaine, Parris Island

MELONS
  Cantaloupe   Ambrosia, Classic, Harper, Saticoy, Bush Star
  Honeydew   Earlydew, Venus
  Watermelon   New Hampshire Midget (AAS), Sugar Baby, Royal Sweet

OKRA   Annie Oakley, Clemson Spineless, Emerald, Blondy (AAS)

ONIONS (storage)
  Seed   Spartan Banner, Gringo, Sweet Sandwich, Carmen (red)
  Sets   Stuttgarter, Golden Mosque, Yellow Ebenezer, Yellow Globe

ONIONS (bunching)   White Portugal, Beltsville Bunching, Southport
NOTE: Granex and other southern short-day types do not do well here.

PARSLEY   Banquet, Paramount (AAS), Emerald, Darki, Dark Green Italian Plain

PARSNIPS   Harris' Model, Hollow Crown, All America

PEAS
  Green (Sugar)   Wando, Knight, Early Frosty, Sparkle
  Edible podded   Dwarf Gray Sugar, Mammoth Melting Sugar, Snowbird
  Snap   Sugar Snap (AAS), Sugar Bon, Sugar Ann (AAS), Sugar Daddy, Super SugarMel

PEPPERS
  Bell   Bell Boy (AAS), Lady Bell, Park's Whopper, Pro Bell II, Golden Bell, Golden Summer, Orobelle
  Other Sweet   Big Bertha, Gypsy (AAS), Cubanelle, Key Largo, Sweet Banana, Pimiento Select
  Hot   Hot Portugal, Hungarian Hot Wax, Anaheim, Long Red Cayenne, Jalapeno

POTATOES   Irish Cobbler (early), Bliss Triumph (red skin), Kennebec, Katahdin
NOTE: Check also local sources for seed potatoes.

RADISHES   Cherry Belle (AAS), Champion (AAS), Comet (AAS), Sparkler, Icicle

RHUBARB   McDonald, Valentine, Victoria (green)

SPINACH   Melody (AAS), America (AAS), Tyee, Fabris, Bloomsdale Longstanding, Winter Bloomsdale (fall), Gold Resistant Savoy (fall)

SQUASH
  Summer (bush)
    Zucchini   Aristocrat (AAS), Ambassador, Zucchini Elite, Seneca Gourmet, Gold Rush (AAS) (yellow), Eldorado (yellow)
    Crookneck   Goldneck, Sundance, Tara
    Straight neck   Goldbar (AAS), Golden Girl, Seneca Butterbar, Multipik
    Scallop   Peter Pan (AAS), Patty Pan, Sunburst (AAS)

SQUASH
  Fall and Winter   Table King (AAS), Sweet Mama (AAS), Gold Nugget, Buttercup, Waltham Butternut

TOMATOES

Slicing	
Indeterminate	Supersonic, Pole King, Jet Star, Better Boy, Big Girl, Park's Whopper, Super Beefsteak, Lady Luck
Determinate	Celebrity (AAS), Floramerica (AAS), Independence, Better Bush, Del Oro
Yellow	Sunray, Lemon Boy
Italian type	Roma VF, Royal Chico
Small fruited	Small Fry (AAS), Sweet 100, Pixie Hybrid II, Presto, Patio

TURNIPS

Tokyo Cross (AAS), Purple Top White Globe, Just Right (AAS) (fall only)

NOTE 1: Where there is a choice the selection of a hybrid will reward the gardener with improved yields of superior quality.

NOTE 2: The cultivars listed are available from a number of sources including one or more of the following: W. Atlee Burpee & Co., Warminster, PA 18974; Harris Seeds, 961 Lyell Ave., Rochester, NY 14606; Park Seed Co., Box 31, Greenwood, SC 29647; Stokes Seeds, Box 548, Buffalo, NY 14240, and Otis Twilley Seed Co., Box 65, Trevose, PA 19047.

How Good Is Your Pesticide?

How long will they last? Chemical pesticides vary in stability. It is not possible to give specific guidelines on bench-life.

If stored in a cool, dark place – preferably a cabinet that can be locked – where they will not be subjected to extremely high temperatures or freezing, insecticides and fungicides formulated as liquids or emulsifiable concentrates should remain effective for at least two years. Wettable powders, flowables and dusts stored in a dry atmosphere will remain stable for five years or more. If they become lumpy they should be discarded.

Most herbicides, regardless of formulation, remain effective almost indefinitely. Natural pesticides and the newer bio-insecticides are relatively stable and may be stored for up to 10 years. An exception is *Bacillus thuringiensis* (BT) which loses its potency after four or five years.

Always read the label carefully and follow manufacturer's instructions.

– Henry E. Allen

Viability of Seeds

When properly stored vegetable seeds should remain viable for one or more years as indicated below.

Vegetables	Years
Asparagus	3
Beans (all types)	3
Beets	6
Brassicas (all types)	5
Carrots	4
Celery	8
Corn	2
Cucumbers	10
Eggplant	6
Leek	3
Lettuce	5
Melons (all types)	6
Okra	5
Onions	2
Parsley	3
Parsnips	1
Peas (all types)	3
Peppers	4
Radish	5
Spinach	5
Squash (all types)	6
Swiss Chard	5
Tomatoes	4
Turnips	5

Table 2. Vegetable Planting Guide for the Greater Washington Area[1]

CROP	Average Planting Dates		Planting Distances (in.)		Depth to Plant (in.)	Days to Germination	Days to First Harvest	Approximate Yield 25 Ft. of Row[4]
	For Spring	For Fall	In Rows[2]	Between Rows				
ASPARAGUS	Mar 20 - Apr15	—	12-18	36-60	6-8	Plant Roots	2-3 yrs.	10 lbs.
BEANS:								
Bush Snap	May 5 - June 15	July 1 - Aug 5	3-4	18-24	1½	6-14	55-70	18 lbs.
Pole Snap	May 5 - June 15	July 1 - 25	4-6	30-36	1½	6-14	60-70	30 lbs.
Bush Lima	May 10 - 31	July 1 - 15	5-6	18-24	1½	7-12	70-85	8 lbs.(shelled)
Pole Lima	May 10 - 31	June 25 - July 10	8-10	30-36	2	7-14	85-90	14 lbs.(shelled)
Pole Broad	May 10 - June 10	July 1 - 25	5-6	24-30	2	7-14	75-90	30 lbs.
BEETS	Apr 1 - June 15	July 1 - Aug 5	2-3	15-24	½	7-10	60-80	25 lbs.
BROCCOLI	Apr 1 - 30	July 15 - Aug 20	18-20	24-36	Plants	—	55-70[3]	15 lbs.
BRUSSELS SPROUTS	Apr 1 - 30	July 1 - 31	18-20	24-36	Plants	—	90-95[3]	8 lbs.
CABBAGE	Mar 15 - Apr 10	July 10 - Aug 20	18-20	24-30	Plants	—	60-90[3]	14 heads
CABBAGE, CHINESE	Apr 1 - 30	July 10 - Aug 10	12-15	18-24	½	4-10	60-90	17 heads
CARROTS	Apr 10 - June 1	June 15 - Aug 1	1-2	15-24	¼	14-21	60-80	25 lbs.
CAULIFLOWER	Apr 1 - 30	July 10 - Aug 20	18-20	24-30	Plants	—	55-70[3]	14 heads
CELERY	Apr 15 - May 1	—	6-8	18-24	Plants	—	100-125[3]	50 stalks
CHARD, SWISS	Apr 15 - July 25	—	4-8	18-24	½	7-10	55-65	20 lbs.
CORN, SWEET	May 10 - July 5	—	10-12	30-36	2	6-10	70-90	25 ears
CUCUMBERS	May 10 - July 5	—	6-10	48-60	1	6-10	50-70	15 lbs.
EGGPLANT	May 15 - June 10	—	18-24	30-42	Plants	—	70-85[3]	50 fruits
ENDIVE	Apr 1 - 30	July 10 - Aug 20	8-12	12-24	¼	5-9	65-90	25 heads
KALE	Mar 20 - Apr 20	July 10 - Aug 10	10-12	18-24	½	5-10	55-75	20 lbs.
KOHLRABI	Apr 1 - May 20	July 10 - Aug 1	8-10	18-24	½	3-10	60-70	35 stems
LEEK	Apr 1 - May 1	—	3-4	12-18	½	7-12	100-130	50-60

Vegetable									
LETTUCE:									
Head	Apr 1 - May 1	Aug 1 - 15	8-10	18-24	¼	4-10	70-85	25 heads
Butterhead	Apr 1 - May 1	Aug 1 - 15	6-10	18-24	¼	4-10	65-80	30 heads
Looseleaf	Apr 1 - May 15	July 15 - Aug 20	5-8	12-18	¼	4-10	45-60	12 lbs.
MELONS	May 10 - June 15	—	24-48	48-60	1	6-12	85-120	variable
OKRA	May 10 - 30	—	18-24	36-42	½	7-12	50-65	20 lbs
ONIONS:									
Sets	Mar 1 - Apr 10	—	2-3	12-18	1-2	—	50-60[3]	25 bunches
Plants	Mar 30 - Apr 10	—	2-3	12-18	Plants	—	60-90	20 lbs.(storage)
PARSLEY	Apr 1 - May 1	—	5-8	15-24	¼	14-24	85-90	2½ lbs.
PARSNIPS	Apr 1 - May 1	—	4-6	18-24	½	15-26	100-120	30 lbs
PEAS	Feb 20 - Mar 20	July 25 - Aug 5	2-3	18-30	2	7-30	60-80	3 lbs.(shelled)
PEPPERS	May 10 - June 10	—	18-24	24-30	Plants	—	60-80[3]	15 lbs.
POTATOES	Mar 15 - May 10	June 15 - July 10	10-12	30-36	4	—	60-90	20 lbs.
RADISHES	Mar 10 - May 10	Aug 1 - Sept 15	1-2	12-18	½	3-7	25-45	12 lbs.
RHUBARB	Mar 10 - Apr 20	—	36-42	36-48	4-6	Plant roots	1-2 years	24 lbs.
SHALLOTS	Mar 1 - Apr 15	—	2-4	18-24	½-1	—	50-60	500 bulbs
SPINACH	Mar 10 - Apr 10	Aug 1 - Sept 5	3-6	12-18	½	6-14	40-60	12 lbs.
SQUASH:									
Summer	May 10 - 30	June 20 - July 10	18-24	48-60	1-2	5-12	50-65	20 lbs.
Winter	May 15 - June 15	—	36-48	60-80	1-2	6-14	90-110	30 lbs.
TOMATOES	May 5 - June 15	—	30-36	36-48	Plants	—	60-90	55 lbs.
TURNIPS	Mar 15 - Apr 30	July 15 - Aug 20	3-5	18-24	1	3-10	35-60	25 lbs.

[1]Planting dates for lower Montgomery County and may vary slightly in other parts of the area.
[2]Distance between plants after thinning, whether in single rows, broad bands or beds. Exceptions are bush snap and bush lima beans which, if planted in broad bands, should be on 6-inch and 9-inch centers, respectively.
[3]Date to first harvest from time transplants are set in the garden.
[4]These are averages for standard varieties and will vary greatly depending upon the cultivar planted.

Based on author's records and information from the Cooperative Extension Services at the University of Maryland and the Virginia Polytechnic Institute and State University.

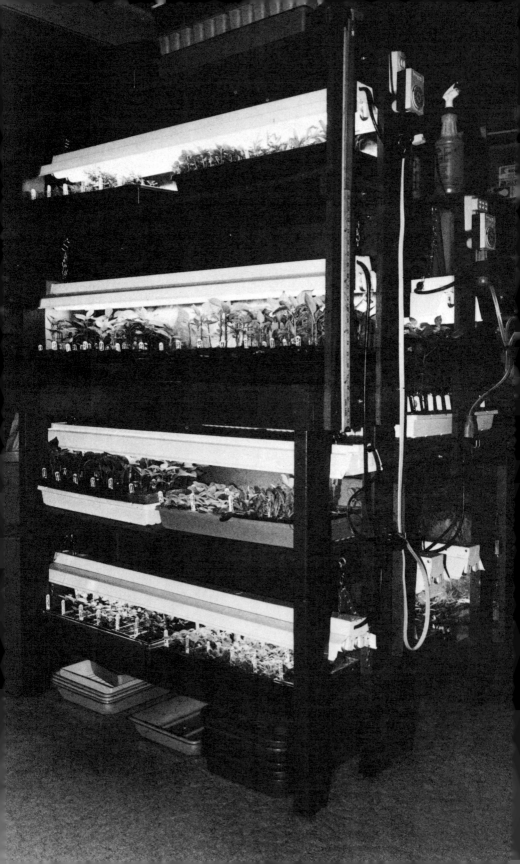

Grow Your Own Transplants

By Henry E. Allen

Why grow your own transplants? There are several reasons. You can start with the best seed. You can be sure of what you are getting – the best varieties for the area, transplants available at the best time for them and for you. You are not bringing in insects or disease pathogens that may plague you later. And you can extend your growing season – earlier in the spring and later in the fall. Finally, there is the personal satisfaction of having a hand in the birth and growth of a plant.

What are the best seed? Hybrid vegetable and flower seed usually are better than open-pollinated seed. Hybrids are bred for top performance – long productivity, resistance to pests and diseases, and vigor and adaptability to our climate. However, some open-pollinated seeds compete well with the hybrids, and at less cost. And not all plants are available as hybrids.

What are the best sources for seeds? Buy seed from a dependable supplier who gives you information on the packets about the rate of germination and the year of packaging, and with packets designed to preserve freshness until opened. You can find them on the seed racks but your chances of finding them – especially if you want that new tomato or petunia – are better in the seed catalogues.

GROWING TRANSPLANTS INDOORS

To start seed indoors, you need a place with adequate light and suitable temperature, good air circulation, and controllable humidity. You may have a place in your basement, attic or spare room; a south-facing window sill may do. Growing under artificial light may be better. And window light supplemented by artificial light gives excellent results. If it's available, "bottom heat" to warm the soil will hasten germination.

If you are growing a lot of plants, you need a table or bench or chest on which to place them after they germinate, and over which you can hang one or more standard 48-inch fluorescent shop lights. Each fixture should be equipped with one "warm" and one "cool" white tube. The combination provides balanced light for growing transplants. Fancy fixtures and expensive "grow" lights are not necessary. The lights should have a timer so young plants automatically get 14 to 16 hours of light at the same time every day. They should be hung so they can be raised or lowered; normally they should be about two inches above the seedlings. Incidentally, if your growing space is limited, 36-inch or even 20-inch fixtures can be used.

Ideally the temperature in this growing area should approximate 68° to 70°F during the day and 58° to 60°F at night. The home gardener may have difficulty in achieving this precisely; the essential point is to have cooler temperatures at night when the light is off than during the day.

PHOTO BY EDMUND C. FLYNN

◄ This center for starting flowers and vegetables indoors began as a work table and was expanded until it now holds seven 48-inch shoplights and space for 16 11-by-21-inch plant trays. The light fixtures may be raised and lowered and are set to provide an automatic 16 hours of light daily. Each holds a "cool" and a "warm" fluorescent tube.

Good air circulation is important. So is adequate humidity. Even with the lower house-heating temperatures, our houses tend to dry out in winter. You can provide humidity by placing your flats or containers on pea gravel and keeping the gravel watered without letting them stand in water unable to drain.

WHEN TO PLANT

Time the planting of your seeds so that you will have good transplants to set out at the proper time. (See Table 2 in "Vegetables for the Home Garden.") If you plan to set out your tomato plants about May 5, count back six weeks and plant your seed about March 24. Peppers and eggplant take longer to germinate so they should be started about a week earlier. Don't start plants too early. They can get tall and "leggy" before you set them out. All this will take some experimenting. Keep records of your planting and germination dates and other information to develop your planting schedules for future years.

PLANT CONTAINERS AND MEDIA

One secret of growing transplants successfully is having sterile containers and media. Almost any container will do as long as it's clean, is at least two and a half inches deep, and has bottom drainage holes. Clay pots, wooden flats or other porous containers should be scrubbed and soaked in a 10 percent Clorox solution for a half hour. Glazed pots, plastic or rubberized containers need only to be washed in the solution. Peat pots need no sterilization.

One of the good "soilless" mixtures is the best medium for starting seeds and growing transplants. Some have a small amount of fertilizer to get seedlings started. Others will need fertilizer added once seedlings develop their true leaves. Moisten the mix before using it. Add a cup of hot water to each quart of mix and work it in well. It will handle better. All these mixes are based on sphagnum peat moss which does not absorb water readily until it has been wet down initially.

If you want to make a bushel of your own mix here is a good formula:

16 quarts well-screened peat moss
16 quarts horticultural grade vermiculite
4 teaspoons complete fertilizer (5-10-5 or 5-10-10)
4 teaspoons horticultural lime
4 teaspoons powdered superphosphate (0-20-0)

Moisten and mix thoroughly before using. You can use this for either starting seeds or potting up seedlings.

If you want to start only a few seeds you may find the use of pellets or similar prepared containers more convenient. These include Jiffy-7 pellets (netted), the smaller Jiffy-9 pellets, or Fertl-Cubes. They will support growth to transplant size and then can be set out with little or no root damage. One caution: If you use Jiffy-7s cut away the netting before planting; it can impede root growth.

In preparing to plant, fill your flat or container with soil to within a half-inch from the top. Press it down gently but firmly. Add more soil if necessary, filling in the corners carefully. A mason's planting trowel is helpful in levelling and firming. Make furrows or drills and plant your seed. Cover with soil except those seeds such as lettuce that require light. Water the container from the bottom by placing it in warm water. When it has absorbed all the water possible, let it drain for an hour. Then cover it with glass or tuck it in a plastic bag.

The soil must not dry out during germination. Moisture under the glass or plastic shows that there is no problem. If the soil should become dry, moisten it with a fine mist or spray over the top. The flat or container should have even heat; bottom heat is best. Most seeds germinate in the dark so the container can be placed in a warm closet, on top of the furnace, refrigerator or other warm place, until germination starts. For most seed the optimum soil temperature for germination is 68° to 86°F.

If you plant more than one kind of seed in the same flat or container, select plants with the same germination period. Don't plant broccoli, which takes from five to eight days, with parsley, which takes from 17 to 27 days. Mark each row or each flat at planting time with the plant cultivar and date. Don't rely on memory. A strip of freezer tape marked with a waterproof pen serves well.

TEMPERATURE AND LIGHT

Most vegetable, herb and flower seeds germinate well in the 68° to 86°F range but some need colder temperatures. The following do best between 55° and 65°F:

Vegetables: celeriac, celery, leek, lettuce, onion, pea, potato, radish, salsify, spinach. Peas and spinach do best in the lower part of the range.

Herbs: chives, rosemary.

Flowers: alyssum, calendula, clarkia, delphinium, hollyhock, gazania, larkspur, lupine, myosotis, pansy, phacelia, tahoka daisy, torenia, viola.

Some seeds require light to germinate. In planting, these seeds should not be covered:

Vegetables: celery, chicory, cress, endive, lettuce, rhubarb, sorrel, husk tomato *(physalis)*.

Herbs: dill, savory.

Flowers: ageratum, alyssum, begonia, browallia, coleus, exacum, gloxinia, helichrysum, impatiens, nicotiana, petunia, primula, salvia, snapdragon, streptocarpus.

CARE OF SEEDLINGS

During the germination period check your seeds daily. See that the soil remains moist. When the first plants emerge, remove the covering and place them under light. Keeping them in the dark too long makes them become weak and spindly. If you place them in a bright window they will tend to lean toward the light so they should be turned every day. If they are under fluorescent lights, keep the light about two inches above the plants as they grow and provide 14 to 16 hours of light daily. Keep the soil moist but not soggy. Use warm water and apply it slowly to avoid disturbing the soil.

When the seedlings develop their first true leaves they can be lifted and planted in pots. If you wait too long before lifting they can suffer unnecessary root dam-

age. For this potting peat pots are ideal. Some people use plastic cell-packs. You can use the same potting medium in which you started your seed or a coarser mix (Pro-Mix BX or similar). The coarser mix encourages root development and good drainage.

As you pot your seedlings, water them with a soluble fertilizer high in phosphorus. This helps root growth and gives the plants enough nutrients to carry them until they are set out.

If your potting mix contains garden soil that might carry pathogens, add Captan 50% WP (wettable powder) to the water at the rate of one teaspoon to a quart. This will discourage any loss of seedlings to the fungal disease known as "damping off." If you grow in a prepared container such as a Jiffy-7 or are seeding directly into pots with a sterile mix this is not a factor.

If you planted two or more seed in each container and more than one germinated, reduce them to one per container. Clip the excess plants off at the soil line with small scissors, thereby avoiding damage to the roots of the chosen plant. If you grow your seedlings to transplant size in the flats in which you started them, you may have to thin them. Use scissors to cut out the weakest, leaving at least an inch between those that remain.

TRANSPLANTING TO GARDEN

Plants should be "hardened off" a week to 10 days before they are set out. This means giving them a gradual adjustment to the environment where they will grow. The simplest way to do this is to move the flats or containers outdoors to a shaded area protected from wind for the first couple of days. Then move them to a place with two or more hours of sunlight and gradually increase the exposure to full sunlight. If frost or high winds are expected at night, protect the plants with covers or bring them inside for the night. As their growth slows, water them at longer intervals. Do not let them wilt or dry out.

All these procedures may seem complicated and time-consuming but if you follow them you'll be rewarded with the best transplants and, as a result, a superior garden.

References

Hill, Lewis: *Secrets of Plant Propagation*, Garden Way Publishing Co., 1985. Charlotte, VT.

Reilly, Ann: *Park's Success With Seeds*, George W. Park Seed Co., 1978.

Janick, Jules: *Horticultural Science*, 2nd edition. W. H. Freeman & Co. 1972. See pages 325-340.

Wells, James S.: *Plant Propagation Practices*. Macmillan Company, New York, 1969.

PHOTO BY EDMUND C. FLYNN

Greenhouses for your home come in many shapes and sizes and for any location you desire. This one is on top of a bar that serves a patio and swimming pool area.

The Backyard Berry Patch

By Rick Heflebower

Growing fruit at home is both fun and rewarding. Strawberries, blueberries, brambles, and grapes may be grown successfully by the homeowner without special equipment or training. In general, "small fruit" have relatively few insect and disease problems compared to "tree fruit" such as apples and peaches. Most "small fruit" will bring a harvest in the first or second season while "tree fruit" will not produce until at least the fourth year.

Select a plant site that is well drained and receives direct sunlight. Plants do not like "wet feet" and heavy clay soils should be improved by working in aged manure or other composted organic matter. Maintain your soil pH at about 5.5 to 6.0, slightly on the acidic side. The only exception to this is the acid-loving blueberry which requires a pH of about 4.5 to 5.0. You can raise the soil pH by adding limestone or lower it by adding sulfur.

STRAWBERRIES

Strawberries grow successfully in a "matted row" system. Set out the plants in early spring, with the roots spread evenly and the crown at ground level, spacing them about one foot apart within an 18-inch-wide row. The plant will form runners, sending out daughter plants to form a "matted row." First-year plants benefit from an application of nitrogen in the spring – about one pound of actual nitrogen per 1,000 square feet just before runner formation.

After the berries are harvested in the summer the plant should be renovated. Mow off the tops about two inches above the crown and cultivate between rows to remove weeds and plants that have de-

veloped outside the intended 18-inch row width. At this time runners and fruit buds are being formed for next season's production. When the plants stop growing – about Thanksgiving in the Washington area – cover them with two or three inches of straw mulch. It doesn't matter if leaves show through; what you are doing is protecting the crown from winter injury.

In addition to the June-bearing types, the home gardener can grow strawberries that produce three crops a season – in late June, mid-summer and fall. One of the best of these is 'Tribute.' It produces a berry of excellent flavor on plants resistant to red stele, powdery mildew and other diseases. Everbearers produce about the same quantity of fruit in a year as the June-bearers.

Another option: runner-less or so-called "alpine" strawberries. The most famous of these is the French *fraises de bois* but more suitable for our climate are 'Alexandria' or 'Ruegen Improved.' They make attractive edgers for perennial beds or vegetable gardens. Culture is the same as for other types. A final option: strawberries from seed. The alpines, including the variety 'Sweetheart,' can easily be grown this way. If started inside in February they may yield fruit the first season.

BLUEBERRIES

"Highbush" and "Rabbiteye" blueberries are the most successful cultivated varieties. "Highbush" is superior in this area. The berries are large, flavorful and overall quality is better than "Rabbiteye," which gets its name because the immature berries are pink. "Rabbiteye" berries like hot weather and are some-

what drought tolerant, and therefore do well in the south.

Blueberries should be planted in acidic soil with lots of organic matter. Plant them about four feet apart in rows eight feet apart. The roots are short and fibrous so remove weeds by pulling or shallow cultivation.

Berries will be borne on the previous year's new wood with the largest berries on the most vigorous wood. So prune blueberry bushes by thinning out the weakest wood at the center of the plant. Where branches become too tall, heading cuts are useful to maintain a low-growing bush. Prune in March when buds are still dormant. Mulching helps hold soil moisture to the fibrous roots.

BLACKBERRIES

Blackberry plants should be planted six feet apart in the row with about 10 feet between rows. The erect thornless types do well in this area but should be trellised for support. About mid-season the weight of vegetation and fruit often will break the brittle canes if not trellised.

Blackberries will bear on the previous season's new growth. When you prune in March remove the older wood – the dark-colored canes that already have fruited. (This is true of all brambles.) Cut off older canes at ground level. The remaining new canes should be cut off ("tipped back") to a height of five or six feet. Blackberries will form fruit on lateral branches from the main canes. Laterals should be left six to 12 inches long depending on their diameter.

RASPBERRIES

Some raspberries are thorny, some thornless. Some have red fruit, some have "black caps." Red raspberries are more popular. Both do well here. Thornless plants are as good or better than

brambles and are easier to handle.

"Black caps" have an erect growing habit and plants should be spaced four feet apart with eight feet between rows. When pruning all dead wood by cutting it at the base of the plant. Remove the top canes and leaves at a height of three to four feet. "Black caps" bear on lateral branches so leave the lateral limbs on the main canes but shorten them to four to six inches to stiffen them.

Red raspberries should be planted three feet apart with about six feet between rows. Prune most red raspberries like the "black caps." Some of the reds bear fruit on the main terminal cane; no pruning at lateral branches is needed.

The exception to this pruning strategy is in the culture of 'Heritage' red raspberries. If you want 'Heritage' to produce as an everbearer follow the normal procedures. However, 'Heritage' is a productive late-summer and fall raspberry. If you want a main crop, cut all the canes to about two inches above the ground in March. The new canes will grow up through the season and produce a beautiful crop beginning in August and lasting until frost.

GRAPES

Grapes do relatively well here. Because of our high humidity choose varieties that have some resistance to powdery mildew and black rot. Set your plants about six to eight feet apart and 10 to 12 feet between rows. Grapes always should be trellised or at least grown next to a fence row where the canes can be attached for support.

The four-arm Kniffen training system is one of the most widely used. The upper trellis wire should be about four and a half feet above ground and the lower wire about two and a half feet. Young, one-year plants should be pruned at planting time to leave only two or three buds. As the shoot develops it should be pinched to stimulate branching as it approaches the upper trellis wire. Two branches should be trained at the upper and lower heights to follow the trellis wires in either direction. The four main branches should be shortened to leave 10 to 15 buds per cane.

PHOTO BY ANGELA SECKINGER

◄ **Six grape vines, each a different cultivar, form the lush arbor that covers this patio. The vines required three years to mature and reach full coverage.**

Each year new canes, about pencil diameter, should be trained to replace the older canes. All other canes should be removed to the trunk with the exception of four or five small ones to be used as renewal spurs. These spurs should have two or three buds and be cut four to six inches from the trunk. They will provide a place for canes to grow that can be trained for the following season.

RECOMMENDED VARIETIES

Strawberry: Allstar, Earliglow, Redchief, Tribute (everbearing), Ruegen Improved (Alpine type).
Blueberry: Berkeley, Bluecrop, Blueray, Spartan (small bush).
Blackberry: Chester, Hull (both thornless).
Red Raspberry: Fall Gold (yellow), Royal Burgundy (purple), Heritage (everbearing), Titan (early summer).
Black Raspberry: Cumberland, Bristol.

Table Grapes: Himrod (white), Canadice (red), Suffolk (red), Lakemont (white), Reliant (red).

References

Fertilizer Recommendations for Fruit Crops, Extension Bulletin HE29-83.
Growing Blackberries. Farmers Bulletin No 2160, U.S. Department of Agriculture.
Growing Raspberries. Farmers Bulletin No 2165, U.S. Department of Agriculture.
Growing Strawberries in Maryland. Extension Bulletin 216, Extension Service, University of Maryland, College Park.
Maryland Commercial Small Fruit Recommendations 1982-83, Extension Bulletin 242, Extension Service, University of Maryland, College Park.

Note: The foregoing excellent references may not be available from their publishers but can be consulted at Extension Service offices.

Childers, Norman F.: *Modern Fruit Science*.

PHOTO BY EDMUND C. FLYNN

Newspapers (black print only) are used most often in the garden as a mulch. Here they also provide a walk through a large planting of strawberries.

Horticultural Publications, Rutgers University, New Brunswick, NJ.

New and Noteworthy Fruits. New York State Fruit Testing Lab, Geneva, NY. 14456.

Pest Control Problems on Small Fruit and Some Ways to Control Them

Many insect and disease problems affect small fruit plantings but they are not as numerous nor as difficult to control in the Washington area as the serious problems that plague the growing of tree fruit. The key to pest control is proper identification since many control measures are very specific.

Insect/Disease	Symptoms	Control
STRAWBERRIES		
Strawberry clipper	Damaged fruit buds	Methoxychlor
Aphids	Pear-shaped insects cause leaf curling	Diazinon
Leafhoppers	Green, wedge-shaped insects cause yellowish discoloration to leaves	Diazinon
Botrytis rot	Grayish mold on fruit	Captan
Powdery mildew	White powdery fungus on underside of leaves	Benomyl
Red Stele	Poor growth, wilting and death of plants in spring	Benomyl

Note: Use only resistant varieties and avoid poorly-drained planting sites.

BLUEBERRIES		
Leafhoppers	Same as for strawberries	Diazinon
Blueberry maggots	Tiny hole in fruit	Diazinon
Japanese beetles	Metallic green beetles chewing irregular holes in leaves	Sevin
Mummy berry	Twigs and flowers wilt and die	Captan plus Benomyl at blossoming

RASPBERRIES AND BLACKBERRIES		
Japanese beetles	Same as for blueberries	Sevin
Powdery mildew	Same as for strawberries	Benomyl
Botrytis rot	Same as for strawberries	Captan
Spur blight	Purplish-brown cankers just below nodes on red raspberry only	Captan

GRAPES		
Flea beetles	Tiny black beetles cause shot holes in leaves	Sevin
Grape berry moth	Webbing on dried brown grape flowers	Diazinon
Black rot	Brown leaf lesions, also dried brown grape clusters	Mancozeb or Ferbam
Powdery mildew	White, powdery fungus on underside of leaves	Sulfur

Grow Your Own Herbs

By Holly Harmar Shimizu

Herbs are at their best when used fresh. So why not grow your own? They're easy to grow and a delight to use. The increasing interest in herbs by gardeners and plant lovers is evident all around us. Commercial plant growers say they cannot supply the demand and new herb-related businesses are springing up all the time.

Traditional herb gardens are designed usually with four squares or rectangles and a center focal point, possibly with a bird bath or sundial. Contemporary designs see herbs mixed into gardens with all types of plants. A raised bed is often ideal; so is an herb rock garden where the Mediterranean herbs like to creep over the rocks, enjoying the heat they absorb on a sunny day. In combination with other plants, herbs add color, fragrance and beauty to your vegetable or flower garden.

Basic Requirements

- At least six hours of sunlight a day.
- Good loamy soil with organic matter added such as leaf mold or well-rotted manure.
- Excellent drainage. You may need to break up heavy clays with either coarse sand or small granite chips.
- Air circulation. It helps prevent serious insect and disease problems.

◄ The author calls this a "representative" herb garden. Here and in an adjacent bed are thyme, basil, tarragon, rosemary, marjoram, oregano, summer savory, salad burnet, costmary, fennel, lavender, hyssop, rue, artemesia, santolina, southernwood, calendula and rose geranium.

- Pruning of established plants to keep them full and compact.

Harvesting and Drying

Harvesting should be done in the morning after the dew is dry but before the sun is too bright. The essential oils in herbs are volatile in the atmosphere during the day. So collect your herbs when their flavor is at its peak. And cut only the amount you need for one day.

Dry herbs in bunches or lay them on screens in a dark, warm, well-ventilated spot. An attic is ideal; closets or dry basements will do. The best temperature is no more than 90°F; if it's too hot the herbs will cook. The time required for drying will vary with the thickness of the plant part.

Store herbs out of direct sunlight to prevent bleaching. Be sure they are well labelled. Most dry herbs will keep for at least a year.

Many prefer to freeze their herbs for use in the winter. This is suitable especially for parsley, tarragon, chives and lovage. Other methods of preservation include their use in vinegars, oils, sauces and jellies.

A Selection for the Washington Area

Perennials

Chives – *Allium Schoenoprasum*. Chives are easy to grow if given full sun and drainage. Closely related to onions, they grow from small bulbs and have thin, hollow stems. Along with culinary uses in salads, sauces and vinegars, chives make an attractive edging.

French Tarragon – *Artemisia Dracunculus*. Be sure you buy the true French tarragon, not the weedy, tasteless Russian tarragon that many growers sell. Tarragon grows best in full sun or partial shade in a moderately rich soil. Young leaves are picked in the spring and are best frozen instead of dried. Tarragon is delicious with chicken, fish and vegetables. Tarragon vinegar is a famous use.

English Lavender – *Lavandula angustifolia.* Lavender is a wonderful, fragrant herb preferring a sunny location and well-drained, sandy, dry soil. It's an excellent edging plant, covering one to two feet in diameter. The flowers are good in potpourri and sachets. The life span of plants is four to seven years after which they must be replaced.

Lovage – *Levisticum officinale.* A tall, hardy perennial, lovage makes a magnificent, towering garden plant. Its growth habit resembles angelica, its flavor resembles celery. The leaves are used to flavor soups and salads. Lovage soup, made the same way as sorrel soup, is superb. Try the hollow stems as straws. The roots can be candied; the seeds are used in baking to flavor breads. It is easy to grow, requiring no special care but a lot of space. One plant is enough for most families.

Mint – *Mentha* species and hybrids. There are many kinds of mint. Peppermint and spearmint are the most common. Some of the fruit-scented ones are delightful. The main concern with mint is to confine it within metal or plastic barriers or plant it where its vigorous growth habit is not a problem. Mints are used for teas, fruit dishes and potpourri.

Catmint (Catnip) – *Nepeta* x *Faassenii.* Catmint is a delightful hardy perennial reaching a height of one to three feet. Cats are attracted by it. The soft grey-green leaves topped with mauve-blue flower spikes give a beautiful show in late spring and will bloom again if cut back after the first bloom. Catmint is used as an edging plant (this cultivar is especially decorative) and to stuff toy mice.

Italian Oregano – *Origanum vulgare* subsp *hirtum.* This is the best of the hardy forms of *Origanum* to use for cooking. It is easily cultivated and requires no special attention. The flavor is strong and peppery. The main use is in flavoring meat, especially important in Italian cookery.

Salad Burnet – *Poterium Sanguisorba.* This is an evergreen herb with the flavor of cucumber. Leaves are used as garnishes for wine or beer, in salads, soups, and chopped in cottage or cream cheese. Burnet prefers a sandy soil in full sun.

Rosemary – *Rosmarinus officinalis.* It's not always hardy in our winters but deserves a place in any herb garden. It has been grown for 3,000 years and there are many fascinating associations. It makes a fine potted herb, thriving with full sun and good drainage. With some protection it may survive our winters. The leaves are used in meat dishes, for teas, in bath mixtures, and for potpourri. Rosemary is an excellent topiary specimen.

Sage – *Salvia officinalis.* Sage is a hardy perennial that can be grown in any good, well-drained soil in full sun. Set plants about two feet apart; if the dwarf form 'Nana' is used set plants about one foot apart. Once the plant reaches a height of six inches leaves may be picked any time during the growing season. Sage lasts only four or five years and must be replaced. It is used in chicken, in stuffing, and in making a pleasant tea.

English Thyme – *Thymus vulgaris.* A woody sub-shrub, English Thyme grows well in warm, light, well-drained calcareous soils. It benefits from a hard pruning in March, removing at least half its growth. Leaves may be harvested throughout the season. Other types of thyme also are suitable for the herb garden and all do well in a rock garden. Thyme has many culinary uses; an ingredient in "bouquet garni," it should be used in small quantities, otherwise its pungent flavor will mask the flavors of other herbs.

Annuals

Dill – *Anethum graveolens.* Plants should be started from seed and grown in place. Dill leaves and seeds are used in cooking and pickling. Once dill produces seed the plants will self-sow if allowed.

Borage – *Borago officinalis.* Borage is a coarse, thick-stemmed herb with drooping blue flowers and will thrive in poor dry soil. It may be grown in place in spring and eventually will self-seed. Leaves have a cucumber taste and are used in salads; flowers are floated in wine cups and used to decorate cakes. Borage is a wonderful plant to attract bees.

Coriander – *Coriandrum sativum.* Coriander is best grown from seed directly in the ground in early spring. The leaves, also called cilantro and culantro, are a popular flavoring in Latin American food and, as Chinese parsley, in Asian foods. Ground coriander seeds are important as a seasoning. Coriander will self-sow easily, often providing two crops a year.

Fennel – *Foeniculum vulgare.* Fennel actually is a perennial but is best treated as an annual. The feathery leaves are topped by clusters of yellow flowers. It grows in place from seed. Its anise-scented leaves and seeds are highly valued in fish cookery and the seeds in herbal teas.

Sweet Basil – *Ocimum basilicum*. Basil is an herb garden "must," a tender annual growing to two feet or more. Plants should be pruned through the summer to prevent flower formation. Basil has a long history and its leaves are famous for use in pesto, soups and salads and are particularly compatible with tomatoes. Many additional forms, such as lemon, cinnamon and spicy are interesting to use.

Sweet Marjoram – *Origanum Majorana*. Sweet marjoram, although a tender perennial, is treated as an annual in Washington gardens. Leaves can be cut when the plants are four inches high but flavor is best when the flower buds appear. Marjoram is used to flavor stews and various kinds of sausage. Combined with fruit juice it is used to make an herb jelly.

Biennials

Angelica – *Angelica Archangelica*. This is a hardy biennial that prefers a moist soil, a cool climate and will grow in some shade. Plants should be set out in early spring. The first year only leaves will be produced; in the second year flowers and seeds will appear. The seeds remain viable for only a short time, so sow them in place immediately to perpetuate the clump. Angelica is used in herbal teas and the stems are candied for use on cakes.

Caraway – *Carum carvi*. Caraway should be sown directly in place in full sun. When seeds appear the following summer they should be harvested when ripe and some should be spread in place to perpetuate the plant. The root is used as a vegetable. The seeds, high in protein and fat, are used on breads, confections, cheeses, vegetables, fish, and in tea.

Parsley – *Petroselinum crispum*. Parsley likes full sun in a rich, deeply cultivated soil. Flower stalks should be cut off when they appear to promote leaf growth. The flat-leaf Italian parsley is best for cooking, the curly-leaf parsley better as a garnish.

Enjoy Your Herbs

There are no set rules about how to use herbs. So creativity is one of the keys to fun and success with these marvelous plants. If you want to learn the flavor of an herb, mix some of the chopped herb with butter or cream cheese and spread it on a cracker. Try making vinegars, jellies, teas, and fragrant mixtures or doing crafts with herbs. Once you start the chances are you will keep on learning and experimenting, and enjoying herbs more and more.

――――

References

Foster, Gertrude B. and Rosemary F. Louden: *Park's Success With Herbs*, George W. Park Seed Co., 1980.
Lowenfeld, Claire and Philippa Back: *The Complete Book of Herbs and Spices*, Little Brown and Company, 1974.
Stuart, Malcolm: *The Encyclopedia of Herbs and Herbalism*, Orbis Publishing Company, 1979.

――――

Sources for Plants

Bittersweet Hill Nurseries, Route 424 and Governors Bridges Road, Davidsonville, MD 21035.
Earthworks, Herb Garden Nursery Company, 923 North Ivy Street, Arlington, VA 22201.
Washington Cathedral Garden Shop, Wisconsin and Massachusetts Avenues, N.W. Washington, DC 20016.

The Gardener's Prayer

O Lord, grant that in some way it may rain every day, say from about midnight until three o'clock in the morning, but, You see, it must be gentle and warm so that it can soak in; grant that at the same time it would not rain on campion, alyssum, helianthemum, lavender, and the others which You in Your infinite wisdom know are drought-living plants – (I will write their names on a little piece of paper if You like) – and grant that the sun may shine the whole day long, but not everywhere (not, for instance, on spiraea, or on gentian, plantain lily, and rhododendron), and not too much; that there be plenty of dew and a little wind, enough worms, no aphids and snails, no mildew, and that once a week liquid manure and guano may fall from heaven. AMEN.

(Note: This gem is reprinted from the winter 1978-79 handbook of the Brooklyn Botanic Garden. The author is the late Karel Capek, the Czech playwright who was famous for his play about robots, "R.U.R.," in the 1920s.)

Techniques for Container Gardening

By Henry E. Allen

Container gardening offers an attractive prospect to gardeners who lack open space. And for those with space it adds flexibility, a range of plant choices, and decorative interest. For the elderly or handicapped it may be more feasible than conventional gardening.

(This article deals with gardening outdoors. For house plants see "How to Grow Plants Indoors.")

Successful container gardening is intensive gardening. It requires daily, at times even hourly attention. The gardener must know the characteristics of containers and soils, be familiar with how plants behave in containers, and keep up with the best cultivars.

Choose the Right Containers

Choose containers that fit the cultural needs of the plants to be grown and suit the decor where they are placed. Suitable containers range from clay pots to terra cotta Venetian and Spanish pots, glazed pots and ceramic ware, and wooden planters and window boxes in various shapes and sizes. Plastic or fiberglass containers are ideal for hanging baskets, wall brackets and window boxes. Some are designed to stack, providing a vertical "wall garden" for small spaces.

Non-porous containers do not have to be watered as often as clay or unglazed terra cotta containers. Plastic pots are useful as liners, cutting down on the frequency of watering and preventing the unsightly buildup of salt deposits like those in clay pots.

Match the containers to the plants you will grow. They should be large enough to allow space for roots, air and water. And pot and soil should be heavy enough to support a fully-grown plant. Small, low-growing plants look best in shallow pots while taller flowers and vegetables look better in larger, deeper pots. For plants that will stay outside during winter, wooden containers provide better insulation for roots and don't crack when the soil freezes. Treat wood containers with a wood preservative that does not contain creosote or pentachlorophenol.

Changing Plants in Window Boxes

Window boxes do not have to be filled with soil. Instead, partly fill them with sphagnum peat moss or shredded bark in which containers can be placed and changed with the season: bulbs and pansies for spring, petunias or marigolds for summer, dwarf chrysanthemums for fall, and herbs or vegetables in their season.

Good drainage is essential. Use containers with holes in the bottom or sides. For patio, balcony or roof gardening set them in saucers or trays to catch water from the drainage holes. Be sure they do not stand long in water. Inadequate drainage can actually drown a plant; standing in water can cause root rot.

Clean containers before using. Those previously used should be scrubbed with detergent and hot water. Porous containers should be soaked for 20 to 30 minutes in a 10 percent solution of Clorox or other bleach. Remember: Cleanliness is a basic for good gardening.

Growing Media Choices

The correct choice of growing media is vital to success. Media range from ordinary garden soil to "soilless" mixes the gardener can buy. Using garden soil can lead to trouble. In a pot it is likely to compact, shutting off air and moisture and impeding root growth. It may contain harmful insect and disease organisms. Soilless mixtures avoid these difficulties and are not expensive. They can be selected or modified to adjust the pH, nutrition and texture for the special need of a particular plant. Some contain no plant food so the gardener must supply it. Available brands include Jiffy-Mix, Nova-Mix, Redi-Earth, Super Soil, Pro-Mix BX and Metro-Mix 200. The last two are prepared specifically for container gardening.

If you want to make your own, here is a good basic mix (for one cubic foot) that is satisfactory for most flowers, vegetables and shrubs:

13 quarts screened sphagnum peat moss

7½ quarts horticultural vermiculite

7½ quarts medium fine perlite

4 tablespoons 5-10-5 or 5-10-10 fertilizer

1 tablespoon powdered superphosphate (0-20-0)

1 tablespoon horticultural limestone

Mix well and moisten. (Dry peat moss repels water and must be damp before using. Hot water works best.) The dampened mix can be stored in a clean plastic bag or trash can. If it dries out before being used, wet it down again.

This formula should have a pH of 6.4 to 6.8. If you are going to grow acid-loving plants, eliminate the lime and use an acid fertilizer. For larger azaleas or rhododendrons, a nitrogen-stabilized or composted fine pine bark can be substituted for half the peat moss. If more weight is needed, substitute coarse builder's sand for half the perlite.

Soils for Year-Round Containers

For plants that stay outside all year, use a soil mix that is rich in organic materials, high in lignins, which are the natural binders in woody tissue, and with an aggregate that will permit water movement yet retain enough moisture for normal plant growth. Vermiculite, which is expanded mica, should not be used in these long-term mixes. Its structure collapses within a few months, causing shrinking and compacting of the soil. Per-

PHOTO BY FISCHER GERANIUMS

Geranium zonals make an impressive display in a container of rough natural wood against a wall of old brick.

lite, which is a volcanic rock that has been expanded by being subjected to very high temperatures, is excellent for all mixes that are not exposed to freezing. It tends to break down and become powdery with alternate freezing and thawing.

A long-term mix should comprise one-third by volume of a good loam topsoil. It provides the trace elements that might otherwise be lacking. Another third should be nitrogen-stabilized or well composted bark. The final third should be composed of aggregate. Coarse builder's sand has been used for this purpose for years. However, if weight is a problem, one of the new light-weight aggregates such as Hadite or Solite can be used. They are derived from shale and do not break down under extreme cold as does perlite.

Choose the composition of nutrients you want, their time of release, and the pH to suit the plants you want to grow. Some slow-release fertilizers release their nutrition only when the soil is warm and damp, and are exhausted in three to four months. Others release food over two years. "Natural" fertilizers vary in providing food. Bonemeal (usually 0-11-0) does not make food available for several months, then releases it slowly for a long time, providing phosphorus and tending to raise soil pH. Others are low in nutrients but continue to release them over a long period of time. Composted animal manures do more for soil texture than for nutrition; they also may foster disease.

If you use large containers place them in their permanent locations before you plant. Place a shard, wire screen or piece of nylon stocking over the drainage holes. Fill the container with mix from a half to two-thirds of its capacity, and press down gently but firmly. Remove the plant from its growing pot or flat, spread out the roots and place it on the soil in your container. If the plant is root bound, cut or pull apart the roots in the lower third to half of the plant so they can be spread out on the soil. Cover them with more soil, filling in no higher than the base of the stem. If you are growing tomatoes or cole crops, they benefit from being planted a bit deeper. Again, gently firm the soil and water with a balanced starter solution high in phosphorus such as Peters' 5-50-17. There should be an inch of space between the rim of the pot and the soil level, two inches in larger containers. A mulch of shredded bark, wood chips or pebbles will help save moisture, keep soil cooler, and, most important for container gardening, prevent soil from splashing onto plants.

If your plants are going to a sunny or windy location, adapt them to that environment gradually by placing them in a shady, calm area for a few days. Watch them closely. If they wilt, water them before you try to place them again in their permanent location.

Don't overcrowd plants. If you put too many in one pot, they will compete with each other for food and water. Visualize each plant as full grown. One 'Scarlet Ruffles' zinnia will fill out a 10-inch pot. Three impatiens will do well in a 12-inch hanging basket. One 'Pixie' tomato will need a 12-inch pot.

In growing vegetables use the high-yielding types like beans, beets, carrots, lettuce, peppers, radishes and some cultivars of tomatoes and summer squash. Most can be seeded directly. To get a jump on the season, however, start them early indoors. (See "Grow Your Own Transplants.")

Continuous Fertilizer Supply

Plants need a steady supply of nutrients. Frequent applications of small amounts of fertilizer are more beneficial than less-frequent applications of larger amounts, much of which will be leached from the soil by frequent waterings.

Fertilizers come in many forms. Choose those that best suit your needs. If you are growing plants principally for foliage, a high nitrogen content such as in Rapid-Gro (23-16-19) is desirable. Flowering and fruiting plants benefit from more phosphorus and potash. However, a balanced fertilizer such as Peters' 20-20-20 is good for virtually all plants.

Start your fertilizing program about three weeks after planting. Use your fertilizer at about one-third the rate recommended for outdoor plants or the rate recommended for indoor plants by the manufacturer. Continue applications at the same rate at about two-week intervals. You may not have to use fertilizers as soon or as often, however, if you add slow-release fertilizers to your soil mix at planting. Let your plants tell you when they are hungry.

Watering is critical to plants in containers. Their roots cannot spread beyond their confines so they depend

PHOTO BY DEREK BROOKS

An apartment balcony garden – seven by 27 feet, nine floors up and south facing – was the setting for this springtime daffodil show. The containers were wrapped in a four-inch foam insulation during the winter to keep the bulb roots from freezing.

upon you for water. As the growing season progresses, and plants mature, you may have to water once a day or more often to prevent checked growth or wilting. Avoid watering in the evening if possible. As dusk comes, food making slows down. The plant has no immediate need to take up water so roots can remain soggy for hours. This is ideal for the growth of fungi and bacteria.

Always check the soil surface before watering. If the plant needs water, flush the container until water runs out the drainage holes. If your pots can be watered from the bottom by filling their saucers, do this until the surface is moist. Then dump out the water remaining in the saucers. If soil has dried to the point where it has pulled away from the side of the pot, submerge the entire pot until the soil fills out again.

If you are going to be away from home,

Common Problems in Container Gardening

Problem	Cause	What To Do
Plants wilt although obtaining enough water	Insufficient drainage and aeration	Use lighter soil mix. Increase number of drainage holes. Use mix with higher percent of organic matter.
Leaf edges die or "burn" turning dry and brittle	High salt content	At regular intervals, leach container by watering until water drains from drainage holes.
Plants spindly, "leggy," and unproductive	Not enough light	Relocate plant to area receiving more light.
	Too much nitrogen	Use a fertilizer with lower nitrogen content and allow water to drain through.
Plants yellowing from bottom, lack vigor, poor color	Too much water	Water less frequently and check for good drainage.
	Not fertile enough	Use fertilizer with higher levels of nutrients.
Plant leaves with spots, dead dried areas, or powdery or rusty areas	Grown at temperature that is too low	Move container to a warmer area
	Low phosphate level	Increase phosphate in base solution used for fertilizing
Leaves with small holes or that are distorted in shape	Insect damage	Use insecticides suited to the type of insect causing the problem.
Plant leaves with spots, dead dried areas, or powdery or rusty areas	Plant diseases	Remove diseased portion of plant and use fungicide. If problem is severe, discard entire plant.

How Much Will It Take?

One cubic foot of soilless mix will fill the following pots:

Size and Type	Number
3" standard	100 - 115
6" standard	15 - 18
4½" geranium	30 - 40
4" azalea	50 - 60
6" azalea	15 - 18
8" azalea	6 - 7
8" hanging	9 - 10
10" hanging	5 - 6
1 gallon	11
2 gallon	5
5 gallon	2

even for a day, it may be wise to arrange for a plant sitter to check your plants and water them when necessary.

Removing spent blossoms encourages plants to continue blooming. Some such as pansies and petunias benefit from pruning if they get "leggy" or if they spread out of bounds. Remove all dead or yellowing leaves. This not only improves appearance but may ward off disease. Inspect your plants regularly for any sign of harmful insects. Some pests, such as aphids or spider mites, can be washed off with a strong stream of water.

Check for Pest Damage

For any suspected pest damage be sure you know what you are dealing with. Your Cooperative Extension Service often can help. When you know your target, go after the specific problems. One advantage of container gardening is that affected plants can be isolated while being treated.

Trees and shrubs in containers benefit from periodic root pruning and rejuvenating of the soil. Late fall is a good time for this. Turn and aerate the soil well without damaging roots. Add slow-acting renewal substances such as well-rotted compost, leafmold or ComPro. (ComPro is alkaline and will raise your pH.) In spring, when the soil is not too wet, cultivate again and add a balanced slow-release fertilizer. If the root system is too heavy, this is a good time to cut away any dead or diseased roots or any encircling the root ball. Replace part of the soil mix into which new roots can grow.

A whole new field is developing in container gardening. New soil mixtures, fertilizers, containers, and plants adapted to container growing are being introduced. If you've never gardened in containers, try it. You'll be delighted with the results.

_____

References

MacCaskey, Michael: *Award-Winning Small Space Gardens*, Ortho Books, 1979.
Taloumis, George: *Container Gardening Outdoors*, Simon & Schuster, 1972.
Ortho editorial staff (project editor, Ken Burke): *Gardening in Containers*, revised edition, Ortho Books, 1985.
Yang, Linda: *Terrace Gardener's Handbook*, Timber, 1982.

Paint That Wound?

For many years we have been told to seal that cut when you remove a branch from a tree. Research in forestry in New England shows that sealing with pruning paint or whatever is/not needed and may even be harmful. It is more important to make the cut correctly – that is, cut smoothly and close to the trunk or branch but without damaging the collar of tissue around the area where the pruned branch grew out. Be sure the tree is in good health. It will heal itself naturally.

Roses are a different story. Most rosarians recommend that you seal a cut of a branch, say a half-inch or larger, with something like Elmer's glue or orange shellac. This will reduce dessication and, more importantly, prevent the entry of boring insects such as sawflies that will ream out the cane. If you think sealing is too much of a chore, you can deter borers by using a systemic insecticide and live with any dessication.

– **Charles A.H. Thomson.**

Patio and Balcony Gardening

By Wallace F. Janssen

A lot of gardening can be done around a patio. Some people can do a lot on an apartment balcony – or on a roof. One of our Club members even had a flower garden in a closet under fluorescent lights.

Patios offer opportunities to garden in raised beds or containers. A balcony or roof garden calls for containers. (See "Techniques for Container Gardening.")

Patio and balcony gardening is like any other gardening in many ways but in some ways it's different. There are special do's and don'ts. If you don't want mud washing over your patio every time it rains, the beds should be enclosed and preferably raised a little for good drainage. Containers also must have a way of getting rid of excess water through drainage holes and saucers. Landscape timbers, stones and brick are good for curbing.

Mulching is important for mud control and to keep soil from splashing up on leaves and flowers. Shredded pine bark is good looking with an attractive color and texture. And pebbles can do what mulches do: add interest to your "decor." Good soil preparation is a must. Commercial mixes are preferable to amended garden soil. Money spent for plants is wasted if growing conditions are not favorable.

Weed Control Important

Success in patio and balcony gardening calls for three things: (1) plant selection, (2) artistic arrangement, and (3) excellent care. The last is critical. A big garden can put up with a few weeds, but not patio or balcony gardens. With less to care for, you can do it better. A look of perfection is what you want in these special settings.

Plan your patio from inside your house: the way your outside living room will look as an extension of your inside living room. Think of it as a theater stage with your plants as the performers. Also you have an opportunity here for creative lighting that can give you spectacular results.

Your arrangement or design can be achieved in many ways. It requires consideration of such factors as location and exposure – will it have morning or afternoon sun? – and the kinds of plants that are suitable. Your garden can be arranged to display a plant collection or planned for particular plants – a rose collection, for example. You can go for a lush, tropical effect or a trim, formal look. Avoid crowding your plants. This is a special temptation in the small garden that it is worthwhile to resist. Allow for growth and room to care for anything you plant.

Plants Can Be Moved Around

Plants in clay pots around a patio can be sunk in beds and moved easily to new locations as desired. Be sure, of course, that your portable plants are in pots the right size and are kept watered. Glazes or plastic pots will not dry out as fast as clay pots but are not as suitable for sinking in beds because they will not transmit moisture from the surrounding soil. Wood tubs are good to make large plants portable.

Many patios and balcony or roof gardens offer protected locations and favorable micro-climates – warm walls is one reason – so you may be able to grow tuberous begonias, gloxinias, hibiscus, oleander, camellias or lantana. The

PHOTO BY GEORGE TALOUMIS

This patio garden reflects one requirement for success: "excellent care." The author observes that with a smaller garden to care for, "you can do it better." This one features azaleas, rhododendrons and pieris with vinca as a ground cover.

Japanese art of bonsai is a promising hobby for the small garden.

Avoid large, fast-growing shrubs like forsythia. And you will not want vigorous ground covers like ivy or pachysandra which take over from other plants, although there are always exceptions. Do plant small azaleas and rhododendrons and boxwoods, which are slow growing. Avoid fast-growing annuals and perennials that take up a lot of space. Instead, grow dwarf cultivars. And look for unusual plants.

Trees? Yes, with care in selection and location. One dogwood or one dwarf pear or apple is enough. A sour cherry can be rewarding (in pies and preserves) until it gets too big, say in five years.

Growing Vegetables

Is it worthwhile to grow vegetables? Yes, if you have enough sunlight. Flowers and vegetables can be mixed with handsome results. In fact, you can make it all vegetables and get worthwhile production from a space as small as 20 by 20 feet, or in a battery of containers. Many vegetables and herbs are worth growing.

At the top of the list are lettuce, radishes, onions and cucumbers (on a trellis) and herbs such as chives, parsley, oregano and basil. Peppers make interesting background or specimen plants.

Be sure to try the dwarf tomatoes. Among the best are 'Patio,' a medium-sized tomato of excellent flavor; 'Pixie Hybrid II,' smaller than 'Patio' but larger than the cherry types, and 'Small Fry,' one of the best cherry tomatoes with good resistance to disease.

The small garden is ideal for the plant hobbyist. You can go in for miniature roses, herbs, espaliered fruits or ornamental vegetables. Some may like a "miscellaneous" garden but this calls for caution. Usually the best results are achieved by specializing. The really impressive miniature garden has a planned look or theme. The plan you draft, incidentally, controls the amount of work your garden will need. You can plan for little maintenance or for hours of rewarding recreation every day.

Seasonal plantings will keep your garden blooming 10 months or more of the year. Around Washington spring bulbs start showing in February and fall-blooming Sasanqua camellias are beautiful until December. (Incidentally, now that recent hard winters have made the conventional growing of camellias chancy, a gardener who can control the climate may be able to enjoy these choice plants.) In between, three crops of flowers are standard procedure, starting with bulbs and hardy perennials and annuals, going to tender ones, and ending with chrysanthemums and fall-blooming bulbs.

Climate and Balcony Gardening

The balcony gardener must give special consideration to climate. Does your apartment face north, south, east or west? This affects your choice of plants. Protection from wind may be a factor. And on some balconies weight must be considered. Plants are heavy.

Given a north exposure, potted dwarf azaleas and rhododendrons do well. Several varieties of ferns, including the maidenhair, also like the climate and can

stay outdoors in their pots the year round. So also do clumps of lily of the valley and several evergreen bonsai. When winter cold comes on, the balcony garden can be protected from drying and chilling winds by attaching heavy plastic sheeting to the railing so its bottom is over the balcony floor, held in place by the pots. Plants left outside are watered sparingly. Snow is no problem, and ferns are dormant and the junipers like it. Tender plants are brought inside or discarded.

Sun-loving Plants

For a south-facing balcony, sun-loving plants of all sorts are obvious choices, not forgetting vegetables and herbs. You can try starting these inside from seed. (See "Grow Your Own Transplants.") Some kind of shade may be needed to reduce extreme light or heat. One choice could be roll-up wood-slat shades. Also, morning glories or other vines can be grown for both shade and flowers on wires or cords.

But remember, just because you like a plant is no reason to suppose that it will like your balcony. And if you are going away, don't forget to arrange for a plant sitter to do the daily watering.

You can say this about patio and balcony gardening: a small space can pay big dividends. Good gardening!

References

Grasby, Nancy: *Imaginative Small Gardens*, Hearthside Press, New York.

Brookes, John: *The Garden Book*, Crown Publishers, New York, 1984.

Do's and Don'ts

DO bring your house plants inside, after being outside during the summer, when night-time temperatures begin dropping into the low 50s.

DO buy flowering plants during the blooming season. Then you won't be disappointed if the flowers are not to your liking.

DO buy good garden tools. The cheap ones end up being expensive.

How to Grow Plants Indoors

By Pamela Marshall

The secret of growing beautiful indoor plants is to select the right plant for the environment. If you have a room with bright diffused light, high relative humidity and good air circulation – and if you pot your plants in soil with good drainage and water them properly – your plants can be the envy of the neighborhood.

Unfortunately, most of us do not have the best growing condition in our homes. We grow plants under circumstances that are less than favorable. These plants are under stress – and we become stress managers. To reduce the stress we must know what a plant needs to grow.

Light. Light is usually the most limiting factor in growing plants indoors. There are three things to consider: intensity, duration, and quality.

Intensity refers to the relative amount of light. In an open field on a clear day in July you can measure between 10,000 and 15,000 foot-candles of light in the Washington area. In the center of a room the same day you can find the light intensity as low as 50 foot-candles.

North windows get less light than other exposures and are cool. East and west windows get about the same amount; east windows are cooler than west windows. South windows get the greatest amount of light and are hot. As a rule of thumb, a plant growing in a north window, or more than eight feet from an east, west, or south window, is in low light. Four to eight feet from an east, west or south window is medium light. Less than four feet is high light. Light in a room can be reduced by drapes, blinds, tinted glass, shade trees outside, and cloudy days. In winter, with the sun at a lower angle and days that are shorter, light intensities decrease.

If you increase the duration of the lighted period you compensate to a degree for low intensity. Placing your plants under a reading lamp for three or four hours in the evening helps.

Quality refers to the wave-length of light received by a plant. Natural sunlight contains all wave-lengths used by plants and is the best and cheapest source. Artificial light may be deficient in the blue, red or far red wave-lengths.

Incandescent light bulbs are rich in the red and far red areas and poor in the blue. Fluorescent light is high in blue and low in red and far red. The special horticultural fluorescent lights of today are designed to provide both red and blue light. Deluxe "cool white" fluorescent tubes are best for foliage plants. Wide-spectrum "warm white" tubes are better for flowering plants. Grow your plants close to lights – eight to 24 inches.

Water. A plant usually will need more water the higher the light, temperature and air circulation and the lower the humidity. A plant with a lot of leaves growing in a small pot needs more watering than one with few leaves in a large pot.

For most plants it is time to water when the surface of the soil is dry to the touch. In a six-inch standard pot the top inch of the soil should be dry. In a larger pot the soil should be allowed to dry deeper. In a shallow pot (a bulb pan) the top half-inch of the soil should be dry.

The most common way to water a plant is from above. Apply the water at room temperature. Try to avoid getting any in the crown of the plant. Water on leaves or in the leaf stem and crown for long periods increases the chance of disease.

Use enough water so some runs out the bottom. Water equal to 10 percent of the volume of the pot should drain out; for a six-inch pot that holds 10 cups of water that means one cup should drain out. This drainage helps to prevent the buildup of soluble salts that can injure the roots. When a plant is weakened it is more susceptible to attacks from insects and disease. Leach the plant every four to six months. You leach a plant by pouring water on the soil – equal to twice the volume of the pot – and letting it drain completely.

Relative Humidity. Plants prefer a relative humidity of between 50 and 75 percent. Plants with small leaves generally need a higher humidity than those with thick, waxy leaves. Some plants such as ferns need a higher humidity than most others.

One way to increase humidity is to use a pebble tray, filling a saucer at least as wide as the plant with pebbles. Water is added to just below the top of the pebbles. The pot sits on the pebbles, not the water. Evaporation increases the humidity around the plant.

Temperature. Most indoor plants will grow in temperatures from 50° to 80°F. Some like African violets prefer the warmer side. Many flowering plants like cyclamen prefer the cooler side. No plant likes to be blasted with cold air or have its tender leaves touch a cold window pane. At the same time, high temperatures can be just as damaging. Direct sunlight can burn leaves and the problem is intensified if the plant is under stress from other sources.

Potting Soil or Media. A well-drained potting medium is vital to the health of a plant. Many commercial potting soils are too heavy and need to be lightened with peat moss, sand, or perlite. Many mixes hold nutrients and water while providing air for roots to breathe. One standard mix calls for equal parts of peat moss, heavy potting soil, and perlite. For each four quarts of mix, add one level teaspoon of dolomitic limestone and one of 5-10-5 fertilizer.

Fertilizing. Plants grow best if they get a constant source of nutrients. You can achieve this by giving them a small amount of fertilizer from time to time. Indoor plants like a balanced fertilizer. Plants in high light use more than those in low light. The numbers on the label such as 5-10-5 refer to nitrogen, phosphorus and potassium. For flowering plants pick a fertilizer where the first and third numbers are about equal, although the third, potassium, may be higher than the first, nitrogen.

Plants with leaves turning yellow between the veins on the older leaves may need magnesium. You can provide this by adding Epsom salts to the watering, one teaspoon per gallon. Once a year use a fertilizer that includes micro-nutrients such as iron, zinc, magnesium, copper, molybdenum and boron. Do not overfertilize. Your plants can become leggy and soluble salts can build up.

Repotting. It is time to repot when the soil breaks down or the plant becomes root bound. Sanitation is important. Be sure the pots are clean and use a fresh, clean, moist soil mix. Do not shift to a pot that is a lot bigger – more than an inch in diameter for plants in pots less than six inches, or more than two inches for plants in larger pots.

Water the plant the day before repotting. Take it out of the old pot, carefully pulling any circular growing roots out to their full length. A sterilized fork will help with this and with breaking up the edge of the root ball. Trim off the roots so they do not extend beyond the ball. If there are signs of high soluble salts, soil insects or root disease, remove as much of the old soil as possible without injuring the roots.

Cover any large drainage hole in the new pot with a shard, a piece of broken pot, or a layer of gravel. Place enough moist potting soil in the bottom so the original soil ball will be from a half-inch to an inch and a half from the top of the pot. Fill in around the sides with the moist potting soil. You want this to be firmly in

---

**Common Problems
of Indoor Plants**

**Over-watering
Not enough light
Poor soil
Insects
Disease
Highly soluble salts
Root-bound plant
Improper repotting
Low humidity
Temperature stress**

---

place but not compacted tightly. Loose soil is better as long as there are no large air holes. When you finish, the plant should be at the same level as before, never deeper. Water it. If it sinks, repot it.

Pruning, Pinching, Training. Plants may need to be pruned, pinched or trained to maintain their shape or form. Pinching means removing the growing tip of the stem. Pruning is more severe and means removing a section of a stem. For this use a sharp, sterile knife. Plants respond to pruning and pinching in different ways. Bushy plants such as coleus are pruned to encourage branching and side growth but branching is discouraged in African violets. On a palm the growing point is at the tip of the stem; if you prune that you will kill the plant.

You encourage branching when you prune or pinch above a node, the point where a leaf joins the stem. Many plants have a tiny bud just above the node. Be careful not to remove it.

Dust. Plants should be washed occasionally to remove the dust buildup on the leaves that lowers the light level and is unattractive. Most plants can be washed with a mild solution of soapy water at or slightly above room temperature. A soft paint brush can be used to dust off hairy-leaved plants.

Insects. Do your best not to bring infested plants into your home. Wash all new plants with soapy water and isolate them for a month. Watch any plant for

signs of insects. Fungus gnats, which look like fruit flies, often indicate that the soil has been kept too wet. Aphids and spider mites can be controlled, if found early enough, by repeated washing with soapy water. Scale and mealybugs, if caught in the early stages of infestation, may be removed with a cotton swab dipped in alcohol. If these methods fail you may have to resort to pesticides. Be sure that you use only the pesticide approved for your plant and for the pest you have identified. Follow label instructions.

Disease. Buy healthy plants and make every effort to keep them healthy. Remember that plants growing under stress are more susceptible to disease. Water sitting on the leaves or leaf stems, in the center of the plant, or on top of the soil promotes disease. Plants that are watered too much or fertilized too much or are potted in poor soil also are candidates for disease.

Recommended Plants
for Low Light Areas

Snake Plant, Mother-in-law's Tongue – *Sansevieria trifasciata.*
Gold-banded Sansevieria – *S. trifasciata* 'Laurentii.'
Bird's-nest Sansevieria – *S. trifasciata* 'Hahnii.'
Comments: Don't over-water sansevierias or let water stand in the center of the plant. Will tolerate heat, drafts and low humidity.
Spathe Flower, Peace Lily – *Spathiphyllum* species.
Comments: Will also bloom in medium to high light levels. Must have good drainage. Sizes range from 1 to 2 feet.
Commutatum – *Aglaonema commutatum.*
Pewter Plant – *A. crispum.*
Chinese Evergreen 'Silver King' – *A. modestum* 'Silver King.'
Comments: Exudation from leaf tips may occur, especially in *A. modestum.* Cuttings will survive for a long time in water. Will tolerate low humidity. Other aglaonemas also are available including new patented cultivars.
Barroom Plant, Cast-iron Plant – *Aspidistra elatior.*
Comments: Withstands dry air, drafts, prefers humidity and higher light. Sensitive to fluoride. May develop leaf spots.

Signs of Stress in Indoor Plants and Possible Causes

Reduced growth	Extremes in temperature, light, water, or pH, root injury, insects or disease
Wilted plant	Over-watering, lack of water, high temperature with low relative humidity, high salts, heavy soil, injured roots, root mealybug
General yellowing over entire plant	Extremes in temperature or light, sudden environmental change, transplant shock, root rot, root mealybug, scale, whitefly
Bottom leaves yellow, may drop off	Low light, over-watering, chronic under-watering, nitrogen or potassium deficiency, heavy soil, high salts, root injury, old leaves, spider mites, whitefly
Dead leaf tips and/or edges	Low humidity, high temperature and low humidity, over- or under-watering, strong air movement, cold drafts, fluoride injury, root injury, spider mites
Dead spots within leaf	Cold water injury, sun scorch, disease
Yellowing between veins	Magnesium deficiency (lower or middle leaves), iron or other micro-nutrient deficiency (top leaves), virus, insects, disease
Sticky leaves	Scale, mealybug, whitefly, aphids (honeydew produced by sucking insects)
Mushy spots in leaves or on leaf edges	Sudden cold or freezing, very cold water, early sign of high-temperature injury during shipping, bacterial rots
Waxy cottony masses on leaves or stems	Mealybug
Mottled leaves (especially older leaves, with or without webs)	Spider mites (webs), scale, whitefly, mealybug (no webs)
New growth small or mis-shapen	Aphids, extremes in temperatures or pH, herbicide damage, micro-nutrient deficiency, broad mite, gas injury
Cupped or mis-shaped leaves	High light with low humidity, rapid changes in moisture, sudden changes during leaf development, micro-nutrient deficiency, herbicide damage, cyclaman mite, insects
Insect like fruit fly flying around plant	Fungus gnat
Stem rot or breakdown	Repeated use of cold water in poorly-drained soil, poor drainage, plant potted too deep, injury to stem, fertilizer placed on or near stem, high salts.
Weak, thin stems	Low light, high temperatures, excessive fertilizer
Roots very shallow	Soil kept too wet, drip plate not emptied, poorly aerated soil, compacted soil
Roots slow to develop	High or low temperatures, over-watering, high salts, poor soil structure, poorly aerated soil, compacted soil
Root rots	Soil kept too wet, high salts, poor soil aerations, root insects, disease
White cottony masses in soil	Root mealybugs

Pest Control in Your Landscape

By Stanton A. Gill

Protecting the garden and landscape from devastating insects and diseases is a concern of most Washington area gardeners. Instead of using routine blanket cover applications of pesticides to protect valuable plants in your landscape, you might try the Integrated Pest Management approach.

This combines key strategies: i.e. selecting pest-resistant landscape materials, being aware of predator and parasite activity, and integrating natural, biological, mechanical and selective chemical controls to maintain the beauty of your landscape and the health and quality of your fruits and vegetables.

Integrated Pest Management (IPM) puts responsibility on the home gardener. Instead of automatically reaching for the sprayer, gardeners must educate themselves about plants and pests so damage can be prevented whenever possible. Then, if an outbreak does occur, only the most selective control tactics should be used. With the Integrated Pest Management approach, pesticides are not totally foregone, but they are used only as a last resort rather than a first action. Those pesticides that are used are as specific as possible to the pest and least harmful to beneficial insects and the home environment.

One of the simplest and most effective steps you can take in avoiding or reducing pest damage is to select landscape plants that have natural built-in resistance.

Through time and evolution, some plants have produced natural chemical and physical barriers to harmful insects and diseases. These plants have developed a natural repellency which makes them unpalatable or indigestible to insects. Some species or cultivars are especially high in these natural defenses, often much higher than closely related species.

Azaleas and Rhododendrons

Years of monitoring in suburban communities where IPM has operated have shown that azalea lacebug is one of the most common insect pests in the Washington area. Lacebugs are small sucking insects found on the underside of the leaves. Foliage damaged by lacebugs does not manufacture a plant's food efficiently.

Heavily infested plants are usually located in full sun, beside driveways in sun, or in open exposed areas. It often is found that where one variety of azalea is grown in full sun and the same variety is grown in shade, the lacebug population tends to be lower and feeding damage less in the shade.

Rhododendrons are more susceptible to *Phytophthora* root rot than most other woody ornamentals grown on the east coast. Rhododendrons may develop this rot in our heavy clay soils. They will show wilting of new growth, and eventually all leaves will droop. By the time foliage symptoms develop, a reddish-brown stem discoloration may be evident at just below the soil line.

The IPM approach to control *Phytophthora* problems is to plant resistant varieties in well-drained soil. In a University of North Carolina study, 336 hybrids and 198 species of rhododendron were tested for resistance to root rot. The most resistant hybrids were: 'Martha Isaacson,' 'Caroline,' 'Professor Hugo de Vries,' and 'Red Head.' 'English Roseum' was moderately resistant.

A common evergreen shrub used in the

Metropolitan area is the Japanese euonymus *(Euonymus japonica)*. This is a tough little shrub that grows well in poor soil. Unfortunately, Japanese euonymus is often damaged by the feeding activity of the euonymus scale. This insect slowly kills the plant over three to four years. It can be controlled with repeated insecticide treatments but the problem will recur and will have to be dealt with throughout the life of the plant. You can use natural plant resistance by planting *Euonymus Sieboldiana* rather than *Euonymus japonica. E. Sieboldiana* is a little larger shrub but its resistance to insect damage makes it a good selection. It can be kept in bounds by pruning.

Looking toward the future, a successful attack on euonymus scale has been made by USDA's Agricultural Research Service. ARS has introduced two beetles from South Korea – *Chelocorus kuwanae* and *Cybocephalus nipponicus* – to fight the scale. And it has disappeared from infested plants where they've become established. This research, however, is not yet available to the home gardener.

Crabapples

Crabapples *(Malus)* are popular landscape trees, grown for their profusion of flowers in spring followed by ornamental fruits, which are attractive to birds. All too often you will see crabapples losing 20 to 60 percent of their foliage by July. Close examination will reveal olive-green spots on the foliage and the fruit. This is from infection by the apple scab fungus. To prevent this fungus from devastating the beauty of susceptible flowering trees, three to five chemical fungicide applications are needed early in the spring.

There are crabapple varieties that have natural resistance to this disease. Why not replace disease-susceptible crabapples with disease-resistant ones? The following varieties of crabapple are recommended for the Washington metropolitan area because they are resistant to apple scab, fireblight, mildew and rust.

'Sargentii' – a small crabapple eight feet in height and with a 12 foot spread that is low and spreading in shape. White flowers and red quarter-inch persistent fruit.

'Adams' – medium-sized crabapple 20 feet in height and a 20 foot spread with dense rounded growth habit; flowers are pink and it has five-eighths inch persistent fruit.

'Donald Wyman' – size and shape is similar to 'Adams' but the flowers are white and the fruit is small, only three-eighths inch and persistent.

'Baskatong' – larger crabapple that reaches 25 feet in height and a 25-foot spread. This tree has arching branches, a reddish flower and red-purple fruits.

Other crabapple varieties with good disease resistance are: 'Floribunda,' 'Liset,' 'Robinson,' 'Veitchii,' 'Zumi var. Calocarpa,' 'Pink Spirea,' and 'Beverly.'

Hawthorns

Hawthorns *(Crataegus)* are another popular plant in the landscape. Selecting the wrong hawthorn may mean repeated spraying to keep it healthy. A common disease, rust, causes peculiar round leaf galls, twig galls, cankers and dieback of branches. To avoid seasonal spraying of fungicides, put only rust-resistant varieties in the landscape.

A rust resistant hawthorn is 'Cockspur Thorn' – *Crataegus crus-galli*. Highly rust susceptible hawthorns to avoid are:

'Downy' – *Crataegus mollis*
'Lavalle' – *Crataegus* x *Lavallei*
'Winter King' – *Crataegus viridis*

Here is a list of other plant materials that have good insect and disease resistance:

Trees
Gingko – *Ginkgo biloba*
Atlas Cedar – *Cedrus atlantica*
Stewartia – *Stewartia pseudocamellia*
Cedar of Lebanon – *Cedrus libani*
Sourwood – *Oxydendrum arboreum*
Golden-rain tree – *Koelreuteria paniculata*
Shrubs
Wintergreen Barberry – *Berberis Julianae*
Winged Euonymus – *Euonymus alatus*
Fragrant Sarcococca – *Sarcococca ruscifolia*
Viburnum varieties (deciduous)

Controlling Insects

While insects can cause damage and spread disease, certain diseases can be used to control insects and certain beneficial insects are widely used to control other insects.

Two well-known and easily available bacterial insecticides are *Bacillus thuringiensis* (BT), sold as Dipel, Thuricide or Biotrol, and *Bacillus popillae* that causes milky spore disease of Japanese beetle grubs. These bacteria are harmless to humans and are specific in killing insects while not affecting desirable predators and parasites.

BT is effective against many caterpillars, including bagworms, tent caterpillars, gypsy moth larvae, oak caterpillars and cabbage caterpillars, if it is used when the caterpillars are in an early stage of development.

When a feeding caterpillar ingests the bacterium, its crystal ruptures the insect's intestine. Caterpillars stop feeding one or two days later and die within a week.

BT is now being improved; a cleaner product with longer effectiveness is now on the market. The San Diego strain, marketed as M-1, is effective against the larvae of the Colorado potato beetle and the elm leaf beetle, a defoliator of shade trees.

Bacillus popillae, responsible for milky spore disease, affects only Japanese beetle grubs. It has no effect on the mature beetles. Unfortunately for the individual homeowner, it is expensive and should be spread on a community-wide basis. Moreover, it takes several years to build up to its full insecticidal potential in the soil.

So the gardener must resort to timely means to control current infestations. These range from hand picking of the adults and winter cultivation of beds to expose larvae, to the use of traps (sometimes attracting more beetles than are caught). As a last resort the gardener might use a chemical insecticide, paying careful attention to the time of application (so as not to kill bees or other beneficial insects), time of biodegradation (if used on vegetables), and label instructions.

Insects versus insects have been used for a long time, and there is intensive research to discover new ones and how best to use them. Lady-beetles versus aphids is the classic case. Preying mantis are an example of a wide-spectrum insect killer, with tastes ranging from other mantis to bumble bees. Syrphid flies and trichogramma wasps, although hard to see, are constantly at work controlling noxious insects, and the gardener must be careful in using IPM to understand how they work and how not to destroy them.

In recent years several insect predators have been introduced into areas of Rockville and Gaithersburg, gaining moderate success in suppressing gypsy moth caterpillars and mature Japanese beetles. Survivability of the predators has been a problem; efforts are now proceeding to find those that will survive better in our climate. However, these predators alone probably will not be able to control these pests, and other methods must be deployed.

Mechanical methods can be used, but timing is vital. To control the gypsy moth caterpillar attacks on especially valuable trees, the gardener in late April can place sticky bands, such as Repellum II around the trunk. These bands will capture the small caterpillars as they try to ascend the trees to feed. Then in May, he can put a skirt of burlap around an affected tree, monitor it frequently and kill any caterpillars so intercepted. If they are not killed, the burlap can protect them from predators. In July and August, after eggs have been laid in their fuzzy masses, the gardener should scrape off any he finds and drop them into alcohol.

None of these methods is effective against a mass infestation. Intervention on a community-wide basis is called for.

Last Resort

When Integrated Pest Management is used, a chemical pesticide is only introduced when insect populations have reached an intolerable level, exceeding aesthetic or economic thresholds. Before resorting to chemicals, keep in mind that the natural enemies of a pest need a little

What You Should Know About the Gypsy Moth

"There is no practical way to eradicate the gypsy moth." These grim words are from Dr. John A. Davidson, entomologist at the University of Maryland (Fact Sheet 242, Cooperative Extension Service). In its caterpillar stage, the gypsy moth is a threat to oak trees in the eastern half of the United States. It is now found throughout Maryland, in the northern counties of Virginia, and as far south as North Carolina.

There are control measures, however, aimed at holding down the pest population to a manageable level and saving the trees. Outlined here are the four stages of the gypsy moth life cycle in terms of our calendar, showing its periods of vulnerability.

GYPSY MOTH LIFE CYCLE

January, February, March. Stage One, the egg masses: Laid the previous June and July, the egg masses have been around since August. They are tan or brown colored, about the size of a 50-cent coin, each containing 500 or more tiny eggs. They are found in trees or sheltered places around houses – under gutters and window sills and on fences. Destroy them whenever possible. Scrape the masses into a container and soak them in ammonia or kerosene for 15 minutes.

April, May. Stage Two, the caterpillars: The eggs begin hatching as it warms up after April 1, releasing hundreds of tiny caterpillars that crawl to the treetops to feed. As they grow, the larger caterpillars come down to hide during the day and then, at dusk, to climb back up and feed all night. Apply a sticky barrier tape on the tree bark. Above it, band the tree with burlap, 12 inches wide, tied around the tree and folded over. Caterpillars, descending, will not cross the sticky barrier and start to climb again, only to find a hiding place under the burlap fold. Here is an onerous task: It is essential that someone inspect the burlap daily, picking the caterpillars and dropping them into soapy water or detergent to kill them.

June. Stage Three, the pupa "cocoon": The mature caterpillars are now about two inches long. From late June through July they seek a sheltered place to change into the pupal stage, shedding their skins to become an inch long, smooth, dark brown and motionless. The only effective control here is to pick them off by hand and soak them in ammonia or kerosene.

July. Stage Four, the adult moths: They appear in July. Females are white and cannot fly. Males are tan to brown and will fly miles, lured by a sex attractant called pheromone, to find a female.

August. Stage One again: The females lay their eggs in sheltered places near where they emerged from their pupal stage. Pheromone traps to trap males, preventing them from fertilizing female eggs, have not proved effective.

September, October, November, December. Continue looking for egg masses and destroying them. Keep a record of the number you destroy for official monitoring. You have a long time for this – until April 1.

CONTROLS

State and county spray programs are based on special criteria: To be eligible for spraying, an area must be at least 25 acres in size with a tree canopy of 50 percent and 50 percent of that in oak. There must be at least 250 egg masses per acre by actual count.

The best time to spray is in May. The bacterial insecticide, *Bacillus thuringiensis* (BT) is a favorite of home owners because it is non-toxic, but it must be used early in the life cycle to be effective. Dimilin *(diflubenzuron)* is a growth regulator that disrupts the life cycle enough to keep the pest from reaching maturity; it is generally non-toxic. Sevin *(carbaryl)* is very effective but highly toxic to bees.

Spraying, whether state, county or private, is carried out in early morning before most people are up and about and before the caterpillars have climbed down to seek shade for the day.

For additional information about control of the gypsy moth, call your local extension service.

– Robert E. Melville

time to catch up as the pest population increases. If a pest is reaching unacceptable levels, however, the gardener should use a control that does the least harm to its predators. Choose the chemical that is the most species-specific and the most rapidly bio-degradable. Your local Cooperative Extension Service is a good source for this information.

Timing is also important in controlling bagworms. The control must be applied when the worms are outside their protective bags. A new synthetic pyrethroid, Maverick, is so irritating to the worms that when applied in early August, they emerge from their bags. This timing is important because the worst defoliation occurs at this time. Once the worms are safe in their bags for the winter, the gardener must hand-pick those he can reach.

Safer Insecticides

Dormant and summer oil sprays: Oil sprays are effective in suffocating scales, mites, and aphids. Oils have been with us for years but in 1983 a newly-refined oil came on the market that can be used when plants are in full leaf, and not cause foliar burn *if used at recommended rates and times*. These summer application rates are very effective on aphids and spider mites. For scale insects, the oils are only effective when applied in early spring (before leafing) at the dormant rate. Oils act as an ovicide, smothering eggs. Timing is critical, especially in summer when the oil can evaporate in 48 hours.

Soaps: The utility of soap sprays for insect control was demonstrated as early as 1842. As the more effective synthetic organic insecticides were developed, research on soap as an insecticide was largely discontinued. In the last 10 years there has been a renewed interest in soaps as a safe control of some insects.

The fatty acids in the soap kill the insects by disrupting their metabolism. A special blend of fatty acids, very toxic to many pests but harmless to most other organisms, is Safer AgroChem Insecticidal Soap. Another insecticidal soap found on the market is Bio-Soap.

Soaps can be used on indoor plants, and outdoors to manage aphids, psyllids, thrips, and spider mites. While insecticidal soaps that are labelled will suppress pest populations they hit directly, they have no residual effectiveness. Repeated applications are needed if the pests persist. If used in higher concentrations than recommended, foliage burn may result. So pre-test the pesticide first on an inconspicuous part of the plant, observe results for four or five days, and adjust concentration accordingly.

Horticultural Oils: Horticultural oils are most effective against small, soft bodied, sucking pests such as spider mites, aphids, mealybug, scale insects, whiteflies and psyllids. These sprays have a minimal effect on the predators and parasites of pests. Some caterpillars and plant bugs can also be controlled if they receive adequate contact with the spray. Dormant season sprays in late winter (March through early April) kill overwintering eggs and inactive forms. Summer sprays kill actively feeding forms and eggs. Many homeowners would benefit from the use of summer rate oil sprays to control serious spider mite problems on susceptible landscape plant material.

Books

Carr, Anna: *Rodale's Color Handbook of Garden Insects*, Emmaus, PA, 1979. Excellent for identification and life cycles.

Kite, L. Patricia: *Controlling Lawn and Garden Insects*, Ortho, San Francisco, 1987. Has a good chapter on "Additional Methods."

Jordan, W.H.: *Windowsill Ecology*, Rodale Press, Emmaus, PA, 1977. A good simple description of how biological control works, with suggestions for biological control on indoor plant pests.

Do's and Don'ts

DON'T use a downward motion when removing snow and ice from shrubs and trees with a broom. Do use an upward motion to avoid adding strain on the branches.

How to Read a Pesticide Label

By William M. Hoffman

So, all your other pest management techniques have failed to control that pest in your garden and you have decided you must use a pesticide to protect that prize bloom, fruit or vegetable you have nurtured so carefully. Nobody likes to use pesticides. Many of them are toxic or harmful but now you believe stern measures are needed to control many unwelcome insects, mites, nematodes, weeds and fungi.

Because pesticides can be dangerous, the federal government has passed laws affecting their use. These laws try to balance the need for pesticides against the need to protect people and the environment from their misuse. In 1972 Congress completely revised the Federal Insecticide Fungicide and Rodenticide Act of 1947 (FIFRA). The new act changed the federal responsibilities from the registration of materials used to control pests to both the registration and the enforcement of rules governing pesticide usage. The latter authority is plainly stated in the words from the act that appear on every pesticide label:

> It is a violation of Federal law to use this product in a manner inconsistent with its labeling.

Such authority thus demands closer scrutiny of the label. This chapter explains the information on a label and how it can help you to use a pesticide safely and correctly.

What a Label Tells You

Each time you buy a pesticide, you receive instructions telling you how to use it. These instructions, called "the labeling," include: the label printed on or attached to the container; and brochures, flyers and any other written information supplied by the manufacturer.

The label means many things: *To the manufacturer*, the label is a "license to sell." *To the state or federal government*, the label is a way to control the distribution, storage, sale, use, and disposal of the product. *To the buyer or user*, the label is the main source of facts on how to use the product correctly and legally. *To the user*, the label gives special precautions needed when using the product.

Some labels are easy to understand. Others are complicated. But all tell you how to use the product correctly.

A Make-Believe Product

This is an exercise to explain what you can learn from the label. I am using a label from a make-believe pesticide, "My-Own Triple-Action Rose and Flower Care." (See illustration on pages 164 and 165). The numbered passages below refer to the sections numbered on the label.

1. Name and Address of Manufacturer

The law requires the maker or distributor of a product to put the name and address of the company on the label. This is so you will know who made or sold the product. If you have a problem with the pesticide, you should contact that company. Some companies buy pesticides in large quantities, and package them for distribution in smaller containers. They are responsible for what they sell.

2. Registration Numbers

A registration number must be on every pesticide label. This number shows that the product has been reviewed by

⑨ → **PRECAUTIONARY STATEMENTS**
Hazards to Humans & Domestic Animals

⑧ → **WARNING:**

May be fatal if swallowed, inhaled or absorbed through the skin. Do not breathe dust. Do not get in eyes, on skin, or on clothing. Wear clean rubber gloves, and freshly laundered protective clothing when handling. Wash thoroughly after handling and before eating or smoking. Use only with adequate ventilation. Remove contaminated clothing and wash before reuse.

⑫ → Environmental Hazard

This product is toxic to wildlife and fish. Use care when applying in areas frequented by wildlife or adjacent to any body of water. Birds and other wildlife feeding on treated areas may be killed. Cover or incorporate granules which are spilled during loading and which are visible on soil surface in turn areas. Keep out of lakes, streams, or ponds.

DIRECTIONS FOR USE
⑬ → GENERAL CLASSIFICATION

It is a violation of federal law to use this product in a manner inconsistent with its labeling.

⑮ → **STORAGE AND DISPOSAL**

Do not contaminate water, food, or feed by storage, disposal, or cleaning of equipment. Do not reuse empty container. Wrap container and put in trash collection.

Guaranteed Fertilizer
Analysis

Total Nitrogen	8.000%
5.6% Ammoniacal Nitrogen	
1.1% Urea Nitrogen	
1.3% Water Insoluble Nitrogen	
Available Phosphoric Acid (P_2O_5)	12.000%
Water Soluble Potash (K_2O)	4.000%
Total Available Primary Plant Food	24.000%
Chlorine, not more than	3.100%
Derived from Urea, Ureaform,	
Ammonium Sulfate, Ammoniated	
Superphosphate, Ammonium	
Phosphate and Muriate of Potash	

Calcium (Ca)	(as CaO—14.0%)	10.000%
Magnesium (Mg)	(as MgO Total-16%,	
	Water Soluble—0.8%)	1.000%
Sulfur (S)	(as SO_3—23.7%)	9.500%
Boron (B)	(as B_2O_3—0.07%)	0.02%
Iron (Fe)	(as Fe_2O_3—0.6%)	0.4%
Manganese (Mn)	(as MnO—0.07%)	0.05%
Molybdenum (Mo)	(as MoO_3—0.0012%	0.0008%
Zinc (Zn)	(as ZnO—0.06%)	0.05%
Derived from Superphosphate Magnesium		
Oxide, Magnesium Sulfate, Ammonium Sulfate,		
Iron Sulfate and Fritted Sources.		

Potential Activity 600 lbs. Calcium Carbonate Equivalent per ton.

MY-OWN ③ TRIPLE ACTION ROSE AND FLOWER CARE

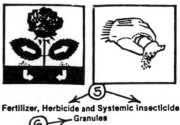

Fertilizer, Herbicide and Systemic Insecticide
⑥ → Granules

④ →

Active Ingredients: By V
*O, O-diethyl S-[2-(ethylthio) ethyl] phosphorodithioate 1.000
trifluralin (a, a, a-trifluoro-2, 6-dinitro-N, N-dipropyl-p-toluidine) 0.174
Inert Ingredients: 98.826
TOTAL: 100

*SECTOFF ← ③

Equivalent 20 lbs. SECTOFF per ton.
Equivalent 3.48 lbs. trifluralin per ton.

KEEP OUT OF REACH OF CHILDREN

⑧ ———→ **WARNING:**

STATEMENT OF PRACTICAL TREATMENT ← ⑩

IF SWALLOWED—Drink 1 or 2 glasses of water and induce vomiting by touching the back of throat. D give anything by mouth to an unconscious victim. Get medical attention.

IF ON SKIN—Wash skin immediately with soap and water. Get medical attention.

IF EYES ARE CONTAMINATED—Wash with plenty of water for at least 15 minutes. Get me attention.

IF INHALED—Remove to fresh air. If not breathing, give artificial respiration, preferably mouth to mouth medical attention.

NEVER GIVE ANYTHING BY MOUTH TO AN UNCONSCIOUS PERSON

NOTE TO PHYSICIAN—SECTOFF is a cholinesterase inhibitor. Atropine is antidotal.

SEE SIDE PANEL FOR ADDITIONAL PRECAUTIONARY STATEMENTS

① → MY-OWN CHEMICAL CO.
1 SHADY LANE
ROSECITY, VERMONT 05732

② → EPA Reg. No. 100250-103
EPA Est. No. 100250-VT-1

Net Weight 5 pounds 4 ounces ← ⑦

This is a make-believe label for a make-believe pesticide to explain what you can learn from a label. The numbered passages in the article refer to the numbered sections on the label. (Number 11 on physical and chemical hazards is not shown on the sample label.) The author, William M. Hoffman, who had a distinguished career in research in fertilizers and pesticides, is deceased. This article is substantially as he wrote it when this book was planned but has been updated in consultation with EPA and University of Maryland personnel.

⑭ ➤ **DIRECTIONS FOR USE**
CONTINUED

WHEN TO USE
Make first application after cultivating and before weed seeds germinate (when roses have about 1" of new growth). Repeat every 6 weeks or 2 to 3 times each season. Do not apply additional fertilizer for 6 weeks following this treatment.

HOW TO USE
Remove all weeds before treating. Cultivate soil around plant. Apply MY-OWN Triple Action Rose and Flower Care evenly at dosages given below. Work granules into top 1 inch of soil. Water thoroughly. Do not apply in planting holes.

1. KILLS SUCKING INSECTS—SECTOFF, a systemic insecticide, is absorbed into the plant through the root system and then moves internally through the sap stream into the branches, leaves and blossoms. Sucking insects that tap the plant's sap stream for food are quickly killed by the insecticide. Protects against insects for at least 6 weeks. It cannot be washed off by rain or sprinkling, since the protection is internal. All surface areas, including undersides of leaves and new growth, are protected from insect damage.

Roses (established or newly planted rose bushes) for control of aphids (plant lice), leafhoppers, spider mites, thrips, whiteflies.

Apply 4 oz. around each rose bush to cover 9 sq. ft. (3' × 3') area.

Established Bedding Plants, Flowers, and Gladioli for control of aphids (plant lice), lace bugs, leafhoppers, leaf miners, mites, thrips, whiteflies.

Apply 4 oz. to cover a 9 sq. ft. area (2¼ lbs. per 100 sq. ft. [5' × 20']). Do not use when planting seed.

Ornamental Shrubs for control of aphids (plant lice), lace bugs, leafhoppers, birch leaf miners, holly leaf miners, mimosa webworms, spider mites, pine tip moths, whiteflies.

Apply 4 oz. for each 9 sq. ft. (3' × 3') occupied by plant.

2. PREVENTS WEEDS in Roses, Established Bedding Plants, Flowers, Gladioli and Ornamental Shrubs. Provides long-lasting weed control. More than two dozen different kinds of annual grasses and broadleaf weeds (listed below) are killed by trifluralin as they germinate. Trifluralin will not kill established weeds. When used as directed it will prevent the re-growth of weeds from seed.

WEEDS CONTROLLED: Crabgrass, Barnyardgrass, Foxtail, Johnsongrass (from seed), Goosegrass, Annual Bluegrass, Stinkgrass, Bromegrass, Junglerice, Sprangletop, Cheat, Pigweeds (Spiny and Redroot), Carelessweed, Lambsquarters, Carpetweed, Russian Thistle, Kochia, Purslane, Florida Purslane (Pussley), Knotweed, Stinging Nettle, Goosefoot, Chickweed, Puncturevine, Texas Panicum, Sandbur.

3. FEEDS PLANTS—A modern fertilizer that supplies the nitrogen, phosphate and potash plus minor elements to maintain strong, healthy, beautiful roses and other ornamental plants.

USE LIMITATIONS

Do not apply to areas occupied by unprotected humans or domestic animals. Food utensils such as a teaspoon or measuring cup should not be used for food purposes after use with this material. Do not apply to areas where roots of fruit trees, vegetables or other food crops may extend. Do not broadcast applications to lawn. Do not apply around Amaranthus, Celosia, Coleus, Phlox, Portulaca, Ajuga or Periwinkle.

NOTICE: Buyer assumes all responsibility for safety and use not in accordance with directions.

---

the federal government, the Environmental Protection Agency (EPA). The government reviews data submitted by the manufacturer or registrant of the pesticide to determine that, when used correctly, it will not generally be harmful to man or the environment. It is usually found on the front panel of the label and will be written as EPA Registration No. 000-000.

If you find pesticide containers with the registration number written USDA 000-000, these products are older, and have not been reviewed recently by the government. You are most likely to find such numbers on products stored for long periods of time. No product that you purchase should bear a USDA number. You should call your Cooperative Extension Service regarding proper disposal of the chemical.

The establishment number tells what factory made the chemical and would make recall easier if a defect should be found.

In 1981, the EPA stopped routinely reviewing efficacy data (except for public health pesticides), but ordered manufacturers to continue collecting this information so that it would be available if EPA should call for it. They felt that the market place would soon weed out any products not effective. So you as a user should be observant when using any chemical, especially one from an unfamiliar company.

3. Names
Brand or trade name. Each company has these names for its products. It is the one used in advertising. These are almost always on the label in large print. Some examples are Benlate, Sevin or Roundup.

Because the chemical names of pesticides are generally long and complex, most (but not all) are given shorter "common" names for quick reference by users. The ingredients statement will list the common name if there is one. Some examples of common names are benomyl (Benlate), carbaryl (Sevin) and glyphosate (Roundup). On the prototype label, the name trifluralin is a common name for the chemical name which follows in parentheses. You should become familiar with the common names of the pesticides you use because many products sold by different companies will contain the same pesticide active ingredient. Most county or state extension bulletins, pamphlets or recommendation lists use the common name of a chemical in order to avoid showing preference among the chemical companies.

4. List of Ingredients

In comparing commercially-sold pesticides, for say price or convenience, check the common name of the active ingredients so you are comparing the same effective ingredients. Every pesticide label must list the percentage of active ingredients that is in the product. The list is written so that you can easily see what the active ingredients are. The amount of each active ingredient is given as a percentage of weight. If there is a common name, it will be given; if not, the chemical name will be used. The inert ingredients need not be identified but the label must show what percentage of the products they make up. They are substances such as diluents, emulsifiers, fillers, solvents and buffers used to make the active ingredient function more effectively.

5. Types of Pesticides

The label will state the types of pests the product will control. In addition to the well-known insecticides, herbicides, fungicides, and rodenticides, the legislation includes chemicals used to attract or repel pests or regulate plant growth or remove leaves (defoliants). These are not pesticides.

6. Types of Formulations

Active ingredients can rarely be used in the form in which they were synthesized. Other ingredients may be added to make them convenient to handle and safe and easy to apply accurately. These are the inert ingredients. The mixture of pesticidal active ingredients and inert ingredients is called a pesticide formulation. Some are ready to use. Others must be diluted with water or a petroleum solvent. The same active ingredient may be available in more than one formulation. You must select the formulation for your particular pest and site and one that can be used in your particular application equipment. The directions for use will tell you how to use the pesticide formulation you select. The

most common types are:

Liquids

a) Emulsifiable Concentrates (EC or E). They can be mixed with water to form an emulsion and usually need little agitation in the spray tank. They can damage some crops.

b) Flowables (F or L). Sold as a finely ground suspension and mixed with water. They seldom clog spray nozzles, need little agitation, and handle as well as emulsifiable concentrates.

c) Aerosols (A). Liquids that contain the active ingredients stored under pressure in a solvent. They have a low percentage of active ingredients and are relatively expensive. However, they are easy to use and great precision can be obtained when spraying targets.

Solids

a) Dusts (D). They are ready to use and contain an active ingredient ground with other fine or powdered dry substances into fine, uniform particles. They must be dry to be used and application is quite simple. They can drift into non-target areas. It is sometimes difficult to apply them to the right plant surfaces and dusts can be washed off by rain.

b) Granules (G). Most are made by applying a liquid formulation of the active ingredient to coarse particles of a porous material like clay, corn cobs, or peanut shells. They are used dry and are easy to apply and do not drift.

c) Wettable Powders (WP or W). They are dry powders but must be mixed with water. Good agitation is needed in the spray tank to keep the suspension homogeneous. If properly mixed, they spray well and do not usually clog nozzles. They are, however, abrasive to pumps and nozzles.

d) Baits (B). A bait is an edible or attractive substance mixed with a pesticide. The amount of active ingredient is quite low, usually less than five percent. They are used mainly to control insects, snails and slugs, or rodent pests.

7. Net Contents

The net content number tells you how much is in the container. It can be expressed in gallons, quarts, pints, pounds, ounces or other units of measure.

8. Signal Words and Symbols

To do their jobs, pesticides must control the target pest. By their very nature, they are intended to be toxic to the pest. By the same token, some may be hazardous to people. You can tell the toxicity of a product by reading the signal word and looking at the symbol on the

SIGNAL WORDS	TOXICITY	APPROXIMATE AMOUNT NEEDED TO KILL THE AVERAGE PERSON
DANGER	HIGHLY TOXIC	A FEW DROPS TO A TEASPOONFUL
WARNING	MODERATELY TOXIC	A TEASPOONFUL TO ONE OUNCE
CAUTION	LOW TOXICITY OR COMPARATIVELY FREE FROM DANGER	AN OUNCE TO MORE THAN A PINT

label. These signal words and symbols are calculated from the safety data supplied by the manufacturer as a part of registration by EPA and are set by law. Symbols are the best way to catch a person's eye. This is why a skull and crossbones is used on all highly toxic materials along with the signal word DANGER and the word POISON in red. Active ingredients which are highly caustic to the eyes or skin will bear the signal word DANGER but will not have the word POISON or the skull and crossbones. All products must bear the statement: "**Keep out of reach of children.**"

9. Precautionary Statements

This part of the label will tell you the ways in which the product may be dangerous to man and animals. It will also tell you any special steps you should take to avoid exposure to the pesticide, such as the kind of protective clothing or equipment needed. The degree of protection will be directly proportional to the signal word on the label. The more toxic the chemical, the more personal protection required of the user. Remember that the safety of pesticide usage is based on following explicitly the label precautions. In fact, I would err on the safe side. If the precaution statement "do not get in eyes" appears, I would use goggles or a face shield even though this often is not required by the label. To me, it's common sense or living defensively.

10. Practical Treatment or First Aid

If swallowing or inhaling the product or getting it in your eyes or on your skin would be harmful, the label will describe appropriate emergency first-aid measures. It also will tell you the types of exposure that require further medical attention. The pesticide label is the most important information you can take to the physician when you think someone has been poisoned.

11. Physical and Chemical Hazards

This section (not on the sample label) will tell you of any special fire, explosion or chemical hazards that the product may pose.

12. Environmental Hazards

Wrong or careless use can cause undesirable effects. To help avoid this, read and follow the environmental precautions on the label. Some examples are:

This product is highly toxic to bees exposed to direct treatment or residues on plants.

Birds feeding on treated areas may be killed.

Do not apply where runoff is likely to occur.

13. State of Use Classification

The 1972 amendments to FIFRA directed EPA to classify all pesticide products for general use or restricted use. The classification is based on: The hazard of poisoning; the way the pesticide is used, and its effect on the environment.

If the pesticide could cause harm to man or the environment without special precautions or restrictions upon use, it will be classified for "Restricted Use." Many pesticides have the potential to cause harm even when used properly, but such effects can be minimized by restricting the way the pesticide is used, or by requiring training of applicators. If a pesticide is for restricted use only, it must be applied by a certified applicator, who has been specially trained and certified by the state. Such pesticides include a statement on the label indicating that they are restricted to use by certified applicators. Often these pesticides are more highly toxic, or require special equipment for use and protection.

The pesticides that will be available to you will not be restricted for use. If you wish to use restricted-use pesticides, you may take the training offered through your Cooperative Extension Service (under USDA), and become certified as a "private applicator."

14. Directions for Use

The label lists the uses of the pesticide that are approved by the EPA. If your intended use is not on the label, you should not use the product. Any non-labeled use is a misuse and is illegal.

The use instructions will help you choose the proper pesticide and control information for your pest problem. It contains: The pests the product is registered to control (common names for pests are used); the crop, animal, or other item the product can be used on (sites); in what form the product should be applied; how much to use, and where and when the material should be applied.

In this part of the label you may find that other chemicals – pesticides or fertilizers – can be mixed with the main pesticide and sprayed at the same time. Check on compatibility before you mix. The label may also tell you whether injury to non-target plants is likely. Some plants are more sensitive than others to pesticide chemicals. The injury can range from slight burning of the leaves to complete loss of leaves, or to death of the plant.

If the gardener has mixed up more spray for a day's use than he needs, he should not store it, but spray it out on a part of the garden where it will pose no environmental hazards and can be biodegraded by sun, air, and rain. However, once the correct amount has been sprayed on the target site – say rose foliage – do not dispose of excess spray by applying to already-treated sites. As in fertilizing, if enough is good, more is not better at all. Foliage burn or other damage to the plant being protected may be the result.

In cleaning spray equipment, using detergents and rinses, the cleaning liquids should not be put down the sink, but poured out on the ground as suggested for excess spray.

15. Storage and Disposal

This section on the label will tell you how to store and dispose of the product and empty containers. Storage instructions are usually straightforward and adequate. Usually labels will warn against such hazards as freezing or excessive heat. In addition containers should be kept out of the way of children, pets or untrained adults. Many are in child resistant containers, but this does not mean you should be less than vigilant in storage and handling. Labels on the more toxic chemicals advise storage in a locked container. Most pesticides if properly stored will retain effectiveness into a second season. Dusts and wettable powders usually have a longer "bench life" than liquids, and present less hazard if spilled. The gardener would be well advised to use stored materials up first, and then get only enough to take care of second-season requirements. Or he can store the pesticide with a properly-qualified user, and dispose of the container as required by the label.

Unfortunately label instruction for disposal of containers represent minimum procedures. But more rigorous methods such as deep burial in out-of-the-way places away from water supplies, or disposal in landfill approved for disposal of pesticides are not feasible for the home gardener. At least, you should rinse the empty container thoroughly, wrap it in at least three thicknesses of newspaper, and put it in your municipal trash collection. Partially filled small containers of less than a gallon can also be triple wrapped and disposed of in the same manner. On no account should containers be reused.

The information found on the label has passed strict government requirements. EPA reviews and approves each statement on the label. The toxicity warnings come from tests required by the government. The pesticide product and its label are registered by EPA only when it de-

Under the Old Apple Tree (Isaac Newton's)

PHOTOS COURTESY OF CHAPEL VALLEY LANDSCAPE COMPANY, Woodbine, Maryland

To move the Isaac Newton apple tree, a special rigging attached to a crane was devised. The 16-foot-wide root ball, four feet high, was shaped, wrapped and laced, and then hoisted onto a low-boy trailer. The 40-ton load was moved 300 yards uphill and lowered into its new location where the tree flowered and fruited without interruption.

Maybe Isaac Newton didn't launch his study of gravity when an apple fell on his head. But there is great reverence for descendants of the tree under which he is supposed to have been sitting.

Scientists at the old Bureau of Standards – it's now the National Institute of Standards and Technology – had a genuine Newtonian apple tree growing outside their laboratory windows. They had to leave it behind when they moved to their new home in Gaithersburg. Intelsat and the University of the District of Columbia moved into the old complex on Connecticut Avenue. The State Department developed the back acres into its International Center for foreign chanceries. Then it was discovered that the venerable tree grew in the path of the projected International Drive. In January 1981 it was moved to the hilltop where it now flourishes in the block-square park off Van Ness Street and across from Intelsat.

The state-of-the-art techniques used to move the tree demonstrate to the home gardener that new technologies are available to back up his or her gardening. Here is a reminder, too, that any tree or shrub, in being planted or transplanted, responds to intelligent and loving care.

– **J.E.**

termines that applicators, consumers, fish and wildlife will be protected.

When you apply a pesticide to your garden crops, some residue of the pesticide will remain on the crop. The government, in permitting use on that crop, has determined that the residues that remain will not be at unsafe levels for human consumption. Nonetheless, you should always clean or wash garden crops thoroughly before eating or cooking; this will reduce the residues even further.

Getting a single pesticide chemical ready for registration and use may take four to seven years and may cost the chemical company 10 to 15 million dollars. Surely if it takes that much time and costs that much money, the label is worth reading. Additionally and more importantly, it may save you from a serious exposure to a chemical while working in your garden.

Do's and Don'ts

DO shear hedges so that the base is wider than the top. This allows in more sunlight, encouraging the growth below.

New Plants, New Experiences

By Henry M. Cathey, Ph.D.,
Director, U. S. National Arboretum

The U. S. National Arboretum, after more than 60 years of growth, offers many moments of inspiration and education to aid you in becoming a better gardener. Through our plant exploration and research, for instance, we are giving you new and "elite" woody plants for the landscape.

Since 1960, 131 new cultivars have come from our breeding programs. We have introduced – with the cooperation of nearly 1,000 plant people around the world – new mildew-proof crape myrtles (*Lagerstroemia*), a stress-resistant London plane tree (*Platanus*), and cold-tolerant camellias. Many other plants are being evaluated that will be adapted to our stressful and pest-riddled environments.

The Arboretum's educational opportunities for the gardener are found in classes, workshops and tours, and in our frequent and "one-of-a-kind" events. And we have created new gardens for you.

New Gardens to See

In the Court of Honor, north of the Administration building, we are displaying 20 of the new cultivars, including the most widely grown new shrub in the world, the Chinese red-fruited and disease-resistant pyracantha 'Mohave.'

Our world-famous National Bonsai Collection has new plantings and a new entrance named for Edith Gordon Allen, founder of Ikebana International. The largest plant in the space is a reclining Japanese black pine (*Pinus Thunbergii*). Other plants of Japanese origin include *Acer, Chamaecyparis, Deutzia, Ilex, Lagerstroemia* and *Prunus*. Most of the trees and shrubs in the garden show up in the bonsai pavilion where one specimen is

NOTE: The Men's Garden Club has maintained close ties with the National Arboretum through the years. We have watched with keen interest its breeding programs for new plants. Dr. Cathey discusses these programs as a part of the overall research and educational mission of the Arboretum.

more than 350 years old.

Adjacent to the Bonsai Collection is a new Penjing Collection from China. Our 31 penjing include many outstanding specimens ranging from 15 to 200 years in age. A permanent pavilion to house them will be constructed in the future.

Our Asian Valley, coursing down to the Anacostia River, is an 1,800-foot valley of great North American trees underplanted with trees and shrubs of Asian origin. A 500-foot watercourse of five levels and a recirculating pool add sounds and reflections of water in this natural setting. We have placed large boulders on the arms of the valley and landscaped it with large sweeps of Japanese plants (right side) and Chinese plants (left side).

Brand new is a west meadow area where an element of our national history is preserved. Twenty-two sandstone columns with Corinthian capitals that were part of the U. S. Capitol's old east front have been erected in a rectangular colonnade from a design by the late Russell Page. The columns, designed by Benjamin Latrobe, came originally from a quarry owned by George Washington. They were removed from the Capitol's east front during its expansion from 1958 to 1962.

In the future, the Arboretum will continue to expand its programs as befits a

A relic of our history comes alive in this horticultural setting. Twenty-two columns from the U.S. Capitol's old east front are preserved in this new colonnade on the National Arboretum's West Meadow. The sandstone for the columns and their Corinthian capitals came originally from a quarry owned by George Washington.

world-class institution. It will serve as a repository for woody plant germplasm. Staff trained in physiology, pathology, entomology, taxonomy and related fields will interact with geneticists breeding new trees, shrubs and ground covers for the landscape. We will be collecting "elite" native North American plants and hardier plants from Asia and the Andes.

Among natives, we are keenly alert to the existence in the wild of superior fringe trees *(Chionanthus virginicus)*, sourwoods *(Oxydendrum arboreum)*, American hollies *(Ilex opaca)*, and Virginia or Sweet Bay magnolias *(Magnolia virginicus)*. We are interested in using such plants in our breeding programs, building on the traits that characterize our "elite" cultivars – superior hardiness, flower and leaf form, resistance to pests and diseases, and suitability for our gardens.

Our living collections and gardens will demonstrate the best plants for landscape use and we will preserve the germplasm necessary to preserve our horticultural heritage and to enrich our future.

National Arboretum Introductions That Grow Well in Washington

Here are 20 cultivars introduced by the National Arboretum that do well in the Washington area. Check with local nurseries for their availability. Do not call the Arboretum. The Arboretum's breeding programs are financed by the Federal government with some private support. New cultivars are released to the wholesale nursery trade without strings attached. The Arboretum receives no royalties.

Boxwood 'Morris Dwarf' *(Buxus microphylla* var. *japonica)*: Slow-growing, probably to 3 or 4 feet in 20 years. Half-inch leaves yellowish in winter, return to green with warm weather. Irregular or "tufted" bush outline.

Crape myrtle 'Catawba' *(Lagerstroemia indica)*: Compact, to 11 feet high and wide. Dark purple flowers from late July to September. Glossy, dark green foliage is mildew-resistant, turns to brilliant orange-red in fall.

Crape myrtle 'Muskogee' *(Lagerstroemia x)*: Multiple-stemmed large shrub or small tree. Dark-green leaves turn red and yellow in fall, mildew-resistant. Recurrent blooms are light lavender, opening in early August.

Crape myrtle 'Potomac' *(Lagerstroemia indica):* Large, tree-like specimens. Dark green, leathery leaves tolerant of mildew except at end of season. Medium-pink flowers from mid-July to August.

Crape myrtle 'Natchez' and 'Tuscarora' *(Lagerstroemia x):* Both highly mildew-resistant, multiple-stemmed large shrubs or small trees. Natchez has dark cinnamon-brown bark; glossy dark green leaves, turning to orange and red in fall; pure white flowers. Tuscarora has light brown bark; glossy, dark green leaves, red-tinged when young; dark coral pink flowers.

Hibiscus 'Diana' *(Hibiscus syriacus):* Upright, densely-branched, to 8 feet tall and 6 feet wide. Heavy, dark green leaves. White blooms often 6 inches across, heavy-textured, ruffled, long-lasting.

Hibiscus 'Helene' *(Hibiscus syriacus):* Smaller, more compact. Heavy, dark green leaves. Blooms from summer to early fall are fine-textured, ruffled white flowers with dark red eyespot.

Holly 'Sparkleberry' *(Ilex x):* Large, multi-stemmed shrub. Elliptical, finely-serrated leaves. Fruit large, bright red, abundant. Noted for its brilliant winter show.

Magnolia 'Betty': To 10 feet, begins flowering in mid- to late April with abundant, up-to-8-inch blooms ranging from white inside to grayed and red-purple outside.

Magnolia 'Galaxy': Outstanding, single-trunk, upright tree with narrow crown. Blossoms are pale red-purple inside to intense shades outside from ruby red at base to magenta rose toward tip. Rapid grower in early years.

Magnolia 'Susan': Small, to 7 feet high and wide. Blooms mid- to late April with abundant, fragrant flowers, red-purple inside and more intense shades of same color outside.

Pyracantha 'Mohave': Dense, upright-branched, to 14 feet high and as wide. Waxy orange-red fruit ripens in mid-August, darkening to red-orange by mid-winter. Foliage dark green, semi- to evergreen. Resistant to fire blight and scab.

Viburnum 'Alleghany' *(Viburnum rhytidophylloides):* Dense to 11 feet high and wide. Leaves dark green, leathery, deciduous to semi-evergreen. Flowers yellow-white in May and again in September-October. Fruit ripens to red, then turns black. Resists bacterial leaf spot.

Viburnum 'Catskill' *(Viburnum dilatatum):* Compact, to 5 feet high and 8 feet wide. Flowers creamy-white in May. Dark red fruit in mid-August, persists to mid-winter. Small round leaves with yellow, orange and red fall color.

Viburnum 'Cayuga' *(Viburnum carlcephalum):* Compact, to 5 feet high and 6 feet wide. Glossy, dark green foliage highly tolerant to bacterial leaf spot and powdery mildew. Pink buds in late April to white, waxy flowers.

Viburnum 'Eskimo' *(Viburnum x):* Very compact, to only 4 feet. Dark green, glossy, evergreen leaves. Pale cream tubular florets open to pure white in early May. Fruit ripens a dull red in August before becoming black.

Viburnum 'Iroquois' *(Viburnum dilatatum):* Grows to 9 feet high and 13 feet wide. Large, dark green leaves, changing to orange-red to maroon in fall. White flowers in May. Vivid feature is glossy, scarlet-red fruit in mid-August, persisting to mid-winter.

Viburnum 'Mohawk' *(Viburnum burkwoodii):* Compact, to 7 feet high and wide. Dark green foliage turns brilliant orange-red in fall. Notable are blossoms that bud at dark red, open to white with red-blotched reverse. Spicy clove fragrance.

Viburnum 'Shasta' *(Viburnum plicatum f. Tomentosum):* Horizontal growth habit at maturity, twice as wide as high. Dark green leaves become dull, purplish-red in fall. Large white flowers. Fruit red maturing to black.

Area Institutions

American Horticultural Society, River Farm, 7931 East Boulevard Drive (off the George Washington Parkway near Mount Vernon), Alexandria, VA 22308. Telephone: (703) 768-5700.

Brookside Botanical Garden, 1500 Glenallen Avenue, Wheaton, MD 20902. Telephone: (301) 949-8230.

Horticultural Educational Center, Green Spring Farm Park, 4603 Green Spring Road (off Route 236 in Annandale), Alexandria, VA 22312. Telephone: (703) 642-5173.

Maryland-National Capital Park and Planning Commission, 8000 Meadowbrook Lane, Chevy Chase, MD 20815. Telephone: (301) 495-8848.

U.S. Botanic Garden, 245 First Street, SW (at the foot of Capitol Hill), Washington, DC 20024. Telephone: (202) 225-8333.

U.S. National Arboretum, 3501 New York Avenue, NE, Washington, DC 20002. Telephone: (202) 475-4815.

What, a Men's Garden Club?

By Anthony R. Gould and John Edwards

Yes, we are a men's garden club in which women have played an active supporting role. And we've been meeting once each month for more than 40 years except for one March night when a raging snowstorm closed us down.

We were organized in 1946 when Americans were looking to the post-war years for new ideas to improve the quality of their lives. In our area a group of men and women, the Bethesda-Chevy Chase Educational Foundation, stimulated and financed a range of activities from harvest shows to student loans. They broached the idea of a men's garden club in the spring of 1946.

Dr. Fred C. Coe, a prominent radiologist and an enthusiastic gardener, noted that women had their Bethesda Community Garden Club. Why, he asked, should men not have one, too? He said it was important to capitalize on the intense interest men had shown in their wartime victory gardens as well as their ornamental plantings. He offered to show color slides of flowering plants – a distinct novelty then – if a meeting place could be found. Principal Thomas Pyle said his school was available. With that, Nurseryman Ed Stock recalls, "the idea took off like a house afire."

On May 23, a Thursday evening, 25 men interested in gardening met at the Bethesda-Chevy Chase High School. They were called upon to introduce themselves and indicate their gardening interests. They enjoyed the slides, said they wanted more, and organized themselves to meet each month thereafter. Fred Coe, the temporary chairman, became the first President. Edward K. Bender, the County "assistant garden agent," became Secretary-Treasurer.

Decisions Set Club Character

Three decisions that night were prophetic. First, when someone suggested that a committee be formed to draft a constitution and by-laws, Fred Coe objected, "If you do that I'll quit. We're gardeners. We don't want a lot of by-laws." Also arguing to "keep things sim-

Past Presidents

Past presidents of the Club and the year they took office follow (the membership year begins June 1):

Dr. Fred O. Coe, 1946; Fred W. Lang, 1947; George A. Smith, 1948; Edward K. Bender, 1949; Anthony R. Gould, 1950.

Col. Charles A. H. Thomson, 1951; J. H. Bodley, 1952; Preston E. Groome, 1953; Henry E. Allen, 1954; Bernard A. Bang, 1955.

Dr. Jack N. Paisley, 1956; Robert J. Foley, RAdm USN, ret, 1957; J. Philip Shaefer, 1958; Robert Osborn, 1959; J. B. Engle, 1960.

Eugene E. Munn, Jr., 1961; Alexander S. Stevenson, 1962; Edward B. Willard, 1963; Dr. Cyril A. Schulman, 1964; Dr. C. L. Lefebvre, 1965.

Dr. David V. Lumsden, 1966; Dr. Edward Wichers, 1967; Roy Magruder, 1968; Val C. Sherman, 1969; Joe B. Parks, 1970.

Sidney S. Kennedy, 1971; Emerson P. Slacum, 1972; Wallace F. Janssen, 1973; Howard Stagner, 1974; Frederick Jochem, 1975.

Harold B. Wiese, 1976; Robert G. Hill, 1977; Dr. William B. Holton, 1978; Dr. Cletis Pride, 1979; Norton Boothe, 1980.

John Edwards, 1981; Lynn M. F. Harriss, 1982; John G. Shaffer, 1983; Dr. Eugene L. Hess, 1984; Carl R. Mahder, 1985.

Dr. Robert S. Melville, 1986; Sam Shiozawa, 1987; Allan E. Baker, 1988; Charles B. Seckinger, 1989.

THE SATURDAY LEANING POST

THE MEN'S GARDEN CLUB OF MONTGOMERY COUNTY

The masthead of our monthly newsletter, *The Saturday Leaning Post,* pictures our mascot, Joe, who says, "Blessed are those who have nothing to say and the courage not to say it." If you would like to attend a meeting of the Men's Garden Club, or become a member, write: Membership Secretary, Men's Garden Club of Montgomery County, P.O. Box 34863, Bethesda, Maryland 20817.

ple" was Frederic P. Lee, a lawyer and law professor who a decade later would head the charter commission for Montgomery County's new form of government. The same Fred Lee was a distinguished horticulturist who wrote the definitive classic, *The Azalea Book,* in 1958.

The Club supported Fred Coe and Fred Lee and has held to their point of view with a certain pride. We have operated by custom and tradition plus a little common sense for so long that a sort of unwritten constitution has come into being. Our meetings, it is agreed, are for gardening. Most business is left to the elected officers.

Second Prophetic Decision

The second prophetic decision came when Ed Bender proposed that the Club not limit its identity to Bethesda and Chevy Chase but expand to all of Montgomery County. Through the years we have broadened ourselves further with our membership open to the entire National Capital area. It is not uncommon for one of our officers to be a Virginia resident.

Finally, the third decision came when Ed Stock suggested that the Club compile a list of desirable plants and flowers for the area. It was completed in 1948, an 84-page mimeographed document that sold out all of its 1,500 copies. Other Club publications followed in 1955, 1969, 1975, and now 1989.

For the first 30 years the Club met in

the fall, winter and spring on the first Thursday evening of the month. Then a scheduling conflict forced a change to the first Wednesday. We are meticulous about starting on time and, except for an occasional lapse, we have ended on time. Our first half-hour is devoted to gardening matters including a popular question-and-answer period known as "Uncle Chlorophyll." Then we have speakers on a variety of garden and garden-related topics. Sometimes a round-table discussion is scheduled.

From our beginnings one of our most popular annual events has been Ladies Night. Other special occasions include Swap Night when we bring in surplus plants or other items and draw for our favorites – everything from a tomato plant to a choice azalea or a garden tool – and Brag Night, a "show and tell" when we see what interests other gardeners and learn their tricks and short cuts. In the summer months the ladies join us in our visits to outstanding gardens.

Monthly Newsletter

The Club has published its monthly newsletter, *The Saturday Leaning Post,* since 1958. Member services have included a wholesale supply order and a vegetable seed sale. The oldest and biggest service is our Holland bulb project when orders to a leading Holland supplier are made in June for delivery in September. In recent years these orders have totalled nearly 90,000 bulbs a year.

The Club now has five officers: President, Vice President, Secretary, Treasurer, and Membership Secretary. The President and Vice President serve for one year only; the Vice President, who acts as program chairman, usually moves up to the presidency. They are called "annuals" while the other officers, who sometimes stay on their jobs for two or three terms, are known as "biennials" or "perennials."

Our membership grew from 25 men at the first meeting to 62 at the end of the first year. These are known as "charter members" and six of them remain on the rolls today. Our membership has included many with a gardening reputation beyond the area as well as many who have called themselves "beginners." Most members, however, have been average but serious home gardeners, many with specialties such as roses, chrysanthemums, azaleas and rhododendrons, spring bulbs, wildflowers, plant propagation, and vegetables. Our active membership (there also is an associate membership for those who move away) average 175 or more. We hold no membership drives. Guests are welcome at our meetings and if they wish to join they see the Membership Secretary.

In *The Washington Post*, garden writer Charles Fenyvesi described us as "the *Academie francaise* of local garden clubs." The analogy may or may not fit but we like the compliment.

The Home Gardener and the Extension Service

Many home gardeners who seek advice from the Cooperative Extension Service say they'd never heard of it before. CES is a joint undertaking of federal and state governments with nearly every county in the United States, the nation's land-grant colleges and universities acting as the go-between. It was set up by the land-grant act of 1914. And it performed so successfully as a rural educational service that the county agent became almost a cult figure in American life.

Changes in America have seen the family farm, once the backbone of many local economies, gradually disappear in many areas. At the same time the number of home owners with a plot of land increased rapidly. Extension has become an urban as well as rural educational service. If the early county agent was an agronomist, his successor today is more likely to be a horticulturist.

In Maryland, CES works through the University of Maryland; in Virginia through the Virginia Polytechnic Institute and State University at Blacksburg, and in the District through the University of the District of Columbia.

The Cooperative Extension Service always has faced budgetary restraints, more so today than before. So volunteerism has played a crucial role, as it did in our earlier days in the barn raising and harvesting of farm folk and in their later 4-H, homemaker, and farm-demonstration activities. For the home gardener this volunteerism appears today in the Master Gardener program which began slowly in the 1970s and now covers 45 states and the District of Columbia and three provinces of Canada.

Master Gardeners are trained volunteers who provide information on gardening and perform other tasks for the Extension Service. There are 15,000 of them across the nation, and they are backed up by the full scientific resources of the land-grant colleges and universities and the U.S. Department of Agriculture. In our area Master Gardeners work in Extension offices handling the voluminous requests that come in for gardening information – in Montgomery County alone they respond to 10,000 calls a year – and, also, in operating the neighborhood plant clinics.

– J.E.

Where To Go For More

Looking for more information? First, check the references cited in the articles in this book. Then look for the bulletins, fact sheets and leaflets prepared with the specific needs and conditions of the Washington area in mind. These are the publications of local universities, cooperative extension services, state departments of agriculture, and public gardens and arboretums – and they are excellent. The only problem is that sometimes they're hard to come by because of limited printings.

Try the libraries. Because this is the Nation's Capital we are blessed with superb facilities. There are libraries at the National Arboretum and the U.S. Botanic Garden, and supporting them, the huge National Agricultural Library at Beltsville. There are libraries at Brookside Gardens and Green Springs Farm Park, and a little-known gem at the Smithsonian Institution downtown on the Mall. For a general range of garden books most public libraries are well supplied.

Books and Encyclopedias

More garden books are published and sold today than at any time in our history. Every book store has at least a shelf of them. The most widely sold are the first-rate Ortho books which also are found in every garden center. Not as readily available are the Brooklyn Botanic Garden handbooks which are authoritative and inexpensive introductory manuals on a wide range of subjects. You can find them in the Arbor House shop of the National Capital Area Federation of Garden Clubs at the National Arboretum. Or get them directly from the Garden (1000 Washington Avenue, Brooklyn, NY 11225). Especially useful to local garden-

ers is the new edition (1988) by Deborah Fialka of the late Wilbur Youngman's *Washington Star Garden Book*. It will complement and reinforce the information in this book.

Some of the classic garden encyclopedias have been or are being updated. *Taylor's Encyclopedia of Gardening* (1961) is now appearing in a series of specialized volumes, each treating a different subject such as bulbs, roses, perennials and vegetables. The books in the *Time-Life Encyclopedia of Gardening* are being updated from time to time. The latest edition of *Wyman's Gardening Encyclopedia* came out in 1986. James and Louise Bush-Brown's *America's Garden Book*, often used as a college textbook, was last revised in 1980. T. H. Everett's *Illustrated Encyclopedia of Gardening* was published as a whole in 1987.

All these standard references, along with Ortho's *Complete Guide to Successful Gardening* (1983) and the Reader's Digest *Illustrated Guide to Gardening* (1978) share similar strengths and weaknesses. The strengths are their excellent coverage of basics. The weaknesses are their lack of geographic specificity and their inability to keep up with cultivars and pesticide and fertilizer information.

Cooperative Extension Service

Do you have a specific garden problem? More and more the home gardener is turning for help to the Cooperative Extension Service, not only for its gardening publications but for the services provided by its Master Gardener program. Master Gardeners are trained volunteers who answer telephone requests for gardening information and operate

PHOTO BY EDMUND C. FLYNN

A home gardener brings in a branch from a sick plant for diagnosis at a neighborhood plant clinic in Montgomery County. The clinics are operated during the growing season by Master Gardener volunteers from the Cooperative Extension Service. The three here also happen to be members of the Men's Garden Club. The clinic shown is at the Davis Library in Bethesda.

neighborhood plant clinics. They are backed up by Extension professionals and the full facilities of the U.S. Department of Agriculture.

One of your best sources for information about the area are members of the Men's Garden Club and other local garden clubs and plant societies. Garden writers in the newspapers and garden programs on radio and television are another, although the quality and accuracy of information on the radio call-in programs can vary enormously.

Garden Clubs and Plant Societies

Hundreds of garden clubs are active in communities throughout the Greater Washington area. Some are general in scope. Others specialize. There are plant societies that concentrate on matters of local interest but are connected with regional, national and international organizations. Some of long standing cover azaleas, rhododendrons, daffodils, chry-

santhemums, roses, daylilies, true lilies, dahlias, iris, camellias, orchids and ferns among others, and new societies, such as one for hostas, have responded to new interests.

The officers, telephone numbers and addresses of these groups keep changing. For the latest information about a garden club or plant society, call the libraries at the National Arboretum, Brookside Gardens or Green Spring Farm Park. Or phone the National Capital Area Federation of Garden Clubs – (202) 399-5958. The Federation comprises about 148 clubs with 4,500 members in four districts of Maryland, Virginia and the District of Columbia.

Do's and Don'ts

DO prune your spring-flowering shrubs such as forsythia immediately after their flowering. Do cut out up to a third of the older canes at ground level.

Index

Boldface type denotes illustrations

USDA's New Plant Hardiness Zone Map

The long-awaited, revised USDA plant hardiness zone map, the first update in 25 years, was unveiled at the National Arboretum with much fanfare on February 22, 1990.

The occasion was a reception in advance of publication of the *National Arboretum Book of Outstanding Garden Plants*. A limited version of the USDA map, showing only the United States, appeared for the first time as endpapers in the book.

The full map unfolds to four by four feet and shows Canada and Mexico as well as Alaska and Hawaii and is detailed enough to show county lines within the states. It has 11 color-coded zones based on 10-degree Fahrenheit differences in average annual minimum temperatures. On the full map each zone is divided into A and B regions based on five-degree Fahrenheit differences.

Zone 11 is a new, almost frost-free zone on the southern tip of Florida, southern California, all but the mountainous areas of Hawaii, most of the coastline of Yucatan in Mexico, the southern Baja peninsula, and the Gulf of Mexico.

The map, printed on heavy, plastic-coated paper, is available only through the U.S. Government Printing Office (miscellaneous publication 1475, stock number 001-000-04550-4). The price is $6.50.